The Short Oxford History of Europe

General Editor: T. C. W. Blanning

Classical Greece

500–323 BC

Editor: Robin Osborne

OXFORD

UNIVERSITY PRESS

OXFORD

UNIVERSITY PRESS

Great Clarendon Street, Oxford OX2 6DP

Oxford University Press is a department of the University of Oxford.
It furthers the University's objective of excellence in research, scholarship,
and education by publishing worldwide in

Oxford New York

Athens Auckland Bangkok Bogotá Buenos Aires Calcutta
Cape Town Chennai Dar es Salaam Delhi Florence Hong Kong Istanbul
Karachi Kuala Lumpur Madrid Melbourne Mexico City Mumbai
Nairobi Paris São Paulo Shanghai Singapore Taipei Tokyo Toronto Warsaw

with associated companies in Berlin Ibadan

Oxford is a trade mark of Oxford University Press
in the UK and in certain other countries

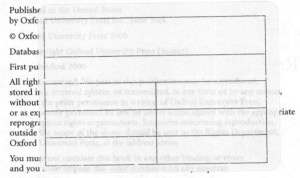

Published in the United States
by Oxford University Press Inc., New York

© Oxford University Press 2000

Database right Oxford University Press (maker)

First published 2000

All rights reserved. No part of this publication may be reproduced,
stored in a retrieval system, or transmitted, in any form or by any means,
without the prior permission in writing of Oxford University Press,
or as expressly permitted by law, or under terms agreed with the appropriate
reprographics rights organizations. Enquiries concerning reproduction
outside the scope of the above should be sent to the Rights Department,
Oxford University Press, at the address above

You must not circulate this book in any other binding or cover
and you must impose this same condition on any acquirer

British Library Cataloguing in Publication Data

Data available

Library of Congress Cataloging in Publication Data

(Data applied for)

ISBN 0–19–873154–X (hbk)
ISBN 0–19–873153–1 (pbk)

10 9 8 7 6 5 4 3 2 1

Typeset in Minion
by RefineCatch Limited, Bungay, Suffolk
Printed in Great Britain by
T.J. International Ltd., Padstow, Cornwall

General Editor's Preface

The problems of writing a satisfactory general history of Europe are many, but the most intractable is clearly the reconciliation of depth with breadth. The historian who can write with equal authority about every part of the continent in all its various aspects has not yet been born. Two main solutions have been tried in the past: either a single scholar has attempted to go it alone, presenting an unashamedly personal view of a period, or teams of specialists have been enlisted to write what are in effect anthologies. The first offers a coherent perspective but unequal coverage, the second sacrifices unity for the sake of expertise. This new series is underpinned by the belief that it is this second way that has the fewest disadvantages and that even those can be diminished if not neutralized by close cooperation between the individual contributors under the directing supervision of the volume editor. All the contributors to every volume in this series have read each other's chapters, have met to discuss problems of overlap and omission, and have then redrafted as part of a truly collective exercise. To strengthen coherence further, the editor has written an introduction and conclusion, weaving the separate strands together to form a single cord. In this exercise, the brevity promised by the adjective 'short' in the series' title has been an asset. The need to be concise has concentrated everyone's minds on what really mattered in the period. No attempt has been made to cover every angle of every topic in every country. What this volume does provide is a short but sharp and deep entry into the history of Europe in the period in all its most important aspects.

T. C. W. Blanning

Sidney Sussex College
Cambridge

Acknowledgements

I am grateful to the Series Editor, Tim Blanning, and to successive History editors at Oxford University Press, Tony Morris and Ruth Parr, for their help and encouragement. I am indebted to John Roberts for kindly reading and commenting copiously and acutely on the first drafts of all the chapters.

Robin Osborne

Contents

List of Illustrations

Maps

List of Contributors

JAMES DAVIDSON is Reader in Ancient History at Birkbeck College, London, and author of *Courtesans and Fishcakes: the Consuming Passions of Classical Athens* (1997) and *One Mykonos* (1999).

LISA KALLET is Professor of Ancient History at the University of Texas at Austin and author of *Money, Expense and Naval Power in Thucydides' History 1–5.24* (1993).

PAUL MILLETT is Lecturer in Ancient History in the University of Cambridge and Fellow of Downing College. He is the author of *Lending and Borrowing in Ancient Athens* (1991).

JOSIAH OBER is David Magie Professor of Ancient History at Princeton University and author of *Fortress Attica: Defense of the Athenian Land Frontier, 404–322 BC* (1985), *Mass and Elite in Democratic Athens: Rhetoric, Ideology and the Power of the People* (1989), *The Athenian Revolution: Essays on Ancient Greek Democracy and Political Theory* (1996), and *Political Dissent in Democratic Athens: Intellectual Critics of Popular Rule* (1998).

ROBIN OSBORNE is a Professor of Ancient History in the University of Oxford and Fellow of Corpus Christi College. He is the author of *Demos: the Discovery of Classical Attika* (1985), *Classical Landscape with Figures: the Ancient Greek City and its Countryside* (1987), *Greece in the Making 1200–479 BC* (1996), and *Archaic and Classical Greek Art* (1998).

ROSALIND THOMAS is Reader in History at Royal Holloway, University of London, and author of *Oral Tradition and Written Record in Classical Athens* (1989), *Literacy and Orality in Ancient Greece* (1992), and *Herodotus in Context: Ethnography, Science and the Art of Persuasion* (2000).

HANS VAN WEES is Lecturer in Ancient History at University College London, and author of *Status Warriors: War, Violence and Society in Homer and History* (1992) and *Greek Warfare: Myths and Realities* (2000).

The creation of classical Greece

Robin Osborne

Classical Greece is both an icon and an enigma.

An icon. The architectural forms and proportions displayed by public buildings of the fifth and fourth centuries BC have become the reference point for all modern western architecture, whether it espouses them or rejects them. The selective naturalism of classical sculpture and its sensuous exploration of the naked human body has put figurative art at the centre of the grand tradition of painting, as well as of sculpture, and has become the epitome of the art of a free and self-confident society. The crises and dilemmas of individual, family, and community, probed and unfolded in Greek tragedy, have been endlessly reinvestigated by successive generations of writers from Roman times to the present day and have acquired archetypal status as the essential expressions of human psychology. The relativism of Heraclitus or Protagoras, the idealism of Plato, the scepticism of Democritus, are still the basic expressions of what are fundamental philosophical positions, and the logic of Aristotle has only recently ceased to confine and control the nature of all philosophical argument. The determination by a community as a whole of its actions and policies through the medium of the popular assembly is still held out as the model of truly democratic practice.

An enigma. The classical Greek world was very different from the earlier great civilizations of Mesopotamia and Egypt. It was a world of tiny, more or less independent 'cities', many of which enjoyed no special resources and whose livelihood was based on agricultural produce which uncertain rainfall rendered highly unpredictable.

Clustered around the shores not just of what is today Greece but also of southern Italy, Sicily, southern France, Asia Minor, the Black Sea, and Cyrenaica, these cities were frequently in conflict; only in the face of invasion on a massive scale from the mighty Persian empire or under the compulsion of a single briefly paramount city, as Athens in the middle of the fifth century, was there any significant degree of collaboration. The Greeks themselves talked of being united by blood, customs, religion, and language, but in each case it is more a matter of similarity than identity: the Greek language included dialects whose structural similarity does not preclude a level of linguistic diversity so high as to make the degree of mutual intelligibility questionable; Greek religion was polytheistic and accommodated any number of gods and heroes worshipped in peculiar local rituals as well as through animal sacrifice whose basic rules were common; Greeks paraded myths of descent that united them with some Greeks (for example as part of the ethnic group identifying itself as 'Dorians') and divided them from other Greeks (the genealogies of 'Dorians' and 'Ionians' had nothing in common), but those myths can be shown to be fictions that both removed and created ethnic distinctions. These salient features of classical Greece certainly distance it from the great civilizations of the Near and Middle East, but they fail to mark it out from other parts of Iron Age Europe. And the subsequent history of Greece, a history of conquest by Rome, is one shared by both the rest of Iron Age Europe and by the Near East. How then are the cultural achievements of classical Greece to be explained?

This volume stands at the head of a History of Europe because of the icon that classical Greece has become. European identity in the two and a half millennia that have passed since has been formed by the processes of comparison and contrast with an image of classical Greece, and every study of subsequent European culture, taking culture in its broadest sense, is a study of response to that classical past. For subsequent volumes the interest lies in the icon, in the manipulation of an image of classical Greece, as the story and the cultural products of the classical Greek city are taken up separately and individually and put to work to social and political ends. This volume is concerned with how those elements which later ages have selected for exploitation hang together; the classic cultural products become themselves part of the evidence as we look behind the images and try better to understand the nature of the enigma, if not to solve it, and put on display the sort of world that produced the art, literature, and philosophy that have determined what art, literature, and philosophy are like for Europeans of all subsequent ages.

The natural world of Greece

The Greek peninsula jutting out into the central Mediterranean consists of small upland and small and larger lowland plains divided by mountains. Communications by land within the peninsula are restricted, and land communications with the rest of Europe to the north very poor. The peninsula's jagged coastline offers numerous landing places and harbours, and communications by sea, whether hugging the coast or making use of chains of islands, are relatively easy. Archaeological evidence suggests that from well back into the third millennium BC communications around and across the southern Aegean were lively. Within the classical period too, it was the sea which enabled Athens to build up the enormous network of alliances that comprised her 'empire'; the rival 'league' of Sparta, the city with the dominant land army, included few cities outside the Peloponnese.

Physical geography conspired with climate to make much of mainland Greece and the islands marginal for agriculture. In a general pattern of long dry windy summers and wet winters, the southeastern part of the Greek peninsula *normally* receives too little rain to support garden vegetables without irrigation (see below p. 28). Marked variation from year to year means that in dry years even less thirsty cereal crops can be totally wiped out in this region, and reduced crop yields are not infrequent in those regions with a generally higher average precipitation. Upland areas enjoy plentiful rainfall, but at higher altitudes areas suitable for cereals are restricted, and their growth, and that of vines, retarded by the cold, while olives, which can survive drought, cannot tolerate mountain winters.

From the Bronze Age onwards Greeks sailed from the mainland and islands of the Aegean and Ionian seas to settle in other regions of the Mediterranean, and part of the attraction of doing so was to secure more favourable agricultural conditions: Sicily is notably wetter than mainland Greece, and the Greek settlement at Cyrene was in the one area of that part of north Africa with good rainfall. In these foreign parts cereal monoculture and production primarily with an eye to the market were possible; in the Greek mainland it was important to combine arable and pastoral agriculture and to grow a little of everything. Hedging bets against what the year might bring, storing some, eating some, and selling some of the produce—this was the essential strategy of any small farmer.

Climate had its effect on communications also. The winters are wet enough—extremely wet in the mountains—to produce seasonal torrents that could be quite impassable, and in ancient as in modern times everyone knew stories of flash floods that had simply washed away villages or fields. Coupled with unpredictable seas, on which none would venture, this severely restricted winter communications: trade and war alike were normally matters for the long summer season. A city could expect to have the months of winter uninterrupted by visitors, and whether for purposes of survival or for purposes of entertainment, residents had to shift for themselves and for each other.

The wild landscape that formed a backdrop to human activities was probably not very dissimilar to what can be seen today. In several pat of Greece there are limestone basins drained through swallow-holes; attempts were made to drain these from the Bronze Age onwards, with sporadic success, but fen and marsh continued to provide an important resource absent from the systematically drained modern landscape. On the other hand claims of massive deforestation since antiquity seem mistaken: Greece today has a greater area of woodland than it had fifty years ago, and the classical landscape may have been less wooded than today's.

The border between the cultivated and the wild fluctuated according to population pressure, and there is some evidence that the fifth and particularly the fourth century saw marginal areas pressed into cultivation. At all times the wild landscape was itself heavily exploited, for fuel and food; the milk products and meat on which cities relied came from animals supported on the uncultivated landscape. Nor was the rough landscape unimportant in inter-city relations: the movement of shepherds through the mountains that divided cities ensured that news spread quickly and widely, and, as the plot of Sophocles' tragedy *Oedipus the King* shows, it was not always the élite who were the best informed.

The pre-classical past: the literary inheritance

There are parts of the circuit wall left, including the gate with lions standing on it. They say this is the work of Cylopes, who built the wall of Tiryns for Proetus. In the ruins of Mycenae is a water-source called Perseus' spring, and the underground chambers of Atreus and his sons where the treasuries of their wealth were.

So Pausanias (2. 16. 4–5) wrote in his guidebook in the second century AD. Monumental remains dating to the second half of the second millennium BC or earlier were visible in various parts of Greece, and graves and grave-goods from the Bronze Age were uncovered from time to time (the 'Treasury of Atreus', named from a mythical ruler associated with Mycenae, was in fact a grave). But the past to which the remains of Mycenae, Tiryns, and so on, were ascribed by classical Greeks was not the past of complex bureaucratic societies, with which the decipherment of the Linear B tablets from late Bronze Age Greece has made modern scholars familiar, but the heroic past known from epic poetry and above all from the poems ascribed to Homer. Between the political and material achievements of the late Bronze Age and the formation of the city-states which flourished so vigorously in the fifth-century BC lay a gulf which we know as the Dark Age; for us it is increasingly illuminated by archaeology, but classical Greeks had no memories of this period and no physical evidence of it remained above ground.

Herodotus' *Histories*, his inquiries into 'the great and remarkable deeds of the Greeks and the Persians and . . . why they went to war with each other' (Preface), written in the second half of the fifth century BC, are our best source for what classical Greeks believed about their past. He claims at one point (2. 53) that it was Homer and Hesiod, whom he places about 400 years before his own time (i.e. in the late ninth century BC), to whom the Greeks owed their knowledge of the gods. The discovery of the names of many of the classical gods in Linear B texts from the late Bronze Age has shown how false Herodotus' belief is. But this only shows the more clearly both the extent to which the world in which classical Greeks lived was a world constructed by literary texts and the limitations of classical memory and oral tradition.

Hesiod, who flourished around 700, was credited with a series of poems of which the two most important were an account of the creation of the world in terms of divine genealogy, entitled the *Theogony*, and a description of how to run a farmer's life properly, known as the *Works and Days*. Homer was credited not only with the *Iliad*, telling of the quarrel between Achilles and Agamemnon and its tragic consequences, and the *Odyssey*, telling of Odysseus' (Ulysses') eventful return journey from Troy to Ithaca, but also with other epics related to events at Troy and with a series of hymns to the major gods. The works attributed to Homer and Hesiod relate systematically the stories of only a few Greek heroes, but they provide an anchorage for a large part of what has come to be known as 'Greek mythology'; more importantly, they offer pictures of a world in which the larger-than-life figures of mythology face and cope with situations comparable to those facing ordinary people within the Greek city.

The form of the *Iliad* and *Odyssey* makes it clear that they are the product of a long poetic tradition stretching back into the Bronze Age; the content of Hesiod's poems, and of the *Theogony*, in particular, seems so closely related to traditions from the Near East as to make totally independent invention unlikely. In this way these foundational texts made fifth-century Greeks the inheritors not simply of a world of small communities with short and parochial histories, but of an extensive, if heavily pre-packaged, prehistory and of stories and ideas with deep roots in the wider Indo-European world to which they also owed their language. Greek politics may owe nothing to the great dynastic kingdoms of the Near East, but Greek forms of thought and means of expression could not have developed without those earlier developments further east.

The heroic Greece of the Homeric poems is already a Greece fragmented into independent city-states. These could he mobilized, partly by means of kinship ties between rulers, into co-operative reaction to a foreign threat (Paris' abduction of Helen, wife of Menelaus the ruler of Sparta), but they were competitive and maintained proud independence—as Achilles does when Agamemnon appropriates his share of Trojan War booty. Political succession in this world was insecure: Odysseus' son Telemachus cannot simply take over his father's power in Ithaca. But even as they quarrelled among themselves the élite kept themselves at a distance from the ordinary troops, as emerges when one of the rank-and-file, named Thersites, tries joining in the criticism of Agamemnon.

Homer's heroes fight above all for their honour, which they maintain by martial valour, by skill in speaking and acuity of political analysis, and by the ability to bestow valuable gifts on others. How one source of honour compares to another is subject to debate: Achilles refuses the recompense that others regard as sufficient repayment for the slight from Agamemnon, and he extorts revenge from the body of Hector for the death of his soulmate Patroclus that is signalled as excessive. Ends can be made to justify the means, and Odysseus' endless deceptions are redeemable by success, but some loyalty to kin and to friends is absolute, and so, when men are away from home, is loyalty to fellow countrymen ('citizens' is not yet the appropriate term).

Homer's account of warfare is highly stylized. At centre stage heroes, whose donning of heavy armour is described in intricate detail, fight duels in which there is space for taunting words, even for the exchange of armour when opposing warriors discover an old link between their families, and to and from which they travel in chariots. Actual encounters tend to be brief, and in many cases a single blow proves immediately fatal. Words and actions compete for attention in this account in which the actions of an individual hero are followed through in detail and the values that are at issue are openly paraded in challenges, petitions, and the ripostes to them. But in the background are the masses of the rank-and-file, raising clouds of dust as they march to battle and sustaining the conflict over a long battle line. This is warfare strongly shaped by convention, but also warfare where numbers count and everyone has a part to play.

Success or failure in war, as in other enterprises in Homer, depends upon the attitude taken by the gods. The gods debate amongst themselves the overall course of events, arguing for their own favourites and harbouring grudges or favour according to past actions which have pleased or displeased them. The gods also intervene directly, disguising themselves as humans in order to give messages and change the course of events, or even entering the battlefield—where they can be wounded. Men repeatedly assume that the gods will intervene on the side of the morally right, but the gods and goddesses are shown to he motivated more by self-interest than by morality; their world, like the world of men, is above all a world in which current actions are undertaken in response to past actions, but where only the cross-cutting interests of others ensure that the reciprocity is even vaguely balanced. When Poseidon wants to punish the people of Phaeacia for helping Odysseus (whom Poseidon hates for his blinding of the Cyclops) get home, Zeus has him turn only the returning Phaeacian ship to stone, and not destroy their whole city, but this does little to mitigate the reader's sense of injustice that a 'good turn' should be rewarded in this way.

Reciprocity similarly characterizes the behaviour of the gods in the poems of Hesiod. This comes out in the *Theogony's* account of the successive generations of gods, in which Cronos, who becomes top god by castrating his father Heaven, who will not allow his children to come to light, is himself ousted by Zeus after he tries to swallow his own children. But it is perhaps clearest of all in the accounts he gives to explain the miserable condition of humanity and why men have to toil to feed themselves when animals do not. Men have to toil for the means of life because Zeus hid it, and Zeus hid it as part of a succession of sanctions against the crafty Prometheus, who had forced the gods to choose between the fat and bones or the meat of sacrificial animals, and had made human retention of the meat useful by recapturing the fire which Zeus had then hidden. Throughout this story, which proceeds with Zeus creating Pandora, the first woman, beautiful but loaded with troubles for men, basic features of human life are explained as the result of a process of give and take with the gods, in which human attempts to alter their lot for the better always risk counter-measures from the gods.

But as in the Homeric poems, so also in Hesiod, the gods who often seem to act in an arbitrary fashion are portrayed within an overall framework that stresses the necessity of moral behaviour, the rewarding of the just and the punishment of the wicked. In the *Odyssey* creatures that are unsociable and obey no rules, such as the Cyclops, or flout the rules, like the suitors for the hand of Odysseus' wife Penelope, get outwitted and punished. In Hesiod's *Works and Days* the poet himself, although very aware that human agents of justice can act crookedly, urges his brother Perses to work hard and time his actions carefully on the basic assumption that prosperity is earned by good sense and hard work and is not a windfall gain. In both Homer and Hesiod, the temptation to believe that the world and its events are as arbitrary as they seem coexists with the desire to believe that there is a system after all. The gods are given an uneasy place between being free and being entirely determined agents.

The profound uncertainty that lies at the heart of Greek tragedy is deeply rooted not just in the text of the Homeric poems but in the world view that those poems and the poems of Hesiod exploit and explore. Many of the plots of tragedy are built around incidents connected with the *Iliad* in particular, and from at least the sixth century some painters of pots had similarly explored the poignant potential for building on the Homeric stories of Achilles, Ajax, and other heroes. Achilles, Agamemnon, and in a different way also Odysseus, are offered to the readers of the Homeric poems as men who combine fine moral qualities with moral short-sightedness: tragedy further explores the characters of Agamemnon and Odysseus in particular, and creates similar moral dilemmas for other heroes who in the archaic period seem to have lived less morally complicated lives. But whereas the Homeric poems explore dilemmas primarily on an individual level, classical tragedy, performed in a different political context, repeatedly makes the interests of the community an element in the moral equation.

In a similar way, classical Greek philosophy can also be seen to grow out of Homer and Hesiod. Out of Hesiod, as it seeks an alternative account of the origins of the world to his divine genealogy, and seeks an original state of the world that can be justified by argument, as Hesiod's own original Chaos (*Theogony* 116) is not. Out of both Hesiod and Homer, as it rejects whimsical gods and, while noting that it is simply because they are men that men think gods must look like men, insists that gods must live up to the moral standards expected of men. Out of Homer's heavy concentration on direct speech, on persuasion, and on the difficulty of knowing whether a speaker is telling the truth or not, as it turns the informal distinctions between types of communication that can be observed in epic into the formal categories that mark the beginning of the study of rhetoric. But here too, as with the development of tragedy, we are not dealing simply with a 'natural' development out of the earlier literature. The political importance of speaking before mass bodies created a new necessity for the analysis of rhetoric, and the frequency of public debate in general quickened the pace of critical thought in natural philosophy, ethics, and theology.

The pre-classical past: oral history

Although Herodotus opens his account of relations between Greece and Persia by putting the great war against Persia of the early fifth century into the context of hostile relations between Greece and Asia going back to such incidents as Paris' abduction of Helen, the great heroes of Greek myth make virtually no appearance in his work. His opening account of abduction and counter-abduction is in fact put into the mouth of the Persians, and throughout his work it is what people say about themselves and their past that provides Herodotus' primary data. And because political behaviour, the decision to fight, is his primary interest, it is stories about politics that dominate his work.

Herodotus is concerned with the big questions of political power and historical causation: what makes a city strong and what weak? what has determined the course of history? His answers to these questions are consonant with the model of the world offered by Homer and Hesiod. Events of today have a relationship with events of the past: no action is taken that does not also have a reaction, and the strong city is the city favoured by the gods which is also the city capable of concerted and regulated actions rather than the city that is disunited and subject to no law. Famously Herodotus suggests that it was giving equal rights to political participation to all (native free-born adult males) that enabled Athens to advance from a minor to a major power among Greek cities.

Herodotus' informants did not necessarily share his agenda. They told stories about the past not in order to make Greek success against Persia comprehensible but for local reasons, perhaps most frequently to justify their current political regime and their current allies and enemies. Cities with monarchs, like the Greek city of Cyrene in Libya, told stories about the remarkable achievements that led to the foundation of the monarchy; cities that had had monarchs and deposed them, like Corinth or Athens itself, adapted those stories to become stories of abuse that justified the deposition. Individual families told stories that claimed glorious deeds by ancestors and defended their past political record in the light of current political preferences.

The pressures on the past from those who told stories about it left it heavily patterned. The patterns in the accounts that have come down to us are partly created by Herodotus himself, partly by his informants, partly by the informants who lie behind the versions of past events we find in later historians, in the Athenian orators, or in the inscriptions which commemorated the past by reproducing what were claimed as past decisions. Every city could point to successes achieved with the explicit support of the gods, consulted through oracles, to rulers whose abuses led to their downfall and/or set-backs for the city as a whole, to acts of deception—in particular false claims to oracular backing or divine support—which had led to short-term but also short-lasting success, to law-givers who displayed their wisdom above all by the paradoxical means by which they achieved their ends. Behind this pattern, as behind the Homeric and Hesiodic poems, is an assumption of order and morality.

In his account of the history of Persia, Herodotus (3. 80–2) tells that after the death of the (bad) king Cambyses the Persians had a debate over whether to continue with monarchy or to adopt either oligarchy, in which political participation was restricted to the well-born or wealthy, or democracy (see further p. 115). The historicity of this debate is dubious, but it does accurately represent the choice that was set up for all Greek cities by the stories told about the past. The trouble with a sole ruler is presented as that he is subject to no control, that power corrupts and leads to savagery, and that the one who should be above envy in fact becomes jealous of the best men in the state. The trouble with rule by the people is that they are ignorant and irresponsible, capable of even greater violence than the sole ruler, and that factionalism inevitably means that one man ends up getting himself installed as ruler. The trouble with oligarchy is that the few who have power compete with each other and that this leads to conflict and bloodshed within the city. The tone of the debate is negative: it is allowed that democracy has the finest of all names, equality of rights, but all that is said in favour of oligarchy is that it is in the self-interest of those nobles who are holding the debate. This negativity is an almost inevitable product of a (Greek) world in which stories of the past are most often told for their cautionary effect.

The negative slant on the past even extends to figures whose own reputations are glowing. The Athenian Solon was responsible for formulating the law code for the city at the beginning of the sixth century which probably first gave some judicial power to the people and may well have transformed Athenian society by eliminating the enslavement of Athenians for debt. But Herodotus presents Solon not as a political reformer but as a wise man whose sagest advice is that no one should be called happy till he is dead.

It is this essentially negative view, not just of politics but of life, that classical Greeks inherited. The glorious past belonged in the age of heroes and was lost beyond recall; the real past was full of trickery, violence and abuse, both within individual cities and in relations between cities. Promises could not be trusted, and nothing was stable. That instability did indeed mean that improvement was always possible: Lycurgus the Spartan lawgiver was held to have turned his city round from being the most lawless to being the best governed, and with good government, success in inter-city relations had followed. But disadvantages were visible in all arrangements, and Sparta's most recent stories were of king Cleomenes (c.520–490), who invented oracles, broke sacred laws, damaged the property of the gods, and ended up mad, killing himself in a gruesome way. However handsome the façade might look at any moment, disaster was always waiting to happen.

The pre-classical past: the monuments

Herodotus (1. 66) tells that Sparta attempted at one time to conquer her northern neighbour Tegea and to enslave her people, as she had earlier enslaved the people of Messenia as helots, before turning to a policy of seeking alliance with her on the basis of common ancestry. He knows this episode to be true because he has seen, in the temple of Athena Alea at Tegea, the fetters which the Spartans had brought with them to use upon the conquered and which the Tegeans, successful in resisting their attack, had then used on their Spartan prisoners of war. The confirmation of a story by an object still visible in his day is a frequent motif in Herodotus: that the poet Arion, when thrown overboard by the Corinthian sailors with whom he was travelling, was carried to shore by a dolphin is confirmed by a statuette of a figure on a dolphin in the sanctuary of Poseidon at Taenarum; the wealth of the prostitute Rhodopis, freed from slavery in Egypt by the brother of the poet Sappho, is demonstrated by her dedication of spits at the sanctuary of Apollo at Delphi; the profit made by a Samian merchant named Colaeus after his ship, bound for Egypt, was blown through the straits of Gibraltar and ended up at Tartessus in south-west Spain, is shown by his dedication of a colossal bronze mixing-bowl at the sanctuary of Hera on Samos.

Because sanctuaries were repositories of dedications made by past generations, they were also repositories of stories. Unusual objects in sanctuaries demanded explanation, and found it in accounts of how they came there. Such accounts might preserve memories of events which would otherwise be forgotten; they might be used to confirm claims about the past which needed reinforcement; they might stimulate the fancy and lead to impressive fictions. One way or another they contributed to the rich resources that classical Greeks had to hand for thinking about the present.

The physical legacy of the past to the fifth century consisted not just of curious objects that had been dedicated to gods but of the temples which dominated sanctuaries and of texts displayed in them. From the first appearance of the Greek alphabet, invented on the model of the Phoenician alphabet probably in the eighth century, sanctuaries had attracted written texts. Men addressed their dedications to gods in writing, put up laws in sanctuaries to ensure divine oversight of them and deposited treaties in the presence of the gods to prevent their being lightly transgressed. Such inscriptions were liable to become difficult to read over time, both because the way individual letters were written changed, and because stones became eroded, but it seems that in Athens reference was still being made in the fifth century to Solon's law code, which was displayed on the Acropolis, and Thucydides (6. 54) tries to prove the correct sequence of the sons of the Athenian sixth-century ruler Pisistratus by reference to the inscription on the altar of Apollo Pythius by which Pisistratus' grandson commemorated his holding of the chief magistracy at Athens, the archonship, in 522/1—an inscription which still survives (Fomara 37).

Most classical cities told stories about how they got their laws, stories that invariably celebrated an individual lawgiver, not infrequently a man brought in from another city or who was held to have drawn ideas from elsewhere. This promotion of the lawgiver served, in part at least, to increase the standing of the laws: the more remarkable the lawgiver the more reluctant ordinary mortals should be to change his laws. Complete rewriting of law codes was rare in classical Greece, and even dramatic changes in constitution tended to be accomplished with the minimum of legislative change; when individuals established themselves as sole rulers they more normally ignored than changed the laws. Old laws were socially conservative, and the relics of old social institutions became embedded in them. Athenian litigants exploited the fact that many laws were old and phrased in peculiar ways in order to insist that the lawgiver really meant something that suited their own case: appeal to the lawgiver's intention became a major tool of legal argument.

Through the laws displayed in sanctuaries, the past reached forward to constrain the actions, and promote the ingenuity, of the classical present. In a similar way the temples and monumental sculptures that dominated those sanctuaries framed the classical view both of the gods and of humanity. Monumental stone temples were first constructed in the seventh century, and during the sixth century virtually every major sanctuary was transformed by the construction of one or more large temples. In Ionia the cities of Samos and Ephesus, and in Sicily the cities of Selinus and Acragas, each built temples more than 100m. long, 50m. wide, and with columns 12–15 m. high (in the case of Samos two successive such temples); Selinus, not content with a single massive temple built five further large temples in the course of the sixth century, with more to follow in the early fifth. Mainland cities were in general more moderate in the scale of their activity, but a temple of 41 × 108 m. was begun (but not finished) at Athens, whose acropolis saw two successive temples to Athena constructed within the sixth century, both richly adorned with sculpture. At the sanctuaries at Olympia and Delphi, widely visited by Greeks to participate in games at both and to consult the oracle at the latter, temple building was accompanied by the competitive building by various cities from the mainland and Sicily of small but ornate treasuries to contain precious dedications.

The architectural form set in the seventh and sixth centuries was to govern the appearance of Greek temples throughout the classical period and be heavily influential also on later Greek and Roman buildings. Temples were gabled buildings on a substantial base, usually oriented east–west, with columns at either end if small and columns all round if large. Within the colonnade was a rectangular structure containing a room in which the cult statue stood, and sometimes a further room in which temple treasures were stored. There were two basic types of column and associated patterns of architectural detailing, known as Ionic and Doric, and the classical period saw some innovation in the forms and combinations of these, but both the 'syntax' and the 'morphology' of classical architectural form were established by 500.

The same could be said for cult practices. Worship of the gods focused upon the altars generally found in front of the east façade of temples. On designated festival days a procession consisting of priests or priestesses and other sacred officials, the animals to be slaughtered, and the group on whose behalf the sacrifice was being offered, made its way to the altar. The animals were made to indicate their consent and then their throats were slit. A butcher divided up the victims, whose innards were grilled and whose flesh was either roasted or boiled, and the assembled group enjoyed the feast, taking away any remaining meat for subsequent consumption. In the case of deities connected closely with the earth, the so-called chthonic deities, no meat was taken away—sometimes the victim was entirely burnt up and there was no meat to be consumed. Already this pattern of religious activity is outlined in the Homeric poems, and the paradox that it is the human participants rather than the gods who get to enjoy the best parts of the sacrificed animal 'explained', as we have seen, in Hesiod's *Theogony*. Religious laws from the classical period arrange the details of processions, victims, and the distribution of meat to participants to achieve political ends, but animal sacrifice continued to have a 'pre-political' function, as both the culminating event of religious festivals and the prime source of meat for the inhabitants of the classical city.

Various rituals further elaborated Greek festivals: cult statues might be washed or adorned with new garments, secret objects might be moved from one place to another or displayed to initiates, and so on. The most important of the elaborations, however, was the addition of competitions in athletic and/or cultural prowess. From at least the eighth century—according to claims by a fifth-century scholar, from 776—races had been part of the festival of Zeus at Olympia, and during the seventh and sixth centuries further athletic events had been added. The quadrennial Olympic games became the biggest event in the calendar for élite families from all over the Greek world, the place at which a city ruler might advertise for a husband for his daughter and the place to show off both individual and city wealth. Victory at Olympia brought no direct financial prize, but it gave enormous prestige; cities gave special rights to citizens who scored success in the games, rights that ranged from free meals to a special place in the battle line. In the fifth century stories were told at Athens of a man who attempted to seize power on the basis of the kudos an Olympic victory had brought him, and of another who first ascribed a victory to the jealous ruler Pisistratus in an attempt to curry favour, and was then secretly executed by Pisistratus' sons when his successes became too persistent. In the early sixth century other sanctuaries had established lookalike games, so that every year there was a major athletic event to which competitors came from all Greek cities.

Festivals provided opportunities not only for competition between cities but for competition within cities. At Athens from the middle of the sixth century the major festival of Athena featured athletic events, including team events, and also competitions for the recitation of the Homeric poems. Later in the century the festival of Dionysus, known as the Great or City Dionysia, acquired a dramatic competition which involved the performance first of just tragedies and then later of both tragedy and comedy over several days. In the later sixth century the Athenians added competitions to more and more festivals, multiplying the number and variety of opportunities citizens had for displaying prowess and earning both reputation and monetary rewards. Classical alterations to festivals—such as the addition of a parade of tribute-paying allies to an Athenian festival in the middle of the fifth century—exploited possibilities that were already there, rather than creating a radically new pattern of activity.

If there was a revolution in the world of the sanctuary, a way in which the monuments of classical Greece broke with the pattern established by the monuments of archaic Greece, it was in sculpture. Some sort of cult statue representing the god or goddess whose sanctuary it was seems to have been found already in the temples of the eighth century. Small bronze figurines of men were also dedicated to deities in that century, along with rather more numerous figures of cattle and sheep, animals which were sacrificed, and birds and horses, animals which were not. From the end of the following century, sanctuaries also saw life-sized or more than life-sized stone figures, partly inspired by Egyptian practices. These standing figures came to be dedicated in very large numbers indeed: we know of more than a hundred at the sanctuary of Apollo Ptoieus in Boeotia.

Most of these large stone statues took a very stereotyped form: the statues of men showed them naked with one foot slightly advanced and their arms by their sides; the statues of women showed them clothed and with an offering in one hand. Although in the course of the sixth century these statues came to make more detailed reference to the precise appearance of men and women, and although when occasionally used as markers on graves statues of this form were in some sense associated with an individual, these *kouroi* and *korai*, as they are called, were never lifelike representations of the appearance of particular men or women. Rather they owed their popularity and usefulness to the rather generalized reference that they made to the males and females of the human species. There were statues of different forms, including men carrying animals to sacrifice and men mounted on horses, but they too were generic rather than specific in their reference.

Classical dedications abandoned the stereotyped *kouros* and *kore* form as they also abandoned stone as the medium. Bronze statues dominated the new sculptural range in sanctuaries, and men might now appear engaged in athletics or music or equipped with helmet and spear. But most importantly, although they did not become portraits, they did become individualized; the detailed reference to taut or slack flesh, the keenness or languidity of eye, the poise and balance of the figure, all encourage the viewer to attribute to the statue the qualities (age, physical fitness) and even the thoughts and passions of a living individual. To enter a sixth-century sanctuary was to enter a forest of symbols; to enter a sanctuary in the middle of the fifth century was to enter a world of living people. Here was an area where the development of new technical resources (in particular through bronze-casting), aided perhaps by the massive destruction of old monuments at Athens as a result of the Persian invasion, made for a real break between the classical Greek world and its archaic past.

City and nation

Few pots made in previous centuries can have been visible or known to Greeks of the fifth century. Pots used in a domestic context got broken and discarded, pots dedicated in sanctuaries got periodically cleared up and deposited out of sight, and pots placed in graves were necessarily invisible. The well-preserved Greek pots of the sixth and fifth centuries in museums today are the ones recovered from graves, and in particular from graves in Italy. Our access to archaic pottery enables us, however, to see more clearly developments that the oral traditions and upstanding monuments from the period rendered less strongly visible to Greeks themselves.

Until into the seventh century production of fine pottery was widespread through mainland Greece and the islands. Archaeologists can distinguish different regional schools of production by their preferences for certain shapes, by their use of certain subsidiary patterns, and by their choice of figure scenes and the way the figures are depicted. Pottery certainly did move about the Greek world; even back in the eleventh century a new pottery style developed in Athens, and known by archaeologists as Protogeometric, had stimulated lookalike rival products in the Peloponnese, the Cyclades, Thessaly, and Asia Minor. But until the seventh century access to other traditions seems simply to have encouraged local endeavours. From the seventh century onwards this changes and Greek pottery begins to pick up motifs from the east as well as from other Greek cities. Corinth, partly by latching onto the fashion for perfumed oil, itself a habit acquired from the east, established itself as the major fine pottery supplier for the rest of the Greek world. A century later Athenian potters, specializing in larger vessels that could be used for drinking parties, captured the market, driving out even Corinthian products. By the fifth century virtually nowhere in the Greek world apart from Athens was producing really fine pottery.

Even the finest pottery was not expensive, and the economic benefit to Athens from the Athenian near-monopoly was probably not great, but this humble product does serve to indicate how the Greek world was coming to be less diverse, more conscious of what cities had in common. A similar story, in which eastern influence plays a major part in establishing a prevailing type, and individual cities cease to produce distinct products, can be told about Greek sculpture and architecture. Greek temple building in stone seems to have been inspired by the cut-stone architecture of Egypt, and the schools of architecture that developed—Doric on the mainland (with a variation played in Sicily and South Italy), Ionic in Asia Minor, a quite distinct Doric style in the Cyclades—were broadly regional, not city-specific. Regional differences can also be noted in stone sculpture from the first appearance of monumental stone statues of standing men and women, again directly inspired by Egyptian work, in the late seventh century, but there is much evidence that both sculptors and their works moved about the Greek world and that the market did not at all respect city boundaries.

The uses of mythology make it clear that cities sought to find a place for themselves as part of a larger whole. Even while promoting distinct styles in fine pottery, the demand seems to have been for scenes which related to stories and heroes with little or no local connection, not for myths of particular local relevance. The great Homeric epics are remarkably lacking in local enthusiasms, even though Ionia claimed Homer's birthplace; any city that chose to make special its major festival by having performances of Homeric epic, as Athens did, was forgoing the chance to promote its own particular history and mythology, and choosing to celebrate Greek rather than, in this case, Athenian achievements.

The diversity and disunity of early Greece is a major theme in the discussion that opens Thucydides' History of the Peloponnesian War between Athens and Sparta at the end of the fifth century. Thucydides argues that that war was the greatest Greece had known because earlier disunity had meant that never before had the whole Greek world been involved in a single conflict. Thucydides accounts for the parochial nature of early Greek history in terms of the early poverty of the land, and the subsequent self-interest of sole rulers whose ambitions were limited to providing for their own comfort. What made fifth-century Greece different was partly the strong constitution and ambitious government in Sparta, which brought about the end of sole rule elsewhere, but more important was the outside threat of Persia, which impelled unprecedented numbers of Greek states to join together to face the Persian invasion.

Greek cities had become aware of the Persian empire and the threat that it posed when the Persians had conquered the kingdom of Lydia in the middle of the sixth century and had become the overlords of the Greeks of Asia Minor. It became apparent that the Persians were actively looking to extend their empire in this direction when they tried to conquer the land of the Scythians to the north of the Black Sea in the penultimate decade of the sixth century. If a not very well co-ordinated revolt by Ionian Greeks against the Persians in the 490s precipitated the first attempt to invade the Greek mainland in 490, it can only have hastened what will already have seemed to many to be inevitable.

Some Greeks had profited from the Persian overlordship of Ionia. Persia liked to work through native agents, and at the end of the sixth century most Greek cities of Asia Minor were controlled by Greek rulers who owed their position to the Persians. For the élite of a small city facing an enormous empire there was effectively little choice: collaboration with Persia offered the only way to preserve personal status. For Persia, working with the willing was preferable to repressing the unwilling, and the internal divisions that promoting a single man or family to pre-eminence were bound to cause would only make a city the easier to rule.

That there is a history of classical Greece to be written, and that that history can be the first volume of a history of Europe, depends, as Thucydides saw, on two momentous events. It depends on the Persian invasions being repulsed by an alliance of Greek cities that was sufficiently large to enable it, when victorious, to present its story as the story of the Greeks as a whole (see below, p. 173). That in turn depends upon the second factor: the development in a body of Greek cities of constitutional government such that individual self-interest could be subordinated to the interests of the whole community (see below, Chapter 3), and a war against impossible odds could seem worth undertaking.

It is at Athens that we know the story of the development of constitutional government best, and it is the story of Athens that has central place in Herodotus' account of how the Greeks defeated the Persians. It is also at Athens that we can best witness the cultural flowering that has inspired classical Greece the icon. Athens—the urban centre, together with its surrounding countryside, known as Attica—was peculiarly large, in area (2,400 square km.) and in population (perhaps 50,000 adult male citizens and 300–400,000 total residents by the middle of the fifth century); Athens was peculiarly rich, by virtue of the silver mines at Laurium in the southern part of Attica (see below, pp. 35–9); Athens was also peculiarly well placed, geographically, to dominate others.

What happened in Athens and what Athens achieved, however, depended crucially on her being part of the wider Greek world. Athens had not been politically or culturally dominant during the archaic period. Socrates and Plato were Athenians by birth, but Heraclitus, Democritus, Aristotle, and Theophrastus were not: Athenians had no monopoly over the development of philosophy (see below, p. 182). Phidias and Praxiteles were Athenian, but the other painters and sculptors who dominate ancient accounts of the history of classical art—Polyclitus, Polygnotus, Zeuxis, Apelles, Scopas, and Lysippus—were not: Athens had no monopoly over developments in the visual arts. All the complete extant tragedies and comedies are by Athenian poets, but the remains of poetry celebrating victories in games are dominated by Pindar, a Theban, and Bacchylides from the island of Ceos, the remains of the showy choral poetry known as dithyramb by Timotheus from Miletus: only part of the song-culture of classical Greece was monopolized by Athenians. Unpicking the enigma that is classical Greece demands that we delve into the history of Greece as a whole, not of Athens alone.

The programme of this book

This chapter has attempted to indicate both the physical nature of the Greek world and the ways in which the achievements of the past and the stories about those achievements encouraged certain attitudes and created certain expectations in the people of classical Greece. In the chapters that follow we explore what Greeks of the fifth and fourth century made of those constraints and opportunities as they secured their material well-being, organized, and theorized, their communal life, both as individual cities and in competition with one another, and forged their distinct lifestyle. In the final two chapters we explore the dynamic created by the complex of interactions between individuals and cities and try to show how events were shaped by and fed back into the culture of the city. If the enigma of classical Greece resists final solution, we hope at least to have taken the icon out of the gallery and put it back into context, so that it ceases to be part of the deadening weight of tradition and becomes once more an effective inspiration.

2

The economy

Paul Millett

The political economy of Attic Oratory

What could be more natural than for a farmer to increase the productivity of his land by grubbing up an old tree stump? The dangers involved in such an apparently uncontroversial act were brought home to an Athenian citizen of the early fourth century who, far from being rewarded for good husbandry, found himself in court facing exile, loss of property, or possibly death. His opponents alleged that he had torn out no ordinary tree, but the stump of an olive tree which was sacred to the goddess Athena.

Scattered through Attica (the rural hinterland of Athens) were sacred olive trees which were supposedly propagated from an ancient tree on the Acropolis, the gift of Athena herself. Complex regulations governed the collection of oil from these trees, destined to be given as prizes to athletes victorious in the Panathenaic Games ([Aristotle], *Constitution of the Athenians* 60; see below, p. 76). Every year, the Council of the Areopagus received reports from inspectors on the state of Athena's olives, with fines for farmers who cultivated too close to them. Even stumps of apparently dead trees were protected in case they produced new growth. It was such a stump, complete with its enclosure, that our citizen stood accused of uprooting and carting away. The case was heard before the Council of the Areopagus, in its capacity as a law-court (see below pp. 126–7). The law of Athens ordained, at least in theory, that the appropriate penalty was death.

In his defence the accused produced as witnesses three previous cultivators who rented the land from him, testifying that there was no such sacred stump (Lysias 7. 9–10). He also protested that any petty financial gain would be far outweighed by possible repercussions against him: his action would have been open for all his neighbours to see—and some of them were at odds with him over his property (7. 18–19). Furthermore, such an act of impiety would have put him at the mercy of his slaves (doing all the hard work on the stump), who could at any time have gained their freedom by informing against him. For the rest of his life, he reminds the jury, he would have had to refrain from punishing them (7. 16). Moreover, the general tenor of his life as a citizen refutes the accusation against him: he has paid his property tax and performed expensive public services (so-called 'liturgies'): equipping triremes, and sponsoring choruses in Athens' dramatic festivals (7. 30–2).

In Athenian courts, litigants presented their own cases in the form of more-or-less extended speeches which were delivered in their own words. Such was the theory of it; but, in reality, those who could afford it, employed a professional speechwriter (*logographos*) who crafted a suitable speech to be learnt by heart. Our defendant was wealthy or desperate enough to secure the services of Lysias, the greatest *logographos* of his day. The source for our litigant's trials and tribulations is the seventh speech of Lysias called (predictably) *On the Olive Stump.*

It is on this and a further 158 speeches, making up the so-called corpus of the Attic Orators, that historians are largely dependent for their detailed reconstruction of economy and society in classical Greece. Other types of testimony, including drama, narrative histories, political pamphlets, philosophy, inscriptions, and archaeology naturally have their parts to play; but the speeches of the Orators (in particular, law-court speeches) form the basis of the exploration of the Greek economy that follows. Although this approach enables economic history to be seen, as it were, in the making, it has clear implications for the scope of our analysis.

1. As the label suggests, Attic Oratory is exclusively an Athenian phenomenon with nothing comparable surviving from any other Greek state. Any account of the ancient Greek economy in practice becomes an analysis of the economy of Athens. Classical Athens was in crucial ways unique and cannot straightforwardly stand proxy for other Greek states. In particular, the experience of empire in the fifth century and the extension of democratic stability (probably interlinked) make for distinctive economic relationships. Where possible, however, contrasts may be drawn with what little is known of other

Greek economies. An idiosyncratic case in point is the Spartan 'command economy', which met agricultural needs through direct exploitation by the Spartiate élite of the state-owned workforce of helots. Money in Sparta took the deliberately cumbersome form of iron spits: accumulated wealth was meant to be conspicuous.

2. Dependence on Attic Oratory places chronological limits on any analysis. Broadly speaking, law-court speeches extend from the late fifth century (*c.*420) down to the destruction of the democracy in 321. Extrapolation beyond these boundaries on the basis of other types of testimony is possible but precarious. Moreover, for any integrated reconstruction to be feasible, there is the necessary but defensible assumption that, between the end of the Peloponnesian War (404) and the ending of democracy, fundamental economic practices and relationships within Athens remained broadly static. As elsewhere in the Greek world, warfare and possibly bad harvests provided the major factors making for short-run disequilibrium and change (see below, p. 97).

3. Speeches of the Attic Orators owe their survival to their status through antiquity as outstanding examples of rhetoric (some 930 speeches were known to the Romans). This has implications for the historian. With few exceptions, the speeches stand in isolation so that we know nothing of opponents' arguments or even the jurors' verdict. Such is the case with *On the Olive Stump*, where we are also left in ignorance of the name of the litigant. We may hope that surviving speeches cover a representative range of subject matter, but litigants who could afford the services of a distinguished *logographos* would tend to come from the upper end of society. The speaker in *On the Olive Stump* is one of many litigants who emphasizes to the jury his expenditure on public services, placing him in the top few per cent of the citizen body.

4. Although we are at the mercy of the litigants as to what they choose to include and leave out, the case as presented (irrespective of innocence or guilt) must have seemed plausible to a jury chosen by lot, normally numbered in hundreds, and broadly representative of the citizen body as a whole (see below, pp. 64 and 136–7). In this way, it becomes possible as it were to 'read between the lines' and draw inferences about socio-economic attitudes and institutions prevailing in fourth-century Athens. So *On the Olive Stump* serves to highlight *inter alia* the use of slaves in agriculture (at least by the Athenian

élite), the importance of neighbours (who, the speaker says, not only know what is open for all to see but get information of what we try to keep hidden), the role of wealthy Athenians in paying direct taxes and providing public services (his liturgies, deployed as evidence of good character), and the possibility of buying and renting land in Athens (not all land is to be thought of in terms of inalienable ancestral estates).

Perhaps most striking is the way in which *On the Olive Stump* combines in a narrow compass key aspects of the life of the polis ('city-state'). Appropriately enough, *oikonomia* (our word 'economics') derives from the business of managing the individual households (*oikoi*) that were the building blocs of the polis. Aristotle in Book One of his *Politics* (an exposition of the nature of the polis-state) builds on the *oikos*, with its family, land, property and slaves, as the primary context for the acquisition and accumulation of wealth. Whatever the realities behind the case in question, the minor economic act of uprooting an olive tree turned out to have religious implications, legal repercussions, and possibly political ramifications: the speaker seems to protest too much in distancing himself from the recent lawlessness of the Thirty Tyrants (7. 27) (for whom see below, pp. 121–2 and 130). All this exemplifies a crucial theme of the Greek polis economy: the extent to which economy, culture, and society were blended to create an economic system that was, in the broadest sense, political.

Back to the land

Our initial encounter with the Greek economy, through the Orators, is deliberately one that involves agriculture, at the heart of ancient economy and society. Although the city of Athens and the associated harbour complex of Piraeus (itself a sizeable town) combined to create the most urbanized community in the Aegean world, perhaps half the total population depended directly on farming for its livelihood. Xenophon in his treatise *On Estate Management* (*Oeconomicus*) chose to manipulate agricultural themes, familiar to his élite readers, as the basis of moral lessons: 'The earth willingly teaches right behaviour to those who can learn' (5. 12). Several of

Aristophanes' popular heroes may loosely be classed as 'peasants' (in *Acharnians, Peace, Clouds, Wealth*). *On the Olive Stump* provides a vivid vignette of the wealthy landowner, beset by hostile neighbours, suspicious of his slaves, and wanting so far as possible (as he puts it) to 'avoid law-suits and public affairs by leading a quiet life'.

Two points of general interest emerge from the speech (7. 24). The speaker refers in passing to 'the other plots of land' which he owns on the plain of Attica. This fragmentation of holdings would seem to be the norm, at least for larger landholders: ownership of several pieces of land, more or less scattered (see below). Any inefficiency, in terms of wasted time, was compensated for by reducing risk of crop losses through exploitation of the local or 'micro-climates' associated with a semi-mountainous terrain. Secondly, the litigant casually mentions how many olive trees are distributed over his various properties. The impression, confirmed by other evidence, is of so-called 'polyculture': making maximum use of available land by growing a mixture of crops (grain, pulses, olives, vines) on the same plot. Again, additional demands on labour time would be compensated for by minimizing the risk of losing an entire crop. The importance of growing a wide range of crops has been confirmed by the comparative evidence of modern practice on the isolated peninsula of Methana in the NE Peloponnese. 'Here we have a little of everything', as one inhabitant put it.

Overriding concern with spreading of risk meant that crop special-ization would be rare. Olives are rightly regarded as a key crop in Greece and Attica. Apart from providing food, fuel for lighting and a substitute for soap, Athenian olive oil, being of superior quality, was exported as a semi-luxury. But, even here, there is no evidence for crop specialization. For at least ten years after planting, until the root system became established, olives needed irrigation; thereafter, extraction of the oil remained labour-intensive. Such may have been the thinking behind the apparently inconvenient scattering of sacred olive trees throughout Attica: some would survive. But even Athenians could not live by olives alone. For evidence of other, staple crops, we turn to a second law-court speech: *Against Phaenippus Concerning an Exchange of Properties*, written by Demosthenes (42) for an unnamed litigant in the mid-fourth century.

The circumstances of the speech illustrate the politicizing of eco-nomic activity characteristic of democratic Athens. A citizen who felt he was being unfairly burdened by a liturgy might nominate a substitute, supposedly wealthier citizen to take his place. If the latter refused, he might be challenged by the former to a complete exchange of properties (*antidosis*). In this way, in theory at least, public services would end up being performed by the wealthiest citizens, without the need for the cumbersome and inaccurate registration of property. In reality, challenges to exchange properties understandably resulted in angry dissent among the Athenian élite: the jurors sat back and enjoyed the fun.

In *Against Phaenippus* the unnamed speaker accuses his opponent of having concealed the resources of his extensive landed estate. In the course of the denunciation, it transpires that Phaenippus allegedly has on his property not one but two threshing floors (42. 6), and has stored up more than a thousand measures of barley and eight hundred of wine to be sold off respectively, he claims (42. 20), at eighteen and twelve drachmas per thirty-kilogram and fifty-litre measure respectively (famine prices!). In addition, a team of six donkeys carries away timber through the year to the tune of twelve drachmas per day (42. 7). The speaker's failure to mention wheat, the other staple grain, may be significant. Although wheat was preferred over barley for consumption, it was a drought-sensitive crop and Attica was one of the driest parts of Greece. In the absence of irrigation (applied systematically only to fruits and vegetables), modern figures for rainfall suggest loss of the wheat crop in ancient Attica one year in four (barley, 1 in 20). Possibly Phaenippus grew and kept wheat for his own table, cultivating for sale the less esteemed but hardier barley; or perhaps it was a bad year (see below, p. 150).

Making allowance for forensic exaggeration, Phaenippus, with an implied annual income of around 30,000 drachmas, emerges as a very wealthy man in a world where a skilled workman might earn two drachmas per day (when work was available). In confirmation, it is stated that he is a keen breeder of horses (42. 24): *the* élite pastime, possible only with access to plenty of good pasture. The city of Athens depended in large but disputed measure on Phaenippus and his like to supply it with food (see below), and to provide, from profits gained in the market-place, public services and property taxes.

Large landowners were, however, in a tiny minority compared with the independent smallholders of Attica (some of them tenants), who are largely invisible in law-court speeches. Perhaps closest comes the unnamed speaker in Demosthenes' speech *Against Callicles* (45), embroiled with his neighbour in the country in a dispute over flood-damage. Otherwise, the rustic characters of Aristophanes' plays, combined with the early archaic testimony of Hesiod's poem *Works and Days* and hints from archaeology, form a fragile basis for generalization about non-élite agriculture (see above, p. 6). It seems reasonable to suppose that, of necessity given the size of their holdings (as little as four or five acres), less use was made of fallow, and the hoe may have taken the place of ox and plough. Although most households will have had the occasional pig, goat, and sheep (essential for sacrifice), larger herds were, like Phaenippus' six donkeys, the preserve of the wealthy. Scope for manuring was correspondingly reduced (see above, p. 4). In other ways, however, large and lesser landholders seem similarly to have combined elementary technology with practices (such as extensive storage of crops) aimed at minimizing risk, but balanced by low yield and high effort (see above, p. 27).

A fair bit of the extra effort was borne by compulsory labour. Commonplace throughout Greece was the exploitation in agriculture of submerged groups in the population; the helots of Sparta (handing over perhaps half their produce) are the best known but by no means the only example: *penestai* in Thessaly, *klarotai* and *oiketai* in Crete, and many more. In Attica, the legislation of Solon, early in the sixth century, had made illegal the formal subordination of poorer to richer Athenians ([Aristotle], *Constitution of the Athenians* 6). This may in part explain the extensive use, unique to Athenian agriculture, of the labour of chattel-slaves, extending (if Aristophanes' plays are to be believed) down through society to poorer landholders. At harvest time, additional labour would be hired and/or use made of neighbours on a reciprocal basis. With different emphases, all cultivators will have aimed at self-sufficiency (*autarkeia*), which paradoxically involved production of a surplus to be exchanged for cash. The élite needed abundant liquid resources to support an appropriate lifestyle (including tax and liturgy payments), and all had to purchase items such as iron tools which were needed for, but not susceptible to, do-it-yourself.

Although there is a natural tendency to contrast urban and rural economies, the distinction in the case of Athens was blurred. In simple terms, a proportion of cultivators may have lived in the city, either (if wealthy) leaving the day-to-day management of their land to overseers, or themselves walking out to work it on a regular basis. In Lysias' speech *On the Murder of Eratosthenes* (1), a wayward wife is able to welcome her lover into the town house because her husband is often away, working on his farm. Problems begin when, one day, he arrives home unexpectedly. Although most smallholders lived away from the city, they congregated in villages or townships ('demes') rather than inhabiting isolated farmsteads (see below, p. 72). The need for mutual support in a potentially hostile environment (to say nothing of the advantage of a secure water supply) made it desirable to have neighbours close at hand. The whole of Menander's comedy *The Bad Tempered Man* pivots on the perverseness of an individual who tries to cut himself off from the wider community; unsuccessfully, as he falls down a well and needs someone to pull him out.

All citizens living in Attica maintained political, religious, and possibly economic links with the city. Apart from serving in the army or navy during the slack season for farming, cultivators might be engaged (possibly with their draft animals) in public building projects. More generally, there was the draw of the city as a political and market centre (see below, p. 72). The philosopher Theophrastus wrote his *Characters* in the later fourth century as an illustration by contraries of acceptable behaviour in the polis. It consists of thirty caricatures of the kinds of disagreeable individuals (all male) who might be met on the streets of Athens; one of whom is the *agroikos* or Rustic (4). Among other things, he is guyed in terms which embrace city and countryside, attending the assembly and making use of city services.

He drinks pungent soup before attending the assembly and swears that no perfume smells so sweet as thyme . . . He doesn't trust his friends and relations but asks advice on the most important matters from his slaves. He describes all the affairs of the assembly to hired hands on his farm . . . In the streets, he doesn't enjoy or gawp at anything, but stands in rapt attention at the sight of a cow, a donkey, or a goat . . .

If he has lent someone a plough, basket, sickle, or bag, he goes to ask for it back in the middle of the night . . . And when he is going to the city, he asks anyone he meets about the price of hides and salt fish . . . and he says right away that, when he gets there, he's going to get his hair cut, have his shoes resoled, get some salt fish along the way from Archias, and have a good sing in the public baths.

From the shop floor

The piece of land of olive-stump fame had, within the space of fifteen years (411–396), four different owners (one for only two months) and three further tenants: one of them a freed slave (7. 4, 9–10). This implies a degree of economic fluidity and even opportunism that gains credibility from the configurations of at least the wealthier households. The speeches written by Isaeus, involving disputed inheritances, are hardly the most readable bits of Attic Oratory; but they preserve valuable details of the composition of the estates at issue. The estates of Ciron (8. 35) and Stratocles (9. 42–3) break down as follows:

Farm at Phyla (15 or so miles north of city)	6,000 dr.
House at Athens (lived in by Ciron)	2,000
House 'near Dionysus in the Marshes' (rented out)	1,300
Slaves (generating income)	– – – –
Three female (domestic) slaves	– – – –
Furniture (value given includes slaves)	1,300
Sums of money ('not inconsiderable') lent at interest	– – – –

Farm at Thria (close to Eleusis, leased out)	15,000 dr.
House at Melite (in the city, rented out)	3,000
House at Eleusis (c.10 miles NW of city; rented out)	500
Furniture, sheep, barley, wine, fruits	4,900
Cash in hand	900
Loans without interest	1,000
Loans at interest	4,000

Notable is the range of income-earning assets: land and houses predominate, but there are also money out on loan and income-earning slaves. This arguably reflects not so much economic rationalism as piecemeal opportunism; an hypothesis strengthened by the physical *fragmentation* of élite households, with property held in various demes across Attica (compare the evidence of the Attic Stelae, below). The pattern is reinforced by the summary, preserved in Aeschines' speech *Against Timarchus* (1), of the estate of the father of Timarchus, whose properties were located as far afield from the city as Cephisia (12 km. NE) and the mining area (50 km. S). Aeschines provides the jury with a blow-by-blow account of how this extensive if scattered estate was broken up and sold piecemeal in order to evade (not avoid) liability for liturgies (1. 97–105). Irresponsible handling of one's patrimony chimed in with the sexual deviance (homosexual prostitution) and incompetence in public affairs of which Timarchus stood accused by his political opponent, Aeschines (1. 30).

Details are forthcoming of the income-earning slaves owned by Timarchus' father: ' . . . nine or ten slaves who were skilled shoemakers each of whom paid a rent of two obols per day and the overseer of the workshop three obols. Besides these there was a woman skilled in flax working, who produced fine goods for the market, and also a man skilled in embroidery' (see below, p. 146). This indicates how larger-scale manufacturing might have been organized. Here, the slaves (at least, the shoemakers) seem to have 'lived apart', organized by a third party and paying over a flat rate to their owner.

The estate of Demosthenes' father was almost unique in containing, at his death, no real property save the family house (valued at 30 minas). His slave manufacturers were part of the household itself and integrated into the family accounts. Says the son, in one of five speeches attempting to recover his embezzled inheritance (27–31), 'My father, men of the jury, left two workshops, both doing a large business. One was a sword manufactory, employing thirty-two or thirty-three slaves, most of them worth five or six minas each . . . The other was a couch manufactory, employing twenty slaves, given to my father as security for a debt for forty minas. These brought him a clear income of twelve minas' (27. 9). Elsewhere he speaks indiscriminately of his guardians 'making the slaves disappear' and 'making the workshop disappear'. In line with opportunist acquisition of assets is the apparently fortuitous way in which Demosthenes' father gained his couch manufacturers—as security on a defaulted debt.

These are almost the largest known holdings of manufacturing slaves from Athens and Greece; Lysias and his brother had, at the close of the Peloponnesian War, a shield-manufactory employing anything up to 120 slaves (12. 19). At the other end of the scale were artisans working either alone or alongside just one or two slaves. One thinks of the shopkeepers and craftsmen in and around the Agora with whom Socrates passed the time of day. Evidence of archaeology suggests for them shops-cum-houses-cum-workshops barely large enough for a small family with a slave or two. In a speech attributed to Lysias (24. 6), a disabled shoemaker appeals to the Council of Five Hundred for a means-tested pension, adducing in support of his poverty that he is 'not yet able' to acquire anyone (meaning a slave) to help him in his work. As with agriculture, slave ownership in the city extended well down the social scale. Considerations of status out-weighed what we might call economic rationality.

Any additional, regular labour over and above the artisan and his immediate family would be supplied by slave- and not wage-labour. 'Those who can afford it buy slaves so that they may have fellow-workers', asserts Xenophon's Socrates, assuming agreement (*Memorabilia* 2. 3. 3). Wage-labour was essentially casual labour, as employed at harvest time (see above). Elsewhere, Xenophon shows Socrates encountering the once wealthy Aristarchus whom the civil war of 403 has robbed of revenues from land and house property (2. 7). Socrates has to exert all his powers of argument to persuade Aristarchus to make ends meet by putting to work as weavers the numerous female relatives who, having sought refuge with him, are eating their heads off. In the course of the dialogue, Socrates lists various Athenians who apparently make a good living by exploiting the non-agricultural labour of slaves (making pearl barley, baking bread, running up capes and cloaks).

What plainly troubles Aristarchus is the notion of free women weaving not for domestic consumption (the norm), but for sale. Once his scruples have been overcome, the household is simply and successfully converted from domestic to petty commodity produc-tion. The ease of the transformation ties in with the rudimentary nature of most manufacturing, exploiting basic technology, which is not to say that a high degree of skill was not involved. Support for this low level of capitalization comes from the circumstances of Hyperides' speech *Against Athenogenes*: a cautionary tale of sex and shopkeeping.

Epicrates, an Athenian citizen, was consumed with desire for a slave boy owned by one Athenogenes, a perfume manufacturer. At the prompting of Athenogenes, the boy, aided and abetted by a siren-like courtesan named Antigone, persuaded Epicrates to buy him along with his father and brother for forty minas: the three of them made up the work-force of the perfumery. Deprived of his work-force, Athenogenes offered to throw in the perfume business, arguing that the value of the raw materials would easily cover any trifling sums owed. In his eagerness to clinch the deal, Epicrates failed (as he disarmingly confesses) to read the small print and subsequently found himself besieged with creditors demanding repayment of five talents. Reading between the lines, Athenogenes' perfume business consisted of the slave work-force, stocks of raw materials, perhaps a stall on the market and little else.

Perfume manufacturers loom surprisingly large in our surviving sources: they had a fixed place in the Athenian Agora where the *jeunesse dorée* congregated (see below). The cultural significance of perfume combined with its status as a luxury good to ensure a profitably elastic demand: you can't have too much of a good thing. Not so, it seems, with mundane goods: the pots, pans, couches, tables, chairs, shoes, clothing, and so on needed in the everyday business of life. Xenophon points to the potential problem of inadequate demand (*Education of Cyrus* 8. 2. 5):

In small towns, the same workman makes chairs and doors and ploughs and tables, and often this same artisan builds houses; and even so he is thankful if he can only find enough employment to support him. And it is of course impossible for a man of many trades to be proficient in all of them. In large cities, on the other hand, inasmuch as many people have demands to make on each branch of manufacturing, one trade alone, and often less than a whole trade, is enough to support a man.

He goes on to cite the case of shoemaking, with different individuals cutting out separate parts of each shoe. Not that this is to be confused with the division of labour in the pin-factory with which Adam Smith's *Wealth of Nations* famously opens. Xenophon is here concerned not with enhanced productivity but the quality of the product. The context of his comment is the superior quality of the food in the palace of the Persian King. Also, Xenophon's argument is based on the assumption that demand would not normally be boosted by access to markets external to the city.

Athens of course qualified as a 'large city': in the classical period, there was none larger; but there were still constraints on effective demand. In our own capitalist society, economies are in large part driven by aggregate household demand. In the Greek world, household demand for purchased goods was restricted by both the drive for self-sufficiency, as noted above, and also by practical limitations. Houses, even of the wealthy, tended to be comparatively small with basic furnishings. As Xenophon puts it, 'When someone has enough furniture for his house, he stops buying it there and then' (*Poroi* 4. 7). Absent were the 'consumer durables' that have become such a feature of our post-war homes. In the Greek world, their place both as status symbols and labour-saving devices seems to have been taken by slaves.

Something of the differing emphasis on real property, slaves, and portable property comes across from the so-called Attic Stelae (Fornara 147). These are a battered collection of inscriptions, found in the Agora, recording the sale of property at auction of the fifty or so individuals (mostly wealthy) found guilty of mutilating the Herms in 415 (see below, p. 193). The fragments which survive are difficult to interpret; items are omitted which did not need to be sold off: cash and precious metals could be added directly to the Treasury. But what remains striking is the gap between the abundance (and value) of land and houses and slaves recorded on the stelae and the seemingly trivial collections of bronze pots, kitchen utensils, and tunics (see below, pp. 146–7). Even the notorious voluptuary Alcibiades could muster only a motley collection of items.

Of course, possession of luxury goods might in part redress the balance, but, at least in democratic Athens, overtly conspicuous consumption was ideologically sensitive. Litigants in law-courts tend to down-play possible manifestations of their wealth. The speaker in Lysias' *On the Murder of Eratosthenes* reassures the jurors that the two-storied house he describes to them is 'just a little one' (1. 9). Theophrastus' Character who is 'Avid for Petty Ambition' (21) is pilloried for having (apart from a grandiose house) a pet monkey, a short-tailed ape, Sicilian doves, Laconian dogs, a jackdaw complete with miniature shield, dice made of gazelle-horn, oil flasks from Thurii, walking-sticks from Sparta, and a Persian carpet.

The silver lining

One category of item missing from the Attic Stelae, no doubt passed direct to the Treasury, was the silverware presumed to have graced the tables of the wealthiest Athenians. For an impression of what might have been (absent also from the Athenian archaeological record), there are the remarkable hoards of silver and silver-plate from Rogozen in ancient Thrace. Other parts of the Greek world (Siphnos, Thasos, Amphipolis) possessed, and had their histories influenced by, deposits of precious metals; but nowhere to the extent that Athens' destiny was moulded by the silver mines at Laurium in SE Attica.

In various ways, mining was an exceptional and even disruptive activity, attracting outsiders into this corner of Attica. Aside from the actual removal of the ore from the ground (calling for shafts and galleries), there was need for extensive surface workings to extract the silver: mortars, grinding-mills, washing tables (with storage of water), and furnaces. Substantial traces remain to this day. Apart from extensive and expensive capital expenditure, plenty of labour was required, skilled and unskilled. A speech of Demosthenes (37, *Against Pantaenetus*) centres on a dispute arising out of ownership of a set of surface installations. The speaker explains how he and his partner lent Pantaenetus 105 minas on the security of a mine installation and thirty slaves. The slave work-force is one of the largest known from classical Athens, and the loan of 105 minas almost the largest from the corpus of the Orators.

Realistic estimates of the total number of slaves involved in mining at its height range from 10,000 to 20,000 (from an overall slave population guessed to be between 80,000 and 100,000). We are specifically told by Xenophon that Nicias, the Athenian General of the later fifth century, owned one thousand slaves in the mines (*Poroi*, 4. 14). So that the great man should not soil his hands, they were rented out to a middleman (Sosias the Thracian), who paid over one obol per day per slave and provided replacements as required. Laurium was one area of Attica where slaves probably outnumbered the free population. As a hint of the dangers, in *c*.135 BC the mining area was the scene of the only known outbreak of mass violence by slaves in Athens. More than one thousand were involved, but the trouble was brutally suppressed before it could spread (Diodorus 34. 2. 19).

Mining operations were largely the preserve of wealthier members of the population: high returns set against high risk. The unnamed litigant whom we earlier encountered, trying to foist his liturgy onto Phaenippus, complains to the jury that he owes the treasury three talents rental over a failed mine (42. 32). Although mines were on private land, ore beneath the surface was state property. Mining concessions were leased out at a rent appropriate to the prospects of profit from the mine, on which royalties were also due. Details of approximately 180 leases survive in inscriptions from the fourth century, and the lessees include a high proportion of Athenians (about one third) known to be wealthy and prominent in other fields, including politics. The father of Timarchus, it will be recalled, owned two workshops in the mining area. Plainly, Nicias was not alone.

The Laurium deposits were being exploited by the Early Bronze Age, but it was with the beginning of the fifth century that the mines played their part in shaping Athenian history, and with it economy and society, through the next couple of centuries. In the late 480s, a major silver strike resulted, we are told, in a windfall gain for the treasury of one hundred talents ([Aristotle], *Constitution of the Athenians* 22. 7). Resisting the temptation to divide up the silver among themselves, the Athenians used the money to build one hundred triremes, which were soon to be instrumental in defeating the Persians at Salamis and establishing Athens as the leading naval power in the Aegean (see below, pp. 107 and 172). Those Athenians who were too poor to serve as hoplites found places as rowers in the fleet on which Athens' supremacy depended (see below, p. 180). As the anti-democratic author of a fifth-century pamphlet (the so-called 'Old Oligarch') grudgingly concedes, it's only right that the common people should have political power in Athens: they are, after all, the ones who power the ships (1. 2). More than that, Athenian naval power underpinned the acquisition of the empire, which in turn funded, through tribute and other revenues, the costly Athenian brand of democracy.

Some figures. Thucydides (2. 13) has Pericles say that the empire at the outbreak of the Peloponnesian War brought Athens an annual income of six hundred talents (credible in the light of surviving Tribute Quota Lists). For the same date, Xenophon gives one thousand talents (a suspiciously round figure) as the sum of Athens' total revenues, internal and external (*Anabasis* 7. 1. 27) (see below, p. 107). It seems safe to conclude that, without the resources of empire, the Athenians could not have funded pay for public office (even the poor could take part) *and* an all-powerful fleet (one talent in rowers' wages alone to keep just one trireme at sea for one month) *and* supported public works (the Parthenon, not including the cult statue, cost about 470 talents) *and* built up a cash reserve of almost 10,000 talents on the Acropolis (Thuc. 2. 13). This last benefit marks Athens off from virtually all other poleis (including Sparta), who ran their public finances on a hand-to-mouth basis (see below, p. 177). In the fourth century, the Thessalian city of Pharsalus used the personal fortune of its most distinguished citizen as a rolling fund to equalize imbalances in income and expenditure from one year to the next (Xenophon, *Hellenica* 6. 1. 2–3).

The notion of fifth-century interdependence of imperialism and democracy in Athens necessarily raises the question of resources in the fourth century. The empire with its revenues came to an abrupt end in 404, and subsequent attempts to revive revenue-raising alliances (notably, the so-called 'Second Athenian Confederacy', 379–55) proved abortive. And yet Athens down to 321 maintained its restored democracy (enhanced from 403 by payment for attending the assembly), deployed a powerful fleet, and intermittently erected public buildings. Replacement funds were presumably provided by the Athenian élite through liturgies, impositions of property and 'semi-voluntary' subscriptions. Pressure was placed on the wealthy gathered in the assembly to compete in contributing sums to the public treasury; at which point, Theophrastus' 'Mean Man' (22) would quietly slip out. Upper-class complaints, particularly from Xenophon (*Symposium* 4. 29–32, *Oeconomicus* 2. 4–8), that burdens on the wealthy made it 'better to be poor than rich' may for once have had some substance. Increasing financial pressures may help explain the élite involvement in mining noted above.

After the strike of 480s, the mines have a low profile in our literary sources until the later fifth century, but modern excavations at the mining centre of Thoricus confirm continuing activity. The Spartan occupation of Decelea in NE Attica in 413 denied the Athenians access to the mines; the 'more than 20,000 skilled slaves' whom Thucydides identifies as defecting to the Spartans may well include many mine workers (7. 27). In 406/5 the Athenians issued a gold coinage and shortly after a copper coinage. Only in 393 was the familiar silver coinage reintroduced. Distribution of mining leases through time suggests an upswing in mining activity around the mid-fourth century (pre-350: *c.*20; 350–40: *c.*130). Confirmation comes from Xenophon's treatise called *Poroi* ('Ways and Means') dated *c.*355, which mentions work in the mines 'restarting only recently'.

Xenophon's *Poroi* is something new in Greek literature: a focused attempt to solve Athens' problems of underfunding in ways which would be painless not only for her wealthiest citizens but also for her disenchanted allies. He canvasses various revenue-raising schemes: attracting immigrants and traders to Athens who will increase the tax base, setting up a state-owned merchant marine, pursuing the peace-dividend; but his main emphasis is on systematic exploitation of the Laurium mines (4). In brief, Xenophon envisages a massive state-owned cadre of mine-slaves to be rented out to private entrepreneurs, giving a clear profit of one obol per slave per day. The scheme is to be built up by stages until there are sufficient slaves to guarantee each citizen an income of three obols per day. To the modern eye, Xenophon's modest proposal seems impossibly flawed: he makes the explicit assumption that the silver will never run out and always retain its value. But a comparison with Book Two of the pseudo-Aristotelian *Oeconomica* with its catalogue of crisis measures for raising cash (through a combination of forced loans, currency debasement, and trickery), highlights the originality of Xenophon's analysis.

Toilers of the sea

In the prelude to his proposals, Xenophon praises (to modern eyes, not altogether accurately) the natural advantages of Athens. In addition to natural fertility and the excellence of the harbour of Piraeus, Athens is (he says) attractive to traders because, in place of a return cargo, they may export silver. 'And this is good business, because they will be able to sell the silver anywhere in the world for more than the original purchase price' (3. 2). In treating Athenian silver as an exportable commodity rather than a means of exchange, Xenophon puts his finger on an economic factor setting Athens apart from much of the Greek world.

Trade was vital for the survival of virtually every Greek polis. Sparta, with access to the extensive area of Messenia, was a possible exception (see below, p. 131). But Thucydides presents the Corinthians, eager for war against the Athenians in 432, as warning their inland allies (including the Spartans?) that losing control of coastal areas would hamper the imports and exports on which they all depended (1. 120). Corinth, situated near the isthmus connecting central Greece and the Peloponnese, owed more than most poleis to revenues derived from trade. Maritime trade was the norm: with few exceptions, bulk transport overland was either impossible or prohibitively expensive. Some exchange was inevitable to compensate for permanent imbalances of raw materials and other essentials of life. Copper, tin, and iron are unevenly distributed around the Mediterranean so that, without ongoing redistribution, most poleis (including Athens) would have remained in the Stone Age. Most slaves were barbarians and necessarily came from beyond the fringes of the Greek world (see below, p. 159). Also, given regional variations in rainfall, staple grains were regularly traded around the Mediterranean to meet temporary shortfalls (see below, p. 44). The importance of these types of trade can hardly be overstated. There was in addition a persistent trade in prestige goods and local specialities. A long list could be drawn up (silphium from Cyrene, frankincense from Syria, ivory from Libya); we have already met a handful of items in the prized possessions of the 'Man of Petty Ambition'.

A limiting factor in the scale of trade (particularly in non-essentials) was the ability of a community to pay for imports in cash or kind. The resources of most poleis stretched little way beyond their land and those labouring on it (see above, p. 26; below, p. 71). Faced with recurring food shortages through excess population (as opposed to poor harvests), the medium-term solution generally lay in exporting people rather than importing food. Not so with Athens. Although the quantities are disputed, for much of the fifth and fourth centuries, Athens was able to sustain a substantial and recurring import bill for grain (mainly wheat) needed to support a population anywhere between 50,000 and 100,000 greater than the 'carrying capacity' of Attica (at most 150,000) (see below, p. 44). Also, a range of authors (the Old Oligarch, Thucydides, the comic poet Hermippus, Isocrates) emphasizes the abundance of goods on sale in Athens from overseas as if a reflection of Athenian power.

The presence of so many luxury goods could in part be explained through Athens' role as an entrepôt (as implied by Isocrates, 4. 42): in which case, no import bill would be borne by Athenians. But Thucydides (2. 38) and the Old Oligarch (2. 7) suggest from their different political perspectives that enjoyment of luxuries was part and parcel of the ideology of democracy in Athens. In any case, grain imported for domestic consumption, along with other essentials, would have to be paid for from Athenian resources. Presumably, the cost would be met over time through a shifting balance between export earnings, imperial revenues, and silver from Laurium. Attention has focused on the disputed significance of painted pottery as the key export from Athens: highly priced luxury cargo, or cheap and cheerful spacefillers (see above, p. 18)? Even if the former, it seems out of the question that trade in pottery alone could offset the grain imports needed to feed as many as 100,000. Whereas Athenian marble gets a mention: 'much in demand by both Greeks and barbarians', says Xenophon (*Poroi* 1. 4), our literary sources are significantly silent about pottery production and producers.

Best estimates suggest that, by the time the population of Athens outstripped its carrying capacity in the mid-fifth century, resources of empire were already available to close the gap. Tribute directed towards public and rowers' pay could be used to purchase imported wheat: *sitos* can mean both grain and pay. In the background, and increasingly prominent in the fourth century, the Laurium mines acted as a massive bullion reserve buried in the ground rather than in the vault of a central bank. Inflationary tendencies inherent in any increase in the money supply through tribute and newly minted silver would have been moderated by expenditure on imports; to say nothing of the practice of hoarding, putting the silver back in the ground.

The only indication of the overall scale of Athens' imports and exports comes from 399 and the speech *On the Mysteries* by the politician Andocides, in which he defends himself against a charge of impiety. He counter-attacks by accusing one of his prosecutors, Agyrrhius, of having a prior grudge against him (1. 133–4). Andocides explains how, the previous year, he broke a ring of tax-farmers, headed by Agyrrhius, who were collusively and corruptly bidding for the right to collect the two per cent tax on imports and exports passing through Piraeus. (Indirect taxes were regularly 'farmed out' in this way.) The sum offered by Andocides and his associates was thirty-six talents, which (he claims) still allowed them a small profit in farming the tax. That would imply a combined value of imports and exports somewhere in the region of 1,800 talents. Uncertainties remain: it is just possible (though unlikely) that the figure may not include the duty on cereals: a later speech refers to 'the two per cent tax on grain' ([Demosthenes] 59. 27). Either way, 1,800 talents remains an impressive figure (at least 350 drachmas for every adult, male citizen); and this with Athens at its lowest economic ebb, in the aftermath of defeat in the Peloponnesian War.

Consideration of how imports were paid for should not imply that the Greeks themselves had any formal idea of a balance of payments; still less any prefiguring of the mercantilist doctrine (a sixteenth-century notion) that the state should intervene to ensure the value of exports exceeded that of imports. Characteristic of Greek maritime trade was its fragmentation and remoteness from state control. In Xenophon's *Oeconomicus* (20. 27–8), Socrates cites as an agreed analogy the behaviour of traders, who

> ... from their passion for grain, sail in search of it wherever they hear it is most abundant, crossing over the Aegean, Euxine, and Sicilian Seas. And when they have got as much of it as they can, they bring it away over the water, stowing it in the vessel in which they themselves sail. And when they are in want of money, they do not dispose of their freight haphazardly, or wherever they happen to be; but wherever they hear that grain will fetch the highest price, and that men set the highest store by it, they carry it there, and offer it for sale to them.

Socrates' words contain an edge of criticism. What might today be regarded as the proper working of the market mechanism (high prices attract suppliers) was viewed with suspicion as traders seemingly took advantage of those in need. Hostility is palpable from conservative thinkers. Aristotle (in his *Politics*, 1258[b]) saw traders as exchanging not in order to gain what was needed (which was natural and acceptable) but unnaturally to make a profit, which necessarily meant deceit in order to buy cheap and sell dear (see below, p. 60). Plato saw traders as a disruptive element from which he wished to insulate his near-ideal community of the *Laws* (952–3). They were to be kept at arm's length and dealt with by specially appointed officials. Those involved in trade had either severed or at least weakened links with their own polis. Typically they were of low status, which made all the more galling their ability to lord it over citizen consumers (see below).

Identifiable, local demand for specialist goods (such as specific types of fine painted pottery) may have encouraged pre-planned voyages. Some 96 per cent of surviving pots made in the later sixth-century 'Workshop of Nikosthenes' in Athens with known findspots are from Etruria in Italy. But the picture of opportunistic 'tramp trading' presented by Xenophon's Socrates remains a reasonable reflection of reality: one man owning a single ship of which he was the master. Not all traders owned their own ships: a merchant (*emporos*) might hire cargo space from a shipowner (*naukleros*). Nor could all merchants and masters afford to buy outright their own cargoes, but were forced to borrow the purchase price (or part of it). In these maritime loans, principal and interest were repaid out of the proceeds of selling the cargo; but only on condition that the ship arrived safely at its agreed destination. Losses through shipwreck or piracy (increasingly a fourth-century problem) were borne by the lender, which gave the transaction an insurance effect. Because of the high risks involved for the lender, rates of interest ranged from 12.5 to 30 per cent or more per voyage.

'The resources required by those who engage in trade come not from those who borrow, but from those who lend; and neither ship nor shipowner nor passenger can put to sea, if you take away the part contributed by those who lend.' So a foreigner called Chrysippus told an Athenian jury in his speech *Against Phormio* (34). As a disappointed lender in a maritime loan, his exaggeration seems pardonable. His is one of four speeches, all attributed to Demosthenes (32, 34, 56), arising directly out of maritime loans, and in the course of which reference is made to a further twenty such loan transactions.

The experiences related by Chrysippus were more or less typical of his fellow litigants. He and his partner (neither of them Athenian residents) lent 2,000 drachmas to the metic Phormio to finance a trading voyage to the Bosporus. Phormio agreed to put on board a ship owned by the *naukleros* Lampis a cargo worth 4,000 drachmas and either to make a return voyage to Athens handing over there a total of 2,600 drachmas, or, if he preferred to remain in the Bosporus, to hand the cash to Lampis for transmission back to Athens. In the event, he stayed behind and the returning ship was sunk with almost all hands; Lampis escaped in the ship's boat. Phormio claimed that, according to the usual terms of maritime credit, loss of the ship absolved him of all obligations. Chrysippus begged to differ, arguing that Phormio never handed the money over to Lampis in the Bosporus.

These four speeches, supported by archaeology, provide much of our detailed knowledge of trading around the classical Greek world (the voyage to the Bosporus seems to have carried perfumed olive oil;

the return voyage, hides and possibly slaves). But they also introduce several of the measures used by the Athenians in the fourth century to boost not exports but imports of crucial commodities: chiefly grain, but also timber, flax, and ruddle for shipbuilding. No longer were the Athenians, as the Old Oligarch put it, 'Rulers of the Sea', able to coerce and control suppliers of raw materials.

Against Phormio is dated to the early 320s. During the previous decade, the Athenians had experienced recurring difficulties in securing adequate grain imports. Against this background, Chrysippus accuses Lampis of carrying grain from the Bosporus not to Athens but to Acanthus in NE Greece: an act punishable for an Athenian resident by death. To compound the felony, Lampis had allegedly taken fraudulent advantage of a long-standing concession by the Bosporan king Paerisades that grain shipped to Athens should be free of export duty. Where possible, the Athenians cultivated with some success good diplomatic relations with kings of the Black Sea region, a major source of imported grain (see below). Chrysippus details how, in contrast to Lampis, he and his partner had, in time of shortage, given the Athenians two talents for the purchase of grain and sold off 10,000 measures of wheat at the 'established price of five drachmas per measure' when it was fetching sixteen drachmas on the open market. The very existence of the speech *Against Phormio* is testimony to Athenian anxiety to attract traders. By a special dispensation restricted to trading disputes, Chrysippus, though not even a metic, was able to appear in court to deliver his accusation in person.

Go a-borrowing, go a-sorrowing?

An Athenian decree, voted by the assembly in 346, praises King Paerisades and his brother Spartacus, 'because they are good men and promise the people of Athens to see to the export of wheat as their father did . . . and the People is to grant Spartacus and Paerisades the privileges which it granted to Satyrus and Leucon and to crown each of them at the Great Panathenaea with a crown of gold worth 1,000 drachmas' (Harding 82). Some fifty years earlier (c.394), a young visitor from the Bosporus had occasion to invoke before an Athenian jury the good name of King Satyrus, then approaching the end of his reign:

My father, men of the jury, is Sopaeus; all who sail to the Black Sea know that his relations with Satyrus are so intimate that he is a ruler of an extensive territory and has charge of that ruler's entire forces. Having heard reports both of this state [of Athens] and of other lands where Greeks live, I desired to travel abroad. And so my father loaded two ships with grain, gave me money, and sent me off on a trading expedition and at the same time to see the world.

Arriving in Athens, the son of Sopaeus was introduced to the banker Pasion, with whom he deposited his money, as much as 1,000 gold staters (c.25,000 drachmas). When he got into trouble for providing a maritime loan on a ship apparently trading with the enemy (Sparta), Pasion found him a citizen guarantor to stand surety for seven talents. Meanwhile, back in the Bosporus, Sopaeus was accused of plotting against Satyrus and suspicion also fell on the son. Moves were made to extradite him and confiscate his money. The son of Sopaeus therefore colluded with Pasion to conceal the existence of his bank deposit and feign poverty by fabricating imaginary loans at interest. In time, Sopaeus was rehabilitated and Satyrus made appropriate amends. Great, therefore, was the son's chagrin (or so he claimed) when Pasion not only denied to his face that any deposit existed but accused him of fraudulently receiving six talents from Cittus, his slave assistant. After repeated attempts to have Cittus tortured, so getting to the bottom of the matter, had been blocked by Pasion, the dispute came to court.

The speech written for the son of Sopaeus by Isocrates (17) is the earliest of six speeches dealing with the banking business belonging to Pasion (Demosthenes 36, 45, 46, 49, 52). Of the twenty or so banks known from Athens, his was easily the most prosperous and durable (see below). Pasion himself was originally a bankers' slave who c.400 gained his freedom, took over his masters business, and eventually bought his way into the citizen body. On his death, he was reputedly worth almost sixty talents (apparently his brush with the son of Sopaeus did him no lasting harm). Incredibly, Pasion's pathway from slavery to citizenship was followed by his own bank-slave, Phormio (not the opponent of Chrysippus). Lest this give a false impression of upward social mobility in Athens, it must be stressed that such rags-to-riches stories are utterly exceptional. Pasion's son Apollodorus never rid himself of the stigma (real or imagined) that he owed his citizenship not to birth but a decree of the people. 'The mouse has just tasted pitch; for he wanted to be an Athenian' is the taunt that, in his paranoia, he attributes to one of his many opponents ([Demosthenes] 50. 26; see below).

Almost all bankers were metics and many were ex-slaves; the detail of Isocrates' speech helps confirm their location on the periphery of polis-society, providing services to those outside the community of citizens. Taking deposits, extending credit and, possibly most import- ant of all, changing money, which was the original function of Greek bankers, are all attested. The Greek word, ancient and modern, for 'bank' (*trapeza*) refers to the moneychanger's table. The son of Sopaeus, never in Athens before, was introduced to Pasion by Pythodorus the Phoenician (34. 4). He seems himself to have acted as middleman in later arranging for Hippolaïdes 'my guest and friend' to borrow from Pasion (34. 38).

The advantage for a trader in having a banker he could trust is shown up in the speech *Against Callipus*, attributed to Demosthenes (52), but delivered (and probably written) by Apollodorus, son of Pasion. He recounts how the Heraclean merchant Lycon, shortly before sailing to Libya, reckoned up his account with Pasion and ordered the sum of 1,640 drachmas to be paid over to his partner, Cephisiades of Scyros. Lycon was killed by pirates, and Callipus, the Heraclean *proxenos* or honorary consul, tried to appropriate the deposit. Despite coming under pressure from Callipus (a high-status citizen) to disregard his obligation to a mere metic, Pasion apparently kept faith and handed over the cash to Cephisiades. The bank itself (or at least a branch) was located in the Piraeus. It was no empty generalization when Apollodorus talked about Lycon using his father's bank 'like the other merchants' (§3).

Citizens, by contrast, would normally have networks of friends, neighbours, and relations to whom they could turn to supply most of the services offered by bankers. Only four citizens are known to have deposited cash with bankers. One was Demosthenes' father, heavily involved in manufacturing, having money with Pasion; another was Epicrates, temporarily depositing with a banker the purchase-price of Athenogenes' three slaves.

Twenty years after Pasion's death in 370, Apollodorus was still try- ing to recover monies allegedly owing to his father. Part of his cam- paign of litigation was an accusation for perjury *Against Stephanus*

(Dem. 45. 69–70), where a character attack on his opponent indicates the ideology of reciprocal assistance between citizens:

You have been better off than you deserved, yet to whom among the mass of the Athenians have you ever made a contribution? To whom have you ever given help? To whom have you done a kindness? You could not mention a single one. But, while lending out money at interest and regarding the misfortune and necessities of others as your good fortune, you ejected your uncle Nicias from his ancestral home, you have deprived your mother-in-law of the resources on which she lived ... No one has ever exacted payment from a man defaulting on the principal as harshly as you exact interest from your debtors.

The implication is that the good Athenian should be prepared to assist his fellow-citizens (and certainly his friends and relations) with interest-free loans. Of course, citizens did regularly lend to each other at interest. In addition to loans at interest in the estates of Ciron and Stratocles, Demosthenes Senior had at his death about one talent lent out at 1 per cent per month, the 'standard rate' in fourth-century Athens. But the underlying ideology was one of reciprocal assistance to those in need; at least, if there was an existing relationship or one was being cultivated for the future.

The 'contribution' mentioned by Apollodorus refers to so-called *eranos* credit: small sums supplied without interest or security to one in need by a plurality of private lenders (friends, neighbours, and the like). Apart from his talent out at interest, Demosthenes' father had a further talent, lent in sums of 200 or 300 drachmas, which have plausibly been identified as *eranos* loans. As often, Theophrastus' *Characters* indicates appropriate behaviour by its opposite. The 'Mean Man' (22), seeing the approach of a friend he knows to be collecting *eranos* contributions, will duck down a sidestreet and go home by a roundabout way.

Some implications of the reciprocal basis of credit and its relationship to friendship emerge from yet another speech by Apollodorus: *Against Nicostratus*, again preserved under Demosthenes' name (53). Apollodorus and Nicostratus were neighbours in the country who helped each other out. 'I came to feel on such intimate terms with him', says Apollodorus, 'that he never failed to win any favour he asked of me; and he, on his part, was useful in looking after my affairs and managing them' (§4).

On the occasion in question, three of the slaves on Nicostratus' farm ran away. He went after them and, by a stroke of poetic justice, was captured by pirates and himself sold as a slave at Aegina, off the coast of Attica. Apollodorus provided Nicostratus' brother, Deinon, with a gift of 300 drachmas to fetch him home. On his return, Nicostratus came to Apollodorus, complained that his relations had let him down, confessed that he needed twenty-six minas to pay off his ransom, and urged him to make an *eranos* contribution. Apollodorus responded with a further gift of ten minas which he raised by offering pledges (cups and a gold crown) to a banker. On to a good thing, Nicostratus a few days later pleaded for an immediate loan of the remaining sixteen minas to pay off the strangers who had ransomed him and were threatening to re-enslave him. He promised, once that threat was lifted, to make an *eranos* collection to recompense Apollodorus. Although Apollodorus readily agreed, he was himself at this time short of ready cash (§13).

Accordingly, I offered my tenement house as security for a loan of sixteen minas from Arcesas of Pambotadae, whom Nicostratus himself introduced to me. He lent me the money at the rate of 1.3 per cent per month. But when Nicostratus had got the money, so far from showing gratitude for what I had done for him, he immediately began to lay a plot against me, to rob me of my money, and become my enemy.

Hence the court case. Although no confidence can be placed on the accuracy of Apollodorus' allegations, key points emerge. There is the potential complexity of credit relations: the initial obligation arising out of the ransom resulted in seven separate loan transactions (far more, had Nicostratus' projected *eranos* been collected). The motive for borrowing, to meet a ransom, was typical of Athenian credit relations; similarly 'unproductive' borrowing embraced funeral expenses, dowries, and (for the élite) funding of liturgies and tax payments. Finally, there is the way in which reciprocity seems to lurk behind not only credit relations but also friendship, and the wider range of inter-personal relations, justice included (see above, p. 8; below, p. 161). Not for nothing did the son of Sopaeus end his speech as he began: with a sharp reminder to the jury of the benefits Satyrus and his own father had bestowed on the Athenians, allowing them grain when other Greeks went without.

The heart of the matter

Our exploration of the Greek economy began in the Athenian countryside. It ends at the very heart of the city, in the Agora. In this handful of acres, formally marked off with boundary-stones, and lustral basins, and lined with civic buildings, the whole life of the polis was concentrated: administration, publicity, justice, ostracism, religion, processions, dancing, athletics, and equestrian displays. Small wonder that 'market-place' might seem an inadequate label for such a highly charged area (see below, p. 167). The Agora was the prime meeting-place in Athens, where citizens and others might go to get information, meet their friends (or enemies), gamble, torture a slave, hire or get hired as wage labourers, accost a prostitute, seek asylum (if a slave), have a haircut, go begging, fetch water, watch cock-fighting, and find out the time from the public water clock. Intermixed with all this was the business of buying and selling, carried on in traders' stalls scattered over the Agora. The comic poet Eubulus highlights the mingling of marketing with the courts (many of the law-suits mentioned above will have been heard in courts in or near the Agora):

In one and the same place you will find all kinds of things for sale together at Athens: figs, bailiffs, bunches of grapes, turnips, pears, apples, witnesses, roses, medlars, milk-puddings, honeycombs, chickpeas, lawsuits, beestings, curds, myrtle, allotment machines, irises, lambs, water-clocks, laws and indictments.

The element of exaggeration need only be slight. It seems possible that the jurors at the trial of Socrates would have sat on stone benches in the open air overlooking all the bustle of the Agora; behind them, on the hill crowned by the Temple of Hephaestus, there was carried on the business of bronzefounding and the hiring of casual labour.

Conservative theorists disliked and devised alternatives for this mixing up of functions. Both Plato and Aristotle present schemes whereby the business of marketing (and its personnel) could be sealed off from more 'dignified' Agora activities like religion and politics (see below, p. 60). In the case of Athens, the assembly-area of the Pnyx was too accessible for their comfort: just a ten-minute walk, south of the Agora. Xenophon has Socrates distastefully imagine a typical assembly as full of clothing-cleaners, shoemakers, carpenters, smiths, peasants, merchants, and 'those who trade in the Agora, who think of nothing but buying cheap and selling dear' (*Memorabilia* 3. 7).

What seems to have aroused particular disapproval was the way the Agora provided civic space within which poorer citizens (and even non-citizens) might legitimately mingle with those of higher status (see below, p. 117). Moreover, the business of the Agora gave scope for subversion (even inversion) of prevailing hierarchies. Epicrates feelingly denounces the perfumer Athenogenes as 'a speechwriter, an *agora*-type and, worst of all, an Egyptian' (§3). Characters in comedy regularly express outrage at ways in which stallholders behave as if the superiors of their natural betters (Athenaeus 6. 224c–227b). 'It's ten-thousand times easier to get access to and a decision from the Athenian General Staff than attention and a civil response from a fishmonger ... So brazen are they in overcharging that, like the Gorgon, their looks turn customers to stone ... Here's one who wears his hair long, claiming it's dedicated to some god; in reality, he's concealing the brand on his forehead showing he's the worst sort of slave. As if to prove the point, he takes the purchase price in one currency and gives change in another, making thereby an extra profit on the deal.'

A market then, but not a market economy. To be sure, money, in the form of silver coinage, was part of every Athenian's life as a means of exchange (perhaps less so as a store of value). From 374, public testers of silver coinage sat daily at designated spots in the Agora and Piraeus. A well-preserved inscription gives details of their terms of reference, including fifty strokes for the tester (a public slave) if he failed to turn up (Harding 45). Prices of staple commodities might fluctuate with supply, especially in time of obvious shortage; but underlying this (and possibly making prices 'sticky') was the notion of an 'accepted price': the five drachmas for which Chrysippus beneficently sold off his grain (see above). The habitual practice of bargaining further modified the idea of market exchange. Haggling in the Agora should be seen not as establishing a price at which the market would be cleared (Adam Smith's 'invisible hand' at work), but rather as an expression of relative power and status. The comic poet Alexis fantasizes about legislation that would prevent fishmongers from bargaining by forcing them to name a fair price at the very outset. 'In this way, old man, old woman, and child will do their marketing at a fifth of the price.'

Alexis imagined protection for the weakest members of the citizen community. The Agora was an area where status could be both asserted and challenged with few holds barred. Provided with 'the knowledge', an individual might tour around the Agora with confidence, knowing not only the specific places where items were sold ('I went around to the garlic and the onions and the incense'), but also the associations of each location. To be avoided by respectable people were 'Cercopes' (allegedly stolen goods on sale) and the 'Women's market' (degrading for a male citizen). By contrast, those wishing to assert high status would frequent the bankers' tables or, aspiring to fashion, the perfumers' stalls. According to the comic poet Eupolis, a peasant who found himself mixed up in the conversation there would feel decidedly out of place.

Envoi

It will not have escaped the sceptical reader that many of the texts referred to in the above discussion of the Greek economy are open to alternative readings. Is it feasible, after all, to talk in terms of industry in Athens? Did wealthy Athenians deliberately maintain a balanced portfolio of assets? Was trade actually geared to sustaining economic growth? Was not the Athenian economy essentially market-orientated and effectively proto-capitalist? It is hoped that the author's view is clear: the Greek economy was neither primitive nor did it foreshadow capitalism; but, as an integral part of a complex culture and society, it possessed its own distinctive sophistication. It was, at the least, all so very different.

The classical city

Rosalind Thomas

The civic model

In the 340s, a woman called Neaera was prosecuted at Athens for fraudulently passing herself off as a woman of Athenian birth and marrying an Athenian man. She was really a foreigner from Corinth, the prosecutor alleged, and, still worse, had been a courtesan and former slave. Yet Stephanus, an Athenian, had married her, presenting her as a fully legitimate Athenian wife and their children as legitimate Athenians, and he had also arranged for Phano, her equally dissolute and non-Athenian daughter, to marry an Athenian who held the office of King Archon. As his wife, Phano had participated in certain secret and special rites of the Athenian festival of the Anthesteria, in which she made offerings on behalf of the city and was given in ritual marriage to the god Dionysus. So still worse, the gods were offended at this non-Athenian presiding over Athenian rituals, a horrible abuse of the most sacred.

The prosecution speech, preserved under Demosthenes' name (Demosthenes 59), charged Neaera with being a foreigner and living in an illegal marriage, but the real target of the prosecution was Stephanus, her 'husband', and it was a serious attack: by Athenian law an Athenian could not marry a woman of non-Athenian birth, and if he fraudulently gave an alien woman to an Athenian in marriage, he would be disfranchised. Children born from a non-Athenian wife could not become Athenian citizens. Neaera's professional activities in Corinth only added to the picture of deception and deceit and heightened the shock the Athenian jury was supposed to feel at this woman's daughter performing the ancient religious rites of Athens. So great was the gulf between the city-states of Athens and Corinth, not very far from each other, which shared a common language, common gods, and a common Greek culture. For all the movement of individuals between these two prosperous cities, Athenian citizens and Corinthian citizens, and their wives, lived in separate worlds, politically and legally insulated from each other.

There was an unbridgeable gulf between the physical mobility of individuals like Stephanus and Neaera and the rigid political realities in each city-state or polis. The Corinthian citizen belonged to an oligarchy, a constitution which gave political rights to a narrow property-based citizen body and political power to a still narrower body, with its own legal regulations. The Athenian citizen was subject to the laws, expectations, and customs of the Athenian radical democracy, a constitution which gave extensive political powers to a large male citizen body and which prided itself on the extent of individual freedom. Each had quite different political rights and a particular range of obligations, laws, and restrictions which amounted almost to a distinct culture. Greek city-states were fiercely independent and often profoundly antagonistic to their immediate Greek neighbours.

Within the city-state it also mattered whether you were a citizen or not: even legal rights and penalties were affected. An extreme and brutally clear case of differentiation by civic status appears in a fifth-century law-code published by Gortyn in southern Crete. The fines for rape and adultery were carefully calibrated according to the civic status of the two people involved (with an extra twist according to relationship). A free man who raped a household slave was subject to a minor fine of merely 1, 2, or 24 obols. But a slave who had the temerity to rape a free person was fined a sum at least a hundred times more (2,400 obols). Adultery with a free woman brought a fine of 600 obols, or 1,200 if the adultery took place in the house of a close male relative; adultery between two slaves incurred a fine of merely 60 obols, a tenth of the lower sum—and so on. We get a chilling sense of the exact 'worth' of each individual in this Cretan city-state: a slave was 'worth' 100 times less than a free person. Gortyn may be extreme, but the general principle is found all over Greece.

The civic model and civic divisions are at the core of Greek society. Our own words 'politics' and 'political' derive from the Greek word *polites*, 'citizen', the active members of the polis (city-state: plural 'poleis'). The polis was a community of citizens, and personal relations were regulated by law by the individual polis for its citizens.

Every polis involved its citizens in some form of active decision-making, whatever its precise political constitution, otherwise it risked not being considered a polis at all: Haemon in Sophocles' *Antigone* (737) retorted to the ruler Creon that a city 'is not a polis if one man rules it'. The mass of surviving literature from the classical period derives from members of city-states; all classical discussions of the ideal state, including Plato's *Republic* and *Laws*, and Aristotle's *Politics*, are premised on the model of the polis. Experimentation in political forms invariably circled around the basic ideal of the polis, though alongside the polis there existed the tribal state or 'ethnos', and leagues and federal states which offered alternatives of varying degrees of permanence and attractiveness to the glorious isolation of the self-governing polis. The influence of the civic model was so strong that sub-groups also mimicked the language and behaviour of the larger polis.

Many city-states inscribed on stone slabs their decrees, treaties, and laws. Athens' inscriptions are most voluminous, for the democracy demanded public accountability and visibility, as well as monumental significance, for the lasting decisions of the democratic institutions and the laws that bound them. But other cities also put written documents on stone: Gortyn in Crete, not a democracy, inscribed its vast law code on the back of its theatre wall for everyone to see. So if we add our literary evidence, our knowledge of the detailed workings of innumerable city-states can often be surprisingly good and very precise.

Inscriptions are a powerful supplement to the narratives of the historians and to the highly articulate political theorists such as Plato and Aristotle, whose analyses of the polis had their own agenda. They also provide invaluable evidence for the many city-states which were less prominent, powerful, or articulate than Athens. Inscriptions reveal minute self-regulation by smaller city-states, often enacted surprisingly early. A law recently found on the island of Thasos in the northern Aegean includes regulations about the public cleanliness of this city-state, an island with its own silver mines, close to the Thracian shore and mines of the north Aegean. It shows an early zeal for urban supervision, and an astute sense of how to persuade officials to collect fines (by fining them instead). Amidst tough regulations and fines about building or digging cisterns, this early fifth-century law continues:

Let every inhabitant keep the street in front of his house clean . . . let him take
up what litter comes from the houses and what is in the road, when the
magistrates order so; whosoever does not do any of these things according to
the law, he shall owe one twelfth of a stater for each day to the polis; the
officials shall exact it [the penalty] and keep half themselves . . . Nobody is
allowed to climb up on the roofs of public buildings in this road to watch [a
procession?] and no woman is permitted to watch from the windows. For
whichever of these things (i.e. crimes) he does, let the occupier owe to the
polis a stater for each offence; the officials shall exact it and keep half themselves. (*SEG* 42, 785)

Such is the kind of regulation that city-states could impose upon
themselves, and consider important enough to inscribe in stone. We
may reckon on at least 750 poleis, large and small, in Greece,
and another 500 in the colonies around the Mediterranean and
Black Sea (Herodotus alone mentions 159 city-states), all of which
decided upon regulations and laws of their own, following local and
particular anxieties and needs.

Citizens and citizenship

If the city-state consists above all of its citizens, what made a citizen?
Citizenship was central to the social, political, and cultural identity of
the Greeks in an active sense which seems remote from the experience of many members of the modern nation-state. Whether or not
someone was a Spartan, an Athenian, or a Corinthian citizen brought
with it profound cultural and political consequences. Being a citizen
of a certain polis slotted that citizen into the small world of a particular community which had enormous power to shape its own politics,
religion, and culture.

In the early archaic period communities seem to have consisted
simply of all inhabitants, the more crucial divisions being between
the free and the slave, or the free and the debt-bondsman, and
between those who were regarded as noble, aristocratic, and the rest.
It is probable that the idea of the citizen became more closely politically defined as the polis and its political system became more refined
and institutionalized. In the eighth century most settlements were
run by a few aristocrats, and the mass of the free inhabitants had

neither political rights nor obligations. 'Citizens' perhaps grew out of what were at first merely the free male inhabitants of a polis, who owned and farmed the land; it was later that the role narrowed to become specifically the free males with political rights. These rights emerged from complex shifts in power and revolution as laws and political structures developed over the seventh and sixth centuries.

The military role of the polis' inhabitants in the hoplite phalanx was crucial, for hoplite fighting was a mode of warfare which from the seventh century onwards gave an equally important role in the ranks of infantry to the ordinary citizen as to the aristocracy (see below, p. 85). With citizen-farmers in the hoplite phalanx, the city-states developed a set of ideals that elevated the courage of the citizen fighting for his city in the front rank. As the Spartan poet Tyrtaeus put it in his military exhortation in the late seventh century, 'This is excellence, this is the best and most beautiful prize in the world for a young man to win, for he brings a common good to the polis and the whole people, the man who remains steadfast unceasingly in the front ranks' (frag. 12). The citizens' military role, their direct and immediate function as defending army against any enemy, almost a standing army composed of the whole citizen-body, meshed with their political status, and identified the individual's honour with his city-state's. Hence the political strength of the citizen body as voters in the citizen assembly.

Citizenship in the classical period was a jealously guarded privilege. Sparta notoriously offered her citizenship to only two members of other Greek poleis in her entire history down to the end of the fourth century despite a catastrophic drop in her citizen numbers by the early fourth century. At the high point of her empire, Athens actually tightened the rules for citizenship in the Periclean law of 451/50, so that citizens now had to have two parents, rather than one, of citizen birth (a further tightening in the fourth century lay behind Neaera's case). It is really only from the 430s on that our evidence indicates that Athens granted citizen rights to wealthy foreigners or non-Athenian benefactors. Such grants were the butt of jokes in comedy in the 420s (see Aristophanes' *Acharnians*, below), but became more common in the fourth century as Athenian confidence waned and her desire to favour rich foreigners grew. But it would have been unthinkable to Athens to offer Athenian citizenship to her fifth-century subject allies as a way of strengthening the alliance. Quite exceptionally, the citizens of the island of Samos were offered Athenian citizenship in 405/4, as the Athenians were losing the Peloponnesian War, as a recognition of their staunch loyalty ('And in return for the benefits they have conferred upon the Athenians and since they now highly esteem them and propose benefits for them, it has been resolved by the Council and the People that the Samians shall be Athenians, governing themselves in the manner they themselves prefer.'). This decree was, at the end of the war, a purely honorific act: the Athenian empire had ridden rough-shod over the autonomy of many of the allied city-states; now when it granted citizenship wholesale to another polis, it carefully assured Samos that she would retain her autonomy. But in the Greek classical world that was almost a contradiction in terms: how could you be loyal citizens of two city-states? We can well see why these wholesale grants were so rare.

Loss of citizen rights was termed *atimia*, literally 'being without honour'. Similarly the expression *achrestos*, literally 'useless', appeared in the archaic period in a Cretan law, in a context where it meant that an individual so punished would be unable to hold office or use his political rights. There is an echo in the fifth century in the Periclean Funeral Speech in Thucydides' *History*, where Pericles declares that the Athenians consider those who are politically inactive to be 'useless' (24. 40. 2). Loss of citizen rights was a devastating punishment. To have citizen rights and not use them was equally despised.

In the *Politics*, in the fullest Greek discussion of citizenship we have, Aristotle struggled to find a single definition of citizenship from all the varieties of citizenships in the Greek world, and eventually settled on a political one: 'A citizen is he who has the power to take part in the deliberative and judicial administration of the polis' (*Politics* 1275^b). By that, he included the power to take part in the assembly, the deliberative gathering of all citizens who then voted on proposals in war, peace, and anything else. But which men were citizens varied considerably from state to state. In general, to be a citizen one had to be a hoplite, and own and farm land: only a radical democracy like the Athenian gave citizen rights even to the landless. A man who had full citizen status in a democracy might not necessarily have it in an oligarchy (literally 'rule by the few'), since citizen rights would then be confined to a smaller body, usually the rich. Sparta at one extreme was particularly rigid, requiring not only birth, but a certain level of land and contributions to the common messes of the city: if these contributions could not be maintained, that is, if the citizen fell below a certain level of wealth, the Spartiate lost his status.

But wealth alone did not make someone a citizen: plenty of very wealthy men born outside Athens lived there but were debarred from citizen rights. Athenian trials and Athenian comedy contain many accusations of barbarian ancestry precisely because this would be a good way of jeopardizing citizenship. Other cities demanded parents of citizen birth for two or three generations. But cities whose citizen population was declining might also make a call for new citizens to 'fill up' the citizen body—the great hope, presumably, for many of the dispossessed. According to the fifth-century Sicilian orator Gorgias, the citizens of Larissa in Thessaly were a 'manufactured article, made, like the kettles which bear the city's name, by the magistrates' (Aristotle, *Politics* 1275^b).

Within the citizen body of a given state, the wealthier citizens tended to have more access to political office than the poorer citizens. An oligarchy might be ruled by a very narrow group who held office within a wider citizen body, as at Corinth, where we hear remarkably little about its assembly. In essence oligarchy was rule by the few and the rich, democracy rule by the people, or as Aristotle puts it, rule by the free. With so much variation in citizen bodies, it is no surprise that Aristotle had such difficulty in finding a single definition of the citizen; the definitions he rejected emphasize a central feature of the polis, that citizenship was fragile and could be temporary.

Citizens expected that their children would be citizens of their polis, and various city-states, Athens most spectacularly, had traditions that they had always lived in the same land, which implied a tight and almost mystical identification between the land and the citizens of the polis. The Athenian tradition connected with their firm belief that they were more civilized because they were more settled and less 'mixed' than other city-states. It gave the whole citizen body something akin to an ancient aristocratic lineage, a long pedigree and a myth of origin (compare the created citizen Apollodorus, above, pp. 45–6), and it may have been a reaction not only to their main Greek opponents like Dorian Sparta, who had rousing traditions of the Dorian invasion of Greece, but also to the fragility of a politically created citizenship.

Citizenship was no inalienable birthright; it was a legal and political creation. It could be redefined in a revolution to give citizen rights to large numbers of new citizens, or to remove citizens, or to reduce the access to political influence of large numbers (compare pp. 121–2 below). It could be lost for other reasons, treason and impiety being the most serious. In fourth-century Athens, Aeschines tried to get his opponent Timarchus, a prominent politician, deprived of full citizen rights on the grounds that he had been a prostitute— and was therefore likely to do anything for money (see above, pp. 31–2). At Sparta those who committed acts of cowardice, or showed other signs of inadequacy, also forfeited their citizen rights (these sub-groups had appropriate names, e.g. 'The Tremblers').

Disfranchisement, enfranchisement, oaths of allegiance: all could be overturned in time of revolution. If revolution involved redistribution of land, as it often did, in most cities that would mean loss of citizen rights, and with mass expulsions in revolutions, there were numerous exiles (the historian Herodotus was one). Citizens could be degraded to resident aliens, or worse. Aristotle, in one of the more convoluted and astonishing sections of *Politics*, is even perplexed by the question of whether a polis remains the same polis when its constitution changes. The question would not arise for a modern nation state: France remained France through revolution, whether its constitution was a monarchy or democracy. What made the question acute for Aristotle was that the polis was so closely identified with its citizen body. With relatively little state apparatus, no permanent 'executive' beyond public slaves, very little bureaucracy, the polis was run by its citizens, even if a narrow élite at the top might hold most offices, and in time of revolution the sense of who was actually an 'Athenian' or 'a Samian' might become problematic.

In the oligarchic coup at Athens in 411, the democracy was persuaded to vote itself out of existence, and power was given over to a far narrower group which labelled itself 'the Four Hundred'. This acted as the council for a body of 'Five Thousand' citizens, and initially tried to ignore the 5,000 altogether, who were all who could furnish a suit of hoplite armour (Thucydides 8. 97) (by contrast, the radical democracy of the fifth century, with around 50,000 citizens, included a lowest property class, the thetes, of which about 5,000 were landless according to one orator). Attica as a territory remained constant under the oligarchy, but 'the Athenians' with full citizen rights were a much reduced body, and decrees issued by the council

in that period, opening without the conventional democratic reference to 'Council and People' (see below), represented a much
reduced body of citizens. No wonder polis stability was a major preoccupation of Greek thinkers.

A further problem was vigorously discussed: whether to accept
into the citizen body those who belonged to certain professions, and
what to do about traders and, often the same people, resident visitors
from other cities (metics). One of the dangers perceived by anti-
democratic politicians and theorists was that the area of the city
where trade was concentrated tended to be more democratically
inclined than the rest. This was the case in Piraeus, Athens' port,
where there was a particularly large concentration of foreigners (see
above, p. 26). It could be seriously suggested that a city might wish to
keep traders out of the main area of the polis, the political 'Agora' or
market-place, and both Plato and Aristotle went so far as to suggest
that there should be a separate agora reserved for trading. In practice
the political and the economic inevitably mixed, and it is only
occasionally that we learn of specific definitions of citizenship that
sought to exclude trade. Several oligarchies had laws against citizens
making money in trade (Aristotle, *Politics* 1316[b]). Thebes had a law
which allowed a man to hold office only if he had retired from
business for ten years (*Politics* 1278[a]) and one can imagine aspiring
office holders rushing to create middlemen for the purpose.

Athens and Sparta

What exactly was meant by political citizenship depended, as we
have seen, on whether a city-state was a radical democracy (such as
Athens), in which the mass of the people held political power, an
oligarchy run by a narrower body, or somewhere on the wide spectrum of possibilities in between. We shall concentrate on Athens as
the best documented of all constitutions, and on Sparta, which can be
treated as an oligarchy even though in formal terms it was a mixed
constitution with monarchic, democratic, and oligarchic elements.
Athenian democracy was radical and exceptional (indeed the most
radical democracy the world has known), and was both criticized and
feared by many non-Athenians.

Athens became a radical democracy in the 460s when the judicial powers held by the old council of the Areopagus were transferred to the popular courts and popular assembly. After the disaster of the end of the Peloponnesian War (431–404), and the emotional and physical horrors of the two periods of oligarchy towards its end, the powers of the assembly were reduced and further power was transferred to magistrates, but the most basic radical elements remained. Those radical features consisted of the very large citizen body, which included 'thetes', men with little or no property; the fact that all political decisions were subject to the will of the demos, the people; that the leaders themselves were held accountable to the people in the Assembly and popular jury courts; and that there was pay for office-holding and jury service which allowed the poorer citizens to play a fuller role in the democracy, or at least not be debarred totally by poverty. As Pericles is made to say in his somewhat lukewarm description of this democratic principle in the Funeral Speech in Thucydides, 'nor does poverty bar the way, but a [poor] man is able to serve the city, despite his lack of authority' (Thucydides 2. 37. 1).

This was direct democracy, in which the people exercised their political power by being present and voting directly on any issue rather than by voting for representatives as in modern (represen-tational) democracy. Most officials were chosen by lot, not election (the generals were an important exception, see below). The citizens expressed their will mainly in the Assembly (*ekklesia*), and in the fifth century all serious business, and much which we would consider minor business for committees, including numerous decisions involving money, came before the Assembly; its vote was final.

In one of the most famous expressions of their sovereignty, the Assembly in 427 made the brutal decision to punish the Mytileneans for revolting by massacring the male citizens, and selling the women and children into slavery. Overnight, however, people began to regret the decision—presumably people were anxiously conferring in the Agora, the houses and streets of the centre of Athens—and an emer-gency Assembly was called the very next day to reopen the question. The arguments for and against such ruthlessness were put to the people, dramatized brilliantly by Thucydides via two opposing speeches by Cleon (for extreme punishment) and Diodotus (calcu-lated mercy) (3. 37–48), and the majority narrowly overturned the previous day's decision. This was what was meant by the authority and sovereignty of the people: the citizen assembly had the power of decision and effectively the power of law in the fifth century, and the decision was reached in debate on the day. It is also illustrates what many saw as the fickle nature of the people, for here was a decision taken on one day, in the heat of the moment, and thought better of the next day, after reflection. It showed the extraordinary confidence and authority which resided in the fifth-century Assembly. In this case the ship conveying the first command had not hurried, and the command could be rescinded before it was too late.

Towards the end of the war the people took the law into their own hands and insisted that they, as the people, had the power to try all eight generals together after the sea battle of Arginusae when they had failed to pick up the bodies of the dead—and all were condemned to death. This was strictly illegal, but who was to say where exactly were the limits of the people's sovereignty? As some citizens claimed, according to Xenophon, 'it was insufferable that the demos should not be allowed to do what it wanted' (*Hellenica* 1. 7). Decisions like these led fourth-century democracy to hive off law-making to a special body of 'lawgivers', who still consisted of ordinary citizens, but who were separated procedurally and emotionally from the heightened excitement of the debates in the Assembly. This might not have prevented war-time decisions like the Mytilene affair, but it gave away the fact that in the fourth century the democracy was more wary of the enormous power the people had in the earlier Assembly.

The body of people who came together in the Assembly on successive days to debate how to punish Mytilene was almost certainly not identical. The assembly-place on the Pnyx could not actually seat the whole citizen body of up to 50,000. Modern calculations suggest that in the fifth century the Pnyx could seat 6,000, in the fourth century slightly more; we hear of quorums of 6,000, which must have been attainable, and 6,000 seems to be seen as equivalent to a full assembly. The powers of the People's Assembly, then, were exercised by a shifting selection of the whole citizen body.

Most of those attending the Assembly at any one time would presumably be those who lived nearest, in the city itself or just outside, who could combine attendance in the Assembly with a visit to the market-place (about one third of citizens lived within six miles of the centre of Athens; Attica itself covered 2,400 square kilometres). Many farmer-citizens spread over the rest of Attica probably travelled in to

an assembly less often, perhaps combining it with some crucial buying and selling. We hear for instance of a barber's shop near the
Agora where men of Decelea used to meet, which implies that not
many Deceleans were in Athens at any one time. The Assembly at any
one meeting can hardly have been representative but that was the
catch of direct democracy: no direct participation without actual
physical presence.

A further result was that ambitious men who sought to persuade
the Assembly to vote their way had to become orators (*rhetores*) for
mass audiences. This called for particular techniques of oratory and
greater professionalism, which again tended to exclude those who
had no access to such skills. The major political leaders were those
with the leisure both to deal with democratic business and to perfect
their skills of persuasion: the fourth-century Athenian word for
politician is *rhetor* (orator). The democracy fuelled the development
of the Greek arts of argument and persuasion.

The Assembly had its agenda prepared by the Council (or *Boulê*).
The Council filtered business before it went to the Assembly for final
decision, vetting proposals for decrees, and also had executive functions; it could act in an emergency and receive ambassadors. Decrees
passed by the Athenians usually start with 'It has been decided by
the Council and the People [i.e. Assembly]', (compare the example
above, p. 57). Amendments could be proposed in the Assembly, but
the Council's role in preparing business had a steadying function
before the spirited and often noisy debates in the Assembly.

The Council was made up democratically of 500 men chosen for a
single year recruited equally from the ten tribes of Athens (50 per
tribe); that tribal contingent was made up of set quotas of representatives from each of the demes, the villages or wards of Attica, the quota
being determined by deme size, so that the largest, Acharnae, sent
twenty-two members to the Council each year, whilst the tiniest
demes sent only one every other year. It is sometimes assumed that
the Council was largely composed of the rich, so that the upper
classes were selecting business to go before the lower classes on the
assembly floor, but it is hard for demographic reasons to see how this
could happen in practice: even if every Council member served
twice—and no one was allowed to serve more than twice—7,500
councillors (who had to be over 30) would be required in the course
of thirty years. There were, by contrast, only about 1,200 Athenians

wealthy enough to contribute liturgies (see above, p. 24). What is more, the final choice was by lot, election being regarded as an oligarchic feature, and this was in deliberate contrast to the principle of the oligarchic council.

For many with a farm to run, a year serving on the Council might be inconvenient, and we can only presume that Council members from the distant demes rented or borrowed somewhere to stay in the city for the frequent meetings. But they were paid, true to the democratic principle. Unless there was massive disregard for the rules, a very high proportion of Athenians must have taken a turn on the Council for a year. As for the ambitious, they will have made the greatest political capital they could out of their year on the Council, as any aspiring politician would, which is why we hear about some very prominent individuals (Cleon, Demosthenes) being on the Council in years which were important to them as politicians. But the ambitious also pursued other avenues of political influence: when wealthy Athenians prosecuted in court appealed to the people for favour, they tended to cite their family's patriotic military zeal and their liturgies, but not the mere fact of serving on the Council.

It was the jury courts which were regarded as most characteristically Athenian, and which embodied the principle of accountability to the people. Juries are addressed by speakers very much as if they themselves are the people and embody the Assembly, and their power was often dreaded. Jury members were called in Greek *dikastai*, literally 'judges', and that is what they were, for there were no presiding judges as in modern courts and no professional lawyers. Drawn from a panel of 6,000 citizens over 30, they were sworn in at the beginning of the year and deployed for separate cases in large and uneven numbers (e.g. 1,001) to avoid a tied vote, again following the principle of decision by large groups. All officials were formally scrutinized before, during, and after their one-year term of office, and if they were prosecuted, they would appear before the courts.

Yet there were risks to going to court as a prosecutor, and these must have deterred many poorer citizens; certain cases carried a financial penalty if they lost and in any case the expenses could be high. The principle was that of equal access to the law, and justice was supposed to be in the hands of all citizens, to lie at the heart of the polis. But with no public prosecutor, the system increasingly depended on semi-professional prosecutors, the much despised 'sycophants', or other citizens who were prepared to take the financial risk of losing a case. Many a speaker in court assured the jury that they had never been in court before, a profession of legal innocence which they hoped would secure sympathy.

Speech-making in fact rapidly became professionalized: by the late fifth century a citizen could pay a skilled speechwriter to write what he would then deliver in court himself, the nearest Greek equivalent to hiring a successful lawyer. This too was something that people did not flaunt, for it too obviously undermined the democratic principle of equal access to justice. One defendant pleaded, 'If I make any mistake in speaking, pardon me and treat it as due to inexperience rather than dishonesty', yet he had paid the clever orator Antiphon to write his defence (Antiphon 5). Thus the more prosperous citizens were better able to use the courts and, unless the jurors were wise to rhetorical tricks, to use them successfully. Many of the speeches we still have, written by skilled orators, are speeches delivered by the wealthy to a jury of ordinary citizens, and they beg for favour on the grounds that they have helped the city financially (as above) or use the democratic arguments that went down well with the jurors. Ultimately the conflict was often between the ordinary citizen and the power of the skilled orator, and by the fourth century this division between the amateur and the skilled orator was increasingly blatant.

Who served on the jury panels—just the poor? the rich? or vicious old men as in Aristophanes' comedy *Wasps*? Their pay was nearer to maintenance payment than lucrative income; and elaborate measures were taken in the fourth century to ensure that the composition of any one court on the day could not be predicted and that the jurors could not be bribed. The extra work and income, however slight (courts sat on five times as many days as the Assembly), would be most useful to the elderly poor, and others without regular employment. But perhaps we should not be narrowly functionalist. The parody of *Wasps* implies that the members of the juries simply enjoyed their power. The Athenians developed a taste for listening to speeches: as the demagogue Cleon is made to say bitterly in the Mytilenean debate by Thucydides, the Athenian people are 'slaves to the pleasures of the ear' and go to hear a speech as if they were attending a public spectacle (3. 38).

One underlying preoccupation in democratic Athens was to limit the power of any individual and make anyone with power accountable to the people. Officials served for one year only and were scrutinized at the beginning and the end. Professionalism was definitely not a primary aim: what is evident is the unwavering distrust and avoidance of any build-up of expertise. Greek states had a long history of distrust of individuals with official power, and we may also be able to connect this with the fear of the larger danger of an individual seizing unconstitutional power and setting himself up as tyrant. The Athenians also developed the weapon of ostracism, by which the citizens voted a single individual into exile for ten years, an election in reverse aimed solely at removing one person rather than a policy or a group. Some of this democratic hesitation about individuals amassing expertise relaxed in the fourth century: Athens' continual financial problems (see above, p. 56) were too great for excessive democratic purism, and a single financial individual was eventually allowed who could also hold office repeatedly.

It is all the more striking that, throughout the fifth and fourth centuries, the generalship could be held repeatedly. Most prominent fifth-century politicians had official power as one of the ten generals elected annually, as well as unofficial influence through their ability to persuade the people in Assembly. Pericles was the most outstanding, re-elected every year after 443 until his death in 429. In formal terms the generalship is the remaining 'oligarchic' element in the midst of the fifth-century democracy: a general could continue indefinitely as long as he was re-elected. The Old Oligarch remarks wryly and triumphantly that the Athenian people make an exception to their rule of choosing officials by lot—far better for the people to elect their generals and have some chance of fighting under someone who knows the job; no one wanted a general selected at random. Generals were therefore precisely what democratic theory sought to avoid, popular leaders with the possibility of repeated tenure of office, extensive power, very often rich and aristocratic. If the generalship could be combined, as it was by Pericles, with brilliant powers of oratory and an ability to instruct, persuade, and lead the demos, then that general could preside over what was close to rule by one man. Thucydides described Pericles' supremacy as 'in fact rule by the first citizen' (2. 65).

The Athenians prided themselves on the freedom of their way of life, the Spartans on their military discipline and moral superiority. The Spartan citizens, the Spartiates, in assembly were more obviously an army at peace than other Greeks. Isocrates called Sparta a military camp (Isocrates 6. 81), and their kings were called by Aristotle 'hereditary generals for life'. In Sparta we see not only an oligarchy, but a political and social system in which the military function of the citizen, present in every city-state, has taken precedence over every other aspect and governs the very development of the city-state's social structure.

The Assembly, for instance, was open to the '10,000' Spartiates, the so-called *Homoioi* or 'Equals'. We hear of them voting on major questions after listening to the speeches presented to them: they voted, for instance, to go to war with Athens in 431. But there is little sign that anyone in the Assembly could contribute to the debate, let alone suggest an amendment from the floor, and it is likely that the effectiveness of the Spartiates as a military machine in the hoplite phalanx, enforced by the hierarchical educational system, discouraged 'insubordination' of any kind.

The Athenians' ideal of accountability to the people is conspicuously absent. There is no sign that the Assembly in Sparta ever had any power or control over officials, or over citizens who were to be prosecuted. Nor were there any popular courts. Indeed Aristotle introduces his definition of the citizen (*Politics* 1275^b) with a comment about Sparta which suggests that he does not think Spartan citizens are covered by it: admitting that his definition of the citizen is 'best suited to the citizens of a democracy', he adds that 'in some states the people are not acknowledged, nor have they any regular assembly, but only extraordinary ones; and law suits are distributed in turn among the magistrates'. Later, he adds that an oligarchic feature of Sparta is that 'the power of inflicting the penalties of death and exile rests with a few persons' (*Politics* 1294^b), and this is borne out by Xenophon's account of the first decades of the fourth century in his *Hellenica*. When a Spartiate named Sphodrias made an unauthorized attack on Piraeus in 378, he was summoned to trial by the ephors, but acquitted even though he failed to appear. King Agesilaus was instrumental in this, declaring that Sparta simply could not afford to lose a man like Sphodrias (*Hellenica* 5. 4. 32). Xenophon, who was in a position to know, mentions that another factor was that Sphodrias' son was having a love affair with Agesilaus' son, and called it 'the most unjust verdict given in a Spartan court' (*Hellenica* 5. 4. 24) (see further below, pp. 204–5).

The ephors, elected annually by the whole citizenry, were the 'democratic' officials of the Spartan state, and in peacetime had great powers over the kings. They are found, for instance, demanding that King Anaxandridas, against his own inclination, take another wife who can bear him children (Herodotus 5. 39–41). They summoned Sphodrias to trial. In so far as they were a concession to the ordinary citizens, they may have helped to keep the state together, but they are also accused of being open to bribes, since they were poor (Aristotle, *Politics* 1270^b), and it is uncertain how much influence they exerted over the kings. The ephors did dispatch troops in secret during the Persian Wars, in a moment of acute diplomatic embarassment (Herodotus 9. 9–11), but they were ordinary men in a system which gave them no formal backing from the Assembly.

The kings and the Council of Elders (*Gerousia)* are relics of an archaic system. The two kings, each of separate families and often in rivalry, are an anomaly in a Greek city-state. Accounts of how their power was limited read as if any restriction upon a king was a remarkable feature for most Greek audiences, and there clearly were tensions as we have seen. But the amount of real power and influence any one king had seems to have depended greatly on his charisma, his military qualities, and his relationship with the other king. Certainly we hear far more about the kings of Sparta than about the ephors, and when our evidence is particularly full, as it is for the late fifth century and first half of the fourth, it is clear that certain kings, above all Agesilaus, had profound effects on Spartan policy (see below, Chapter 8). Kings put issues to the vote in the Assembly, at least, but the Gerousia seems to have been unaccountable. The twenty-eight elders, who were members for life, seem drawn in practice, if not by law, from a narrow range of families in the upper echelons of Spartan society. This was the pure 'oligarchic' element and a narrow one at that: a small council drawn from certain families, with enormous judicial powers, a fine example of an oligarchic council which never became more egalitarian.

Yet paradoxically, Spartan society could be an outstanding example of equality. Certain elements of the Spartan state which may seem to modern observers to involve excessive state control, were regarded by some Greeks as democratic. The state-system of education, for instance, was itself highly aberrant for classical Greece, not only state-controlled but uniform, at least in theory, for rich and poor. Spartan society in its later classical form is described by Xenophon, with a strong input of nostalgia (*Constitution of Sparta*), and by Aristotle (e.g. *Politics* 1294^b), as continuing this same equality. In practice, and especially in the late fifth century and early fourth, we know that rich Spartiates could flaunt their wealth in numerous ways. But on the level of principle and polis ideology, the equality of the hoplite phalanx, the levelling of the military messes, had been extended to the whole citizen society.

Spartan society contains many elements which seem reminiscent of a far older system, and there is always fascination, as there was for other Greeks, with the more wayward, eccentric, or even bizarre elements—the emphasis upon physical endurance, the supposed relics of ancient rituals of fertility and initiation. The constant fear of revolt from the subjected helots in Messenia and Laconia, who were the economic basis of the society (see above, p. 39), may have had a far more profound influence on Sparta's whole development than our evidence indicates. The education of the women, and their apparent freedom, astonished the rest of Greece. Xenophon wrote his *Constitution of Sparta*, which describes so much of this system, with the aim of explaining how Sparta came to be great, but he asserts that it was (in the early fourth century) no longer like this. His nostalgia makes it hard to see where either 'myth' or 'reality' began or ended: Spartan society lived out its invented traditions, and the rest of Greece believed them. However, if one looks at the political structures, the Spartans had a city-state very like many others. Constitutionally Sparta had much more in common with other city-states than Athens did. It was the control of the inhabitants and territory of Messenia, making both possible and necessary a highly developed warrior society, which was truly exceptional.

The polis

Despite the violence of revolution, the ideological antithesis between oligarchs and democrats, the variety in the activity and size of the citizen body, we can isolate certain common features which the Greek city-states shared. Non-citizens and slaves were numerous, and their exclusion set in relief the privileges of the citizens. The general idea that a polis was free and that its citizens had freedom was elevated to a supreme article of faith in Greek superiority over others: this was just as true in Athens where the citizens had more freedom in more areas than any other city-state, as it was in Sparta which thought of itself as the champion of freedom. Sparta freed many cities, including Athens, from their tyrants, fought bravely for Greek freedom from the Persians, and then claimed to be freeing Greece from Athens at the beginning of the Peloponnesian War. The ideal of citizen freedom and equality, egalitarianism, is found across democracies and oligarchies. 'Freedom' here was active, political freedom for a community to run itself, rather than the freedom of individuals to act as they wished in private life.

Respect for law, the idea that the polis should be run according to law and the processes of law, also crossed the political boundaries of oligarchy and democracy. What varied was who or what body administered that law, and what exactly 'law' meant. The primary word for 'law', *nomos*, was significantly and conveniently wide, including regulations which were unwritten as well as written, rules, norms, customs. Athenians prided themselves on being run by 'law' and revered their ancient law-giver Solon. Sparta looked back to her mythical lawgiver Lycurgus, and kept to the laws of Lycurgus which were in fact (conveniently) unwritten. Herodotus suggested it was Sparta's respect for *nomos* that gave it its greatness (Herodotus 7. 104), and here *nomos* included custom, the enshrined habits of the society, its system of upbringing, its discipline. Plato could declare that 'a city without regularly established law courts would not be a city at all' (*Laws* 766d). One of the most striking characteristics of the emerging city-states of the archaic period was the way they attempted from very early on to set up official rules for their running, tough laws to bind their top officials to the will of the polis and to prevent abuse of power—even if these laws were primarily produced by the élite to control their peers.

Each polis was fiercely independent and often had a long-running antagonism to its immediate neighbours, and this does much to explain the vitality of Greek cultural achievement. But this independence can be exaggerated: independence in the area of internal law was not, and could not, always be combined with total independence in external relations. Smaller places inevitably came under the umbrella of larger poleis, whether by means of formal alliances or outright control by the larger city-state. Megara, for instance, on a crucial route between central and southern Greece, was at various times a member of the Peloponnesian League of city-states led by Sparta (which included the powerful Corinth, Tegea, and [at times] Elis, the other cities of Arcadia, and Boeotia). But she frequently fell under the control of Athens (see below, pp. 184, 187). Political independence for Megara, as for many other small city-states, was a mirage.

What smaller city-states tried to do was choose their own allies, rather than be forced into alliances. Plataea, in southern Boeotia, tried to enlist Athens as a protector against its large neighbour Thebes, and became a constant challenge to Thebes' control over the cities of Boeotia through the federal Boeotian League. It was independent enough to be the only city to send troops to help the Athenians at the battle of Marathon. But placed where it was, its allegiance was critical. Thebes sought to bring it into the Boeotian League, seized it at the start of the Peloponnesian war, and eventually destroyed it 'in the ninety-third year after its alliance with the Athenians', as Thucydides put it (3. 68) bringing out its sad end and its long but ultimately unhelpful relationship with Athens.

Just as it is only a half-truth that modern nations are 'independent', so it is only a half truth that city-states were independent: they were certainly not always as independent as they wished. Internally, however, along with individual constitutions and laws, each polis had its own cults, and each was a community of its citizens and could forge its separate culture. Even the form of alphabet used by each polis tended to be regional: Athens, for instance, used a form of the alphabet with only 22 letters until the latter part of the fifth century when she moved over to the Ionian alphabet with 24 letters. The shared and common Hellenism expressed itself through regional and polis variations on the theme.

Athens itself, which provides so much of our evidence, and Sparta were similarly exceptional as city-states. Most poleis had a territory which gave them only their basic necessities of life: yet Athens had the large expanse of Attica, (see above p. 62), which she may have gained partly by expansion early in the archaic period. Within this were many villages (demes), some of which were so large that they could have passed as small poleis in their own right—Rhamnous, Marathon, Thoricus, or Acharnae. Sparta, which had conquered the whole of Messenia in the south-west Peloponnese and Southern

Laconia, had a territory of 8,000 square kilometres. This provided her with a large agricultural territory and the Messenians, enslaved as helots, to work it. Athens and Sparta both also created large and powerful leagues, the Athenian maritime league becoming an empire. In many respects, it is in the less powerful city-states that we see most clearly the remarkable particularism, individuality, the nature of such self-regulating, as well as the strengths and tensions, of the classical city-state.

The conventional translation of polis as 'city-state' is an attempt to convey the fact that all poleis are self-governing, having their own laws, army (the citizen-body), and decision-making processes. That is, they had the trappings of a simple state. But for all but the largest, Athens, the polis was primarily a community, and the sense of community was as strong as, or stronger than, the elements of state apparatus. Most city-states were small, and their inhabitants tended to cluster together in a compressed settlement which a modern observer might prefer to describe as a village or small market town. The model of the medieval city visible in late medieval or early Renaissance paintings, with city-walls, crowded houses within the walls, a few houses outside perhaps, and fields beyond, may give a reasonable parallel, if we add to this a temple to the patron deity, perhaps a defensible citadel, and the political and military identity of the ancient citizen-body. If Athens was unusual; Sparta, traditionally regarded as having ten thousand citizens but in fact declining to little more than a tenth that number, was more typical. To this moderate citizen body we would have to add wives, children, slaves, and resident aliens to arrive at the full population. Luxemburg has a territory of 2,600 square kilometres, almost the same size as Attica; the principalities of San Marino or Monaco would be nearer in size to the medium to small Greek poleis; and the citizen bodies meeting together in a small polis might be equivalent to the House of Commons of the British parliament when the House is packed. The quorum of 6,000 of the Athenian Assembly was uniquely large.

The polis was exceptional in the intensity and particularism of its political life, and above all the emphasis on the citizen body and its duties. It was a community and a state at once: and the citizens were subordinated to the common good of the community. As Aristotle put it, 'man is by nature an animal fitted to live in a polis'—he is 'a political animal' (*Politics* 1253^a). 'Citizen-state' then perhaps translates

'polis' more aptly than 'city-state': at any rate, while Aristotle oscil-
lated between thinking of the polis as the male citizen body alone, or
as the male citizens plus their families and all the other inhabitants,
the emphasis in other Greek writers was upon the polis as a community. The general Nicias could say to his dejected army in Sicily,
about to suffer overwhelming defeat in 413, 'you are a polis wherever
you sit down' (Thucydides 7. 77. 4), and ancient writers habitually
talked of the movers of events as 'the Spartans', 'the Athenians',
rather than the more abstract 'Sparta', 'Athens'. The human citizens
were in first place, and in political terms the polis may as well be the
citizen body. If we consider the wider networks and people necessary
to make a workable community, the women, children, slaves, and
metics, then obviously the polis necessarily involves, and therefore
includes, the larger population. But the narrower political definition
comes first.

So central was the nature of the citizen body in Greek thought that
theorists trying to construct the ideal polis or stable polis found it
hard to think beyond the citizen body itself and assumed that the
polis could be reformed by reforming its citizens. Similar assumptions lie behind the idea voiced several times in Aristotle's *Politics* that
the constitution of a city-state was educational: 'the polis is the
teacher of men' as the poet Simonides put it earlier (frag. 95). If one
says today that the modern citizen is educated by the state, one would
be referring to state-provided education. But state-controlled or even
state-provided education is conspicuous by its absence in ancient
Greece: it was not until the Hellenistic period that some cities took it
upon themselves to provide free tuition for the children of citizen
birth. Sparta was exceptional in the classical period for 'making education the business of the state', as Aristotle puts it (*Politics* 1337ᵃ),
though the education in question was mainly athletic, a training with
a clear military purpose. What Greeks normally meant by saying that
the polis was a teacher was that the city itself, its political institutions,
its constitution, and its laws—and we should add the religious cults
(below)—was educational, was crucial to the maturing of the citizen-
body: it was a culture in itself. Similarly when Thucydides has Pericles
say of the Athenians, 'We are an education to Greece', the idea
expresses well the subordination of the individual citizens to the
general needs and perceived common good.

Aristotle's *Politics*, written in about the 330s or 320s, is sometimes thought to be looking back with nostalgia to a system—the city-state—that was being overtaken by events, the dominant power of Macedon and what was to become the new world of the Hellenistic monarchies. But the very manner in which Aristotle describes the polis system implies that it was in strong health at the time he was writing. That period of tension, rapid change, and threats to some elements of the earlier polis, was an apt time for reflection and for ordering a mass of specific examples and theories into a clear analysis. The polis as an institution continued long after Philip of Macedon's defeat of the Greek coalition against him in 338 and after Alexander's death—though whether any polis would ever again be so powerful is another matter.

Religious activity and the polis

Religious cults articulate, reflect, and reinforce the bonds of the city-state. Many ancient historians (most notably Thucydides) and political thinkers showed little interest in the religious side to polis existence. Perhaps this is because the paramount preoccupation of Greek political thought was the attainment of stability and the avoidance of violent revolution. Or perhaps religious cult was too close a shadow of political secular structures—rather than an alternative power base—for it to be considered central to any study of politics. At any rate, the exclusively secular and political definition and interpretation of the polis in Aristotle's *Politics* has been immensely influential, and it skates over the religious festivals, processions, cults heroic and divine, great and tiny religious rituals, which were all as integral to citizen existence as citizen assemblies. A balanced vision of the classical period cannot do without attention to religion. There may be doubts about whether religious duties or pure political expediency governed any particular political decisions, but the communal life of the city-states was based as much around the rituals of cults as the political institutions such as Assembly and Council. Religious festivals were the occasion for competitive performances of much Greek poetry (including Homer), music, tragedies and comedies, as well as athletics.

Every city-state had temples to its patron deity and shrines and altars to many others. Each temple, each deity, received regular sacrifices according to a detailed calendar and the high points for citizens, in a world without weekends, were the festivals held in honour of one or other deity. Each polis had its own local version of religious observances for the main great deities, a multiplicity of cults and rituals of their own which combined observance of the usual gods of the Greek world with the peculiar details and emphases of each locality. So Hera was the patron goddess of Samos and had a spectacular temple there, along with Samian rituals; she also had an important shrine at Argos, strategically placed on an area of disputed territory, where she was also patron goddess. The patron deity of Athens, Athena Polias, had a cult statue in the Parthenon on the Acropolis, and there were other statues, altars and shrines to Athena.

Athena, Apollo or Dionysus and the other Olympian deities were honoured all over Greece and with rituals specific to each city according to the particular emphasis of their cults. At Athens, the City Dionysia honoured Dionysus with competitions of drama (see pp. 16, 126, 128, 181), and its rituals reflected features of the democracy, hence comedy became political satire. Elsewhere in Greece there were different festivals for Dionysus and even within Attica we find the rural Dionysia and the Lenaea which also included drama. Heroes also had cults, which were often bound to central myths of the city's past and its origins. Sparta had a cult to Menelaus and Helen; Athens revered Theseus, one of their legendary kings and heroes, recovered his bones in the 470s, and established a festival for him, the Theseia, to signal his importance. The polis particularism visible in other spheres was equally visible in cult.

Civic status was crucial, as always, and could be determined or reinforced by whether or not someone participated in certain cults. Cult was thus the backbone to much civic life, integrated closely with politics, and taken for granted to such an extent that changes in political life would be reflected in cult practice. Aristophanes makes a character in his *Acharnians* (146) joke about a Thracian prince, newly granted Athenian citizenship, having the right 'to eat sausages at the Apatouria'. The Apatouria was the festival at which the phratries (brotherhoods) held a sacrificial feast: children were introduced to the phratry at this festival and the phratries played a part in protecting entry to Athenian citizenship, guarding against fraudulent attempts to pass off illegitimate children. Similarly when an Athenian stood for office, he had to specify, as proof of his citizenship, where his family's altars were to Zeus Herkeios, 'Zeus of the front court', and to Apollo Patroos, Ancestral Apollo, and where their family graves were ([Aristotle] *Constitution of the Athenians* 55. 3). Some polis cults were celebrated only by women. The festival of the Thesmophoria, a fertility festival in honour of Demeter, was widespread and usually celebrated solely by citizen women. Wider allegiances, ethnic or tribal, could also be reflected in ritual observances. Herodotus (1. 147) could declare that in his view, Ionians were 'those who participated in the festival of the Apatouria'. Sparta and other Dorian states marked their claim to common ancestry by all celebrating the Carneia, in honour of Apollo, with races, whirling dances, hymns, and musical competitions. Civic identity, community participation, and membership of sub-groups within the polis were symbolized and expressed by cult participation.

The grand Athenian festival of the Panathenaea shows the interweaving of cult practice and political hierarchy and division. The festival took place roughly in August. Every four years it became the Great Panathenaea, and its athletic and musical festival attracted competitors and spectators from all over Greece. The great Panathenaic procession progressed to the Agora, then across the Agora along the designated route up to the Acropolis. The procession included representatives of all Athenians (hence the title of Panathenaea), including old men, Athenian women, young girls from the old aristocratic families. Even some metic women and slaves were apparently present, though in a clearly subordinate role. Women of Athens wove the peplos or robe to be presented to the statue of Athena Polias on the Acropolis, embroidered with a scene of the battle with the Giants. It was a festival of civic display and pride, the various sectors of the polis carefully represented in their proper places, foreigners and metics present to admire. When Athens developed her maritime empire in the fifth century, she began to require her allies to bring a cow and a full hoplite panoply or set of armour to the Panathenaea (and also to parade their tribute at the City Dionysia). Allied subordination and allegiance to Athens was symbolized by these contributions to her main city cults. Similarly the Athenians demanded that their colony Brea in Thrace participate in their mother-city's festivals, bringing a cow and panoply at the Panathenaea, and a phallos to the City Dionysia. Political relations were reflected in cult participation. That the precise relationship of colonists to their mother-city in cult activities should be formally worked out was not unique to imperial Athens. In a well-preserved early fifth-century law (c.500–475) about a colony of East Locrians established at Naupactus at the west end of the Corinthian Gulf, the Locrians lay down under what conditions the colonists can go back if their new life does not prosper: they give up their rights as citizens of East Locris, but they can sacrifice in Locris as foreigners and participate in other ceremonies of the mother city (Fornara 47). Their link with Locris as citizens is cut off, but they retain an association through cult.

Various subdivisions and subgroups in Athens also had numerous other cultic associations—metics from Phoenicia and metics from Corinth, for instance, had their own cults. Alongside the great city cults, which included the whole political community, were tribal cults: the ten new tribal divisions of the citizen body, created by Cleisthenes, celebrated cults of the ten Attic heroes after whom they were named. There were deme heroes, deme cults, and the phratry festival of the Apatouria already mentioned. Cultic activity expressed participation in one or other group or association as well as piety.

The polis regulated the details of cult as of all else. There was no clear separation of 'church' and 'state': the people regulated cultic ritual, decided who should not attend certain rituals and determined how priests were chosen and what their pay and perks should be. Thus the Athenian democracy created new democratic priesthoods alongside the traditional aristocratic ones. A fourth-century Athenian law on the Panathenaic procession meticulously specified how the sacrificial meat was to be distributed amongst the citizen body according to cult and status: for example the sacrifices at the great altar of Athena Polias and Athena Nike are to be distributed only to citizen men, not to the women who had some ritual function, unlike other sacrifices in the festival. When Eretria in Euboea set up a spectacular music festival in honour of the goddess Artemis, in a burst of civic triumph and confidence (c.340), the decree passed by the People and Council opens with the intention to celebrate the Artemisia 'as finely as possible'; prizes, maintenance payments for competitors, processions and sacrifices are all arranged. In this, the most important Eretrian festival, they celebrated their liberation by Athens (this is the period of Macedonian expansion, not Athenian), and the decree ends triumphantly with the decision, 'to write up the decree on a stone stele and stand it in the temple of Artemis, in order that the sacrifice and the musical festival for Artemis happen in this way for all time, while the people of Eretria are free and prosper and rule themselves' (*LSCG* 92).

When metics in the Piraeus wished to set up a cult to one of their home deities, Bendis the Thracian goddess, or Isis from Egypt, they requested permission from the Athenian people. The cult to Bendis became so domesticated that it became an Athenian public cult, though quite why the Athenians felt such a close affinity to this Thracian goddess is unknown. The early celebration of the cult to Bendis forms part of the dramatic setting of the opening of Plato's *Republic* (dramatic date 410). Other non-Athenian (but Greek) cults were introduced by the official approval of the Athenians: Pan was introduced from Arcadia to Athens after he had appeared to the messenger running from Athens to Sparta at the time of the Persian invasion of Attica in 490 and had demanded proper recognition (Herodotus 6. 105); Boreas the North Wind was also established at Athens in return for his help against the Persians (Herodotus 7. 189). Asclepius the healing god, who had a large sanctuary at Epidaurus, arrived in Athens in 420—the tragedian Sophocles gave him his first temporary home. It was also possible to set up a shrine to a deity who was already established, but with a new epithet to create a new shrine and cult: another innovation of the Persian Wars was the sacrifice to Zeus Eleutherios (Zeus the Liberator) after the great victory of Plataea (Thucydides 2. 71. 2).

Matters of cult were a formal item on the agenda of every meeting of the Athenian assembly. Important decisions might be confirmed or checked with the oracle at Delphi, but with the exception of that oracle, we search in vain for religious authority residing in the personnel of shrines and cults. Citizens not only regulated their own religious activities; they also punished those who went beyond the bounds of what was acceptable in religious matters: the formal charge against the philosopher Socrates was that he was introducing new gods and corrupting the youth (see below, p. 129).

Certain city-states attempted to enforce their will and authority upon the citizen body by invoking communal curses or religious sanctions. The city of Teos in Ionia issued communal curses, which they inscribed on stone (*c.*470) and uttered for the collectivity. They called down a curse upon any person and his family who used poison against the Teians, prevented corn imports or exported them again, damaged Teos, betrayed the city or harboured brigands, 'or [if anyone] does harm to the community of Teians and to Hellenes or to barbarians, let him perish, himself and his descendants'. This curse was to be uttered at the three main festivals, the spring festival of the Anthesteria, and the festivals of Heracles and of Zeus. This is an unusually direct and extreme case, but other cities felt perfectly able to invoke a specific god or religious sanctions in order to safeguard political decisions. This practice may have been more common before the Persian Wars but it does not die out completely in the classical period, and is even visible occasionally at Athens. Athenian democracy had such elaborate and effective political means to assert its collective will and authority that it did not need to resort so often to invoking religious sanctions, but Athens was exceptionally developed politically.

Amidst such a multiplicity of cults, large and small, there was bound to be much overlapping. Festivals and rituals point to a series of crossing and interweaving groups which might be larger or smaller than the polis to which they belonged. Some cults created an umbrella over several cities. The Greek traders and settlers given a privileged settlement at Naucratis in Egypt had individual cults for certain of the participating cities (Miletus, Aegina, Samos), but also a shrine called the 'Hellenion', which signified the collective association of Greeks together in Naucratis, as opposed to the separate communities of citizens from each contributing city. The twelve main cities in Ionia had a 'Panionion', a temple where a festival for all Ionians was held and a place where they met to discuss policy (Herodotus 1. 142–3), and it signified their common Ionian identity alongside individual polis rivalries and polis cults.

It is within the polis itself that the multiplicity of cults is most striking. In Attica, an Athenian citizen had his own local deme cults, as well as associations with cults which crossed larger parts of Attica. Take an Athenian who came from the village and deme of Marathon, for instance: Marathon was part of an ancient group of villages called the Tetrapolis ('Four cities'), which had their own impressive calendar and sacrifices to very ancient cults. But our citizen from Marathon would also be associated with the cults of his tribe and his phratry, and with the big city cults in the centre of Athens. In addition there were various private religious associations, for citizens and for non-citizens, connected to the cult and shrine of a hero. Even associations such as drinking clubs often had a ritual element, making sacrifices or libations to a particular deity, though that was hardly their central purpose, and they easily turned into provocative political groups.

Cults of initiation stood apart, transcending the usual civic, polis, and even ethnic divisions. They were voluntary, 'elective' cults, which people joined as a positive individual choice rather than participating automatically as part of a particular polis, tribe, or other group. The cult of Demeter at Eleusis, one of the most important, accepted as initiates men and women, free and slave, Athenian and non-Athenian; the Mysteries of Samothrace, for the Cabiri or 'Great Gods', accepted initiates of any status, though initiates were mostly male. Other cults, often foreign, like the cults of Isis or Dionysus (who was perceived to be foreign) attracted a zeal that far outstepped the bonds of community and polis. But these cults throw into relief the more usual pattern. Cults and sacrifices in classical Greece were intimately linked to civic distinctions and in their staggering multiplicity they also reflect the regionalism and particularism of classical Greek society.

The city at war

Hans van Wees

About two dozen city-states were annihilated in the wars of the classical period. After receiving their unconditional surrender, the enemy cut the throats of the entire adult male population, made slaves of the women, children, and elderly, and sold to new masters those who were slaves already. It counted as an act of humanity to ensure that all prisoners were indeed sold, however difficult it might be to find buyers for them: normally, the slave traders would simply abandon the smallest children and the aged by the roadside to die of starvation and exposure, if they were not killed by dogs or wolves first (Xenophon, *Agesilaus* 1. 21–2). Thousands more died in each of the major battles of the age, which brought together coalition armies of tens of thousands of soldiers from all over Greece. Soldiers fell at an average rate of one in seven on the losing side, one in twenty among the victors. The financial cost of war dwarfed all other public expenditure, including the most monumental of building projects. Greek warfare did not usually have such a devastating impact—much of the time it was confined to brief incursions which did some damage to farming areas and claimed a few victims but had no lasting social, economic, or demographic consequences—yet there was always a risk of escalation into a war threatening the very existence of the state.

The high stakes involved, and the large proportion of men liable for military service during most of their adult lives, meant that warlike prowess was regarded as a vital aspect of being a man, a citizen, and a Greek. So sensitive were Greek men to any slur on their bravery that the orator Aeschines sought to win points in debate by listing his own military credentials, as well as those of his brother and brother-in-law, while accusing his opponent Demosthenes of cowardice: 'I dare not call you a real man, since you were prosecuted for desertion'

(2. 148–51, 167–9). A sense that Greeks collectively were far better soldiers than any nation of barbarians developed early: Homer's *Iliad* already contrasted the obedience and solidarity of the legendary Greek heroes with the chaotic efforts of the Trojans (3. 2–9; 4. 428–38; 17. 364–5). In the classical period, Greek successes against the Persian Empire reinforced such ideas to the point where the historian Herodotus could represent the Persians as not only inferior in skill but incapable of grasping the principles which inspired Greek discipline and courage (Herodotus 5. 49, 97; 7. 101–4, 208–9; 9. 62). War shaped Greek identities no less than Greek political, social, and economic life.

The causes of war

Armed conflict was common: it has been estimated that classical Athens was at war two years out of three. Representations and reminders of war were everywhere: in the ubiquitous memorials and tombs of the dead, in the victory monuments littering sacred precincts, in the sculptural decoration of temples, in dramatic performances, in the orations delivered in assemblies, lawcourts, and at public funerals. Images of war penetrated even the dining-rooms of private houses, where arms and armour were hung on the walls and many a bowl or drinking cup bore a painted scene of battle. Yet the Greeks did not think of war as the normal state of affairs in international relations. When at the beginning of *Laws*, Plato's last dialogue, one of the speakers declares that 'what most people call peace is nothing but a word, and in fact every city-state is always, by nature, in a state of undeclared war with every other city-state' (626a), this state of war is purely theoretical. It is an intellectual's analysis of the underlying tensions in international relations, not the perception of politicians, soldiers, or the general public. Plato himself argued that constitutions should be geared towards peace (628de).

A peculiarity of Greek international relations, which might seem to suggest that peace was indeed seen as an abnormal, temporary condition, is that peace treaties were usually of limited duration: fifty years, thirty years, or less. But most of these treaties did more than merely establish relations of non-aggression: they created alliances, binding the parties to support one another in war, whether defensive or offen-sive. It is hardly surprising that states set a limit on such agreements rather than commit themselves indefinitely to fighting on behalf of their allies. In the fourth century, many attempts were made to forge a common peace, embracing all Greeks, and these multilateral treaties, which did not entail military obligations to any single city-state, were *not* limited in time. Throughout classical literature, the virtues of peace were extolled, and the evils of war denounced. Tragedies such as Aeschylus' *Persians* or Euripides' *Trojan Women* brought to life the terrible consequences of defeat, while comedies such as Aristophanes' *Acharnians* and *Peace* positively glorified peace as a time of celebra-tion and abundance. The sense that war was an unnatural state of affairs was reflected in a proverb: 'in peace, sons bury their fathers; in war, fathers bury their sons' (Herodotus 1. 87).

War was nevertheless common because, as Thucydides has an Athenian say, 'We believe that it is divine, and know for certain that it is universally human, by natural compulsion, to rule whatever one can' (5. 105. 2). The city-states aimed to establish for themselves a recognized position of leadership as a regional power, as ruler of the sea (*thalassokrator*), or as the dominant state in Greece at large. The Athenians, according to Thucydides, gave three reasons for waging wars in pursuit of leadership: they wanted honour or respect (*timê*) and profit (*ophelia*), and were motivated by fear (1. 75. 3, 76. 2). Fear implies that they built up their military resources in self-defence: first against Persia, later against Sparta. In a climate of fierce competition for supremacy, suspicion of others' ambitions was rife and bound to lead to pre-emptive strikes. Hence Thucydides' famous claim that 'the truest cause' of the Peloponnesian War was Sparta's fear of the grow-ing power of Athens (1. 23. 6; 1. 88; see p. 187). As for profit, the outcome of war was usually that the defeated party agreed to become an ally of the victor, which did not usually involve the payment of tribute or any other transfer of resources. Even when a city was des-troyed, a new, independent, community was normally established on its site; direct annexation of land was rare. Greek armies did eagerly seize chances to take booty, but, as a rule, the material stakes for which they fought were small: 'tiny amounts of not particularly good land' (Herodotus 5. 49).

Most remarkable is the desire for honour or respect. Herodotus imagined that the Persians were deeply impressed to find that Greeks 'competed not for money but for excellence' (8. 26). There are strik-ing instances of wars being attributed to more or less symbolic acts of disrespect towards communities or their citizens. When the Corinthians declared war on Corcyra in 433, according to Thucydides the dispute concerned primarily the *hybris* towards Corinth which the Corcyraeans displayed in refusing to grant Corinth its con-ventional ritual privileges and signs of respect (1. 38. 2–3). Xenophon similarly cites Elis' insults to Sparta among the causes of the Elean War; they had, among other things, banned Spartans from competing in the Olympic games, publicly whipped a prominent Spartan for taking part surreptitiously, and stopped a Spartan king from offering sacrifice at Olympia (*Hellenica* 3. 2. 21–2). Much of the value of hegemony and domination lay in the prestige or honour it brought, and a state which felt that it was not being shown the respect to which it was entitled might respond with force, even if its security or resources were not at risk.

The soldiers: military roles and social status

Conscript citizen armies were the norm in classical Greece, and liabil-ity for service was nearly life-long (until the age of sixty). A distinc-tion between civilian and soldier therefore barely existed. The armed forces consisted largely of amateur, part-time soldiers, and social and political statuses within a community were tied to military roles.

Citizen infantry: hoplites and light-armed

In most parts of Greece, the main armed force consisted of hoplites, heavy infantry, each armed with a single thrusting spear and sword, and protected by a panoply of bronze armour (see Fig. 1). The round hoplite shield, measuring 3 ft. (90 cm.) across and made of wood faced with bronze, weighed about 15 lbs. (7 kg.); its weight was sup-ported by a double grip: a handle at the rim and an arm-band in the centre. This shield, and a bronze helmet, were the core of the panoply; less essential items were bronze shin-guards and the corslet, either of thin bronze sheet metal or thick layered linen or leather, lighter and cheaper, yet no less effective.

Figure 1 Hoplites in action recovering the body of a dead comrade from the line of battle, third quarter of the sixth century.

Hoplite service was compulsory for all adult male citizens who met a certain property requirement. The level of this requirement seems higher than what one needed in order to afford the armour and weapons: the hoplite class may have been defined more narrowly than it need have been because military duty and political privilege were linked—the right to hold some offices in Athens, and the right to vote in Sparta, were confined to those who met the hoplite property census (see above, p. 56). From the figures we have for the size of Athens' general levy, we may tentatively deduce that between a third and half the population had the means to provide hoplite arms and armour. Mobilization in self-defence, and for large-scale campaigns against neighbours was by general levy, and included not only the hoplite census class, but everyone capable of laying their hands on any kind of weapon. The presence of light-armed citizens (*psiloi*) in the general levy was so much taken for granted that it is hardly ever mentioned. When the Athenians invaded Boeotia in 424, 'numerous poorly armed men followed, as part of the general levy of available foreigners and citizens', a total of many more than 10,000 (Thucydides 4. 93. 3–94. 1): discounting the foreigners, and the slave attendants who would also have formed part of the levy (see below), they must still have been as numerous as the hoplites. The greater mobility and range of light-armed soldiers gave them certain advantages over hoplites, which might have been put to very effective use. Yet the military potential of the mass of poorer citizens remained untapped, since institutionalizing their role would have given them a claim to political power on a par with the hoplites; as a disorganized mob, not obliged to perform regular service, they could be safely ignored.

As part-time soldiers, citizen hoplites subscribed to a distinctly non-professional ethos. For most of the classical period, training and organization remained rudimentary everywhere except Sparta. The main form of training was exercise in the gymnasia, which may have included some weapons training but primarily consisted of wrestling, running, jumping, and throwing the javelin and discus; it apparently did not include formation drills. Dancing was also seen as a suitable way to improve one's co-ordination in battle, and there was indeed a war-dance, the *pyrrikhê*, which mimicked combat movements. It was left to private initiative how often and how hard a man trained, and whether he took additional instruction in the use of weapons from a private tutor, as some did (Plato, *Laches* 178a–184c). Some communities did, however, maintain crack infantry units, such as the Theban Sacred Band, which consisted of 300 men organized in homoerotically-linked pairs (Diodorus 12. 70. 1; Plutarch *Pelopidas* 18–19).

Only in Sparta was training regimented for *all* male citizens, who exercised regularly and in organized groups from the age of seven. It is likely that the Spartans practised some weapons- and formation-drill, but their training, too, centred on athletics. Tellingly, when king Agesilaus tried to get his troops in top condition, he offered prizes for the best javelin-thrower, the best archer, and the best horseman, but gave the prize for hoplites simply to the man who had the best body

(Xenophon *Hellenica* 3. 4. 16). As elsewhere, the main goal of exercise was clearly general fitness, strength, and agility, rather than more specific combat skills.

Both Sparta and Athens ensured that 18- and 19-year old youths gained some military experience by sending them out to patrol the countryside, before they were eligible to fight in the regular army. In Sparta, this took the form of the notorious 'secret service', the *krypteia*, covert patrols which terrorized the helot population (see p. 133). Athens employed regular patrols (*peripoloi*), which from the 370s at the latest consisted of youths known as ephebes. By the 330s, ephebes received a full year of training in hoplite fighting, archery, javelin-throwing, and catapult-firing, followed by a year of patrol duty.

Cavalry

In most parts of Greece, only the rich could afford the expense of keeping horses. Archaic poetry and art show that those who did own horses had long been in the habit of riding to battle, but dismounting to take their place among the hoplites and fight on foot. At the time of the Persian invasion, the Greek coalition army had no cavalry. Some of the reasons for this were practical. Much of the terrain was unsuitable for horses, which were particularly vulnerable since horseshoes were not used. Also it was not easy to find the steady seat needed to fight from horseback, without the use of saddle or stirrups. Another reason for the late development of cavalry was the notion that its style of fighting—quick charges and retreats, and mostly missile action—was less demanding and dangerous than heavy infantry combat. The élite was reluctant to take on a military role which lacked the prestige accorded to hoplites. This also explains the curious system which Sparta eventually adopted, whereby the wealthiest citizens provided cavalry horses but did not ride them. Instead, the authorities assigned to cavalry service those who were 'physically weakest' and 'least concerned with honour' (Xenophon, *Hellenica* 6. 4. 11): in Sparta, which more than any other community cultivated hoplite values, no self-respecting citizen could be asked to fight on horseback.

The Athenians in the first half of the fifth century were fighting enemies who possessed large cavalry forces, and so, despite these obstacles to the creation of cavalry, they were compelled to establish a cavalry of their own. This reached a size of 1,000 by the beginning of the Peloponnesian War, and proved particularly useful in harassing and containing invading forces which scattered to pillage and burn. Soon afterwards, the Spartans in turn were forced to create a cavalry in order to contain raids into Spartan territory (Thuc. 4. 55. 2). By the early fourth century, most states had at least a small cavalry detachment of their own.

Mercenaries

In the fourth century, mercenary forces were so widespread that some regarded them as a plague threatening the very existence of the citizen soldier (Isocrates 8. 41–8). Such hostile views were exaggerated: to the end of the classical age, mercenary forces were used in addition to, not instead of, citizen hoplites. The conditions which pushed many Greeks into mercenary service had existed for centuries: general poverty; continual faction fighting and *coups d'état* within communities which created large bodies of political exiles looking for new careers; and a spirit of enterprise which led many young men to seek their fortunes abroad despite being well-off and under no compulsion to leave home. The supply of mercenaries had accordingly been abundant since the early archaic period.

A rise in demand, rather than supply, explains why mercenaries played an ever more prominent role in fourth-century Greece. Mercenary troops had two advantages: they could be committed to long and distant campaigns, unlike citizen soldiers who had families and farms to look after, and they could provide specialist skills which citizen soldiers did not possess. Most Greek states had nothing to match the archers of the Persians or the javelin-throwers known as peltasts found in the mountains of north-western Greece, Macedonia, and Thrace. These peltasts could be a serious threat to hoplites. Equipped with a long javelin and short sword, their only armour was a light shield of wicker or hide (see Fig. 2), which meant that they were mobile enough to run forward, throw their missiles, and run back again without giving the heavy-armed an opportunity to defend themselves. Their effect could be devastating when they caught hoplites on their exposed flank or when hoplites tried to give chase, broke rank, and became vulnerable to hit-and-run attacks. The heavy infantry came to fear peltasts 'as little children fear the bogeyman' (Xenophon, *Hellenica* 4. 4. 17).

Figure 2 Lightly-armed warrior known as a 'peltast' from the shape of his shield (*pelte*), shown on a cup of *c.*510.

As with the cavalry, there was a tension between the military need for such specialist light infantry and the social and cultural obstacles to its creation. Greek pride in close combat, and contempt for missile warfare as effeminate, meant that citizens of hoplite status could hardly be asked to train as archers or peltasts. Employing poorer citizens in these roles would have meant giving them the kind of formal military status which hoplites, for political reasons, liked to reserve for themselves. To play the part that some citizens would not play, and others could not be allowed to play, a city therefore needed to recruit outsiders.

In the major wars of the fifth century, the additional manpower and specialist skills were usually provided by *allies* rather than mercenaries, and many distant campaigns, too, could be sustained by locally mobilizing allied troops. The Athenian general Demosthenes owed much of his famous victory over the Spartans at Pylos in 425 to the presence of allied peltasts and archers (Thucydides 4. 28. 4, 32. 2). Fifth-century Athens and Sparta had so many allies in so many places that they rarely needed mercenary support. A minor player such as Corinth, on the other hand, might well recruit mercenaries even before the Peloponnesian War (Thucydides 1. 60. 1). When Athens lost its allies, it too began to hire troops, establishing a unit of up to 4,000 peltasts under Iphicrates which proved highly successful during the Corinthian War (see below, pp. 197–202). The prominence of mercenaries in the fourth century may therefore be explained not only by the growing length and range of campaigns, and the increasing use of specialists, but also by the attenuated nature of alliances at the time. With the collapse of Spartan hegemony in 371, the fragmentation of Greece was such that it became harder to find allies than to hire troops. Mercenaries accordingly featured in just about every war from the 360s onwards.

The fighting skills of the professional soldier were universally recognized. Xenophon, himself once a mercenary commander, went so far as to claim that the quality of citizen soldiers improved when the presence of mercenary troops set a high standard of excellence to emulate (*The Cavalry Commander* 9. 3–4). Nevertheless, many felt that mercenaries would not stand their ground against the odds as citizens would (Aristotle, *Nicomachean Ethics* 1116^{b}) and, of course, that mercenaries would desert for better, or more regular, pay elsewhere. The employment of professionals thus remained inhibited by the citizens' suspicion of their loyalty.

Slaves and the army

Since slaves were not normally allowed to fight as hoplites or horsemen, their role in warfare is often underestimated. Yet it was not confined to crisis situations, when the loyalty of slaves might be bought with a promise of freedom for those who took up arms on behalf of their masters. Nor was it confined to the armies of freed helots (*neodamodeis*) which the Spartans sent to fight all their long-distance campaigns in northern Greece and Asia Minor. Slaves served their masters in war just as they did at home.

The personal slave attendants of hoplites and horsemen formed the bulk of the army's baggage-train. These 'shield-bearers', 'retainers', and 'baggage-carriers' fetched water, cooked, put up tents, and carried equipment, food, and other possessions. They also followed their masters on active duty. That the attendants were armed is evident from Herodotus' claim that at Plataea in 479 there were as many light-armed as heavy-armed, since there was 'one with each man' (9. 29). He can only be thinking of the hoplites' personal servants. On the same occasion, in the Spartan contingent seven light-armed helots were 'stationed with' each hoplite, protecting him (9. 28–9). This probably means that, when Sparta mobilized its large serf population, as it regularly did, these helots were assigned to the service of individual hoplites. We are never told where they are or what they do in battle, but Herodotus' emphasis on their vast numbers, their armament, and their closeness to the hoplites, shows that these men did more than just carry baggage. We can only guess that such attendants stood close behind the phalanx, launching missiles over the heads of the hoplites. If so, their loyalty and their impact on battle must have been greater than our sources care to admit.

Warships and their crews

Citizens, foreigners, and slaves were all found together on board the classical Greek warship, the technologically highly sophisticated trireme (see Fig. 3). Since each trireme had a crew of up to 200, navies required vast resources of manpower. In the early years of the Peloponnesian War, Athens kept 100 ships on semi-permanent guard-duty, while it regularly employed a total of up to 250 ships, or a complement of up to 50,000 men (Thucydides 3. 17).

The captain of the trireme, the trierarch, was not a specialist, but a wealthy citizen who had volunteered or been appointed to take up this prestigious position. In Athens, he was allotted a state-owned ship for a term of one year, during which time it was his responsibility to hire a crew and keep the ship in a seaworthy condition. Serving under the captain were the marines (*epibatai*), normally ten citizen hoplites and four archers, and the ship's officers (a helmsman and a look-out; a rowing-master, assisted by a pipe-player; a purser; and a shipwright to make emergency repairs), all specialists, who might be hired abroad as well as at home.

Figure 3 The *Olympias*, a modern reconstruction of an ancient trireme.

The bulk of the crew consisted of oarsmen, recruited from among anyone willing to serve for pay, whether citizen, metic, or slave. Among citizens, this meant primarily the *thetes*, the lowest property class, who needed the money and were not liable to other forms of military service. A large navy would need to draw not only on citizens, but on metics and on manpower recruited abroad (Xenophon *Hellenica* 6. 2. 12). Rowers might bring their slaves to row on the same ship and earn them extra wages (Thucydides 7. 13. 2). Citizen rowers were usually outnumbered by foreigners and slaves. In the navy of Corcyra as many as 8 in 10 were slaves (Thucydides 1. 55. 1), and while the Athenians were in principle capable of manning a fleet with citizens only, their crews, too, were normally 'bought rather than home-grown', and made up largely of metics and slaves (Thucydides 1. 121. 3, 143. 1–2; 3. 16, 18; 7. 63. 3).

Even if they formed a minority of the crew, many thousands of citizen oarsmen were employed by the larger navies: hence the common people of Athens could be mockingly called *to rhuppapai*, the yo-heave-ho, after the rowers' rhythmic call (Aristophanes, *Wasps* 908–9). Many ancient texts express the greatest contempt for the naval mob. Even the compliments paid to rowers in the earliest comedies of Aristophanes are back-handed: the risk to life and limb is ignored in favour of remarks about the sore bottoms and blisters suffered in the battle of Salamis (*Wasps* 1118–19; *Knights* 784–5, 1366–8). The ideology of infantry warfare thus draws a sharp distinction between the marines who, despite their low social status, fight as hoplites and deserve respect, and the rest of the crew who are despised because they do not actually fight. As in the case of light-armed infantry, there was a political agenda behind this contempt for the crews of triremes: authors who belittle the rowers do so because they are hostile to the idea of letting them have a share in power on a par with the hoplites.

Many, probably most, of the oarsmen, like the ships' officers, made their living primarily from rowing. As individuals, they were professionals; collectively, however, they had to begin training anew every time they joined a ship, since crews were not permanent units but assembled from scratch whenever a vessel was about to be launched. As a rule, it would take a week or so before the crew of a newly manned ship had had enough practice of various drills to be ready for action. The superior quality of full-time rowers became painfully evident when, in a crisis, the rest of the citizens were mobilized for service in the navy. With these inexpert crews normal battle tactics could not be executed (Xenophon, *Hellenica* 1. 6. 31), and when Apollodorus (see above, pp. 45–8) was trierarch he simply dismissed his levied crew as useless and set about hiring replacements ([Demosthenes] 50. 7).

Waging war

Classical Greek war had two faces. Its ideals and some of its customs encouraged waging campaigns and battles as if war were a game played by restrictive rules. In practice, the pursuit of profit and honour knew few restraints and tended towards total warfare. As so often in a clash of values, people liked to think that the ideal had been reality in the past, but abandoned by the present generation. Such nostalgic images have much influenced modern ideas about traditional Greek warfare, but, whatever did change in classical warfare, chivalrous ideals and ruthless violence always coexisted and clashed.

Practical limitations

Demosthenes, in one of his tirades against Philip II of Macedon (*Third Philippic* 9. 47–52), painted a rosy picture of the 'simplicity' of warfare in the days of the Peloponnesian War. His first claim, in which there is some truth, was that war used to be confined to 'its own season' of four or five months of summer. Most campaigns took place between the time of the grain harvest in May and the vintage in September, or the ploughing in November at the latest, when there were crops to raid for provisions and it was possible to camp out in the open. Summer was also the only safe season for sailing. Waging war during the rest of the year was beyond the means of most city-states. However, the few states which did have the requisite manpower and money had long since extended the season for war as far as they could, and, like Philip, 'made no distinction between summer and winter' (Demosthenes 9. 48, 50).

Demosthenes' assertion that armies once confined themselves to ravaging enemy countryside and fighting pitched battles, without attempting to capture cities, is a half-truth. Although sieges were not common, they were far from unknown: already in 491, Athenian troops laid siege to Aegina, and in 489 they besieged Paros for 26 days (Herodotus 9. 75; 6. 135). The short duration and failure of such attempts indicate that the relative scarcity of sieges stemmed, again, from a lack of means rather than a lack of will. Given an opportunity, Greeks rarely passed up the chance to sack an enemy city. Throughout the classical period assaults on cities and other fortified sites seem to have been about as common as pitched battles.

Most misleading is Demosthenes' notion that warfare used to be 'open and governed by custom' (9. 48). The image of battle as a for-mally arranged duel is an extreme idealization. Tradition knew of a few archaic battles fought under formally agreed conditions, but even at the time these were hardly typical. In the classical period, pitched battles were often fought *as if* they had been arranged, because wars tended to follow a predictable sequence: an army would begin ravaging enemy farmland, defenders would march out to stop them, and the forces would come face-to-face in the open plain. The armies might remain encamped opposite one another for a few days, or even a week, waiting for a favourable opportunity to arise, or for the other to make the first move. They might even try to sting the enemy into action by sending out cavalry to taunt them: 'Are you planning to settle here?' (Thucydides 6. 63. 3). The conditions thus superficially resembled those of a duel. But neither time, place, nor conditions were ever negotiated or formally agreed in classical Greece, and few felt inhibited by a sense of chivalry from taking an unfair advantage when they had the chance.

Xenophon urged unequivocally that a commander should 'himself devise a ruse for every occasion, since in war nothing is more profitable than deceit . . . Think about successes in war, and you will find that most of the greatest have been achieved by means of deceit' (*The Cavalry Commander* 5. 9–11). We hear of ambushes, sudden descents on armies still in marching column, and enemies taken by surprise as a result of sudden forced marches, stealthy changes of position, deceptive signals, and deliberate misinformation. Such episodes cannot be attributed to a decline from previously sportsman-like principles. It was, after all, back in 496 that Cleomenes I of Sparta used the herald's call for breakfast as the secret signal to attack, caught the Argive army by surprise, and chased 6,000 soldiers into an enclosure where they were massacred to a man (Herodotus 6. 78; 7. 148). Out-of-season campaigns, assaults on cities, and deception, then, were not forbidden by agonal principles. Morally they were perfectly acceptable, and if they were relatively uncommon, it was because they were often unfeasible.

Religious and moral constraints

Warfare was, however, subject to certain religious and other norms. An army could not move without consultation of oracles and omens. Bad omens were often given as the reason for inaction or retreat, and earthquakes were interpreted as warning signs, causing more than one major expedition to be aborted. Religious scruples required the observance of sacred periods during which warfare was not permitted. Spartans missed the Battle of Marathon because they were not allowed to start a campaign before the full moon (Herodotus 6. 106); they let the celebration of the Hyacinthia festival interfere with their conduct of wars (Herodotus 9. 7; Xenophon, *Hellenica* 4. 5. 11); and they did not fight during the Carneia festival, so that most of the Spartan army missed the Battle of Thermopylae (Herodotus 7. 206;

Thucydides 5. 54). No Greek state was allowed to fight during the truces proclaimed for the celebration of the Olympic and other Panhellenic Games. There is enough evidence for these rules being followed even in the most trying circumstances to show that they were not cynically invoked only when it was convenient. On the other hand, there was a good deal of leeway in applying them. In 419, Argos invaded Epidaurus on the fourth day before the Carneia, but gave itself more time by adding a number of interpolated days to its calendar. Thus Argos was able to fight on while Epidaurus' allies, celebrating their festival at the normal time, were unable to intervene (Thucydides 5. 53–6).

Moral constraints on classical warfare were few, but significant. One important ideal current in the fourth century was that one should not enslave or massacre the inhabitants or destroy the buildings of a captured Greek city. The most evidently agonal rules applied to the aftermath of pitched battle. Mutilation of enemy dead was banned: the victors confined themselves to stripping the bodies of all possessions, before allowing the naked corpses to be recovered by their comrades under a truce. The defeated army, in turn, had to respect the enemy's *tropaion*, a trophy of arms and armour attached to a wooden frame set up to mark the site of a victory, even if this meant tolerating a memorial of humiliating defeat just outside one's own city gates. By custom, the *tropaion* was constructed with perishable materials so that eventually it would collapse and past hostility could be forgotten.

At the conclusion of pitched battle, then, we at last find explicit and widely observed conventions designed to keep hostility within bounds. Their importance is not to be denied, but equally one can hardly escape the conclusion that their scope was limited. Much of what gave classical warfare the appearance of restraint was the result of practical limitations, and warring states were happy to overcome such limitations if they could.

Devastation

Invariably the first hostile action after a declaration of war was to send troops to ravage hostile territory. A war might pass without a pitched battle or siege, but never without an attempt to wreak destruction in enemy countryside. Arguably, to exact revenge or punishment by means of agricultural devastation was the essence of Greek warfare.

The verb to ravage (*deioo*) indicates destruction in the form of trampling down, cutting, or burning crops and trees, smashing agricultural machinery such as olive presses, and destroying farm houses. This was accompanied by what the Greeks called driving and carrying (*agein kai pherein*), that is to say, driving off animals and captives and carrying off movable wealth. How much damage would be sustained by enemy territory depended on the invader's timing, resources, and intentions. Most often, it seems, an invading army would find little to destroy or plunder, since at its approach the countryside had been evacuated. The population sought refuge behind city walls, taking with them 'even the woodwork of the houses themselves' (Thucydides 2.14.1). Livestock were ferried across to neighbouring islands, or herded together in remote peninsulas and mountain regions. Even the crops had usually already been harvested. On the other hand, an invasion could do very great damage if it was entirely unexpected, like Agesipolis' invasion of Argos during a sacred month (Xenophon, *Hellenica* 4. 7. 7). If one could time an invasion to interfere with the harvesting or sowing, it might be as effective as a siege in creating shortages of food (*Hellenica* 4. 6. 13–7. 1).

In any case, it took a long time and a large number of men equipped with axes, swords, and firebrands to do such extensive damage that a whole community suffered economically. Often, cavalry came out to harass enemy armies as they scattered to plunder, slowing down progress even further. Invasions could last only as long as the provisions which the soldiers brought along, supplemented with what they could find in enemy country, and normally food and drink ran out after 2–6 weeks, however austere the military diet. As a result, the capacity for destruction was limited, and only small territories invaded by large armies were in danger of sustaining structural damage. In order to do serious harm to a large city-state, one needed to establish within its territory a fortified position manned by a garrison that could mount raids all year round as well as encourage the desertion of slaves or serfs. This tactic, known as *epiteikhismos*, became a major force during and after the Peloponnesian War.

In certain circumstances, then, agricultural devastation could be severe enough to force the enemy to surrender, but in most circumstances agricultural devastation was much more limited and took on a more symbolic character, as a challenge to come out and fight. Even some token ravaging of enemy territory could thus save face after a major defeat, if the enemy failed to rise to the challenge (*Hellenica* 4. 5. 10; 6. 5. 20–1). For the victims, the consequences of not responding were both loss of resources and loss of prestige; and internal dissension was bound to break out as some lost their livelihoods while others were spared (Thucydides 2. 13, 20–1). If they did respond, a pitched battle would decide the issue.

Battle

A key tactical decision in leading out the hoplite *phalanx* was whether to make the formation wide but shallow, and try to outflank the enemy, or make it deep but narrow, and aim to break through one section of the enemy ranks in the hope of causing a general panic. The Thebans owed their famous victories over the Spartans at Leuctra in 371 (see pp. 206–7) in part to exceptional depths of up to fifty ranks; most armies opted for width and drew up only eight to sixteen deep.

When the charge was signalled by trumpets, the forces began to move at walking pace and sang a *paian*. They gradually picked up speed and ultimately broke into a run. At this point the battle-hymn degenerated into a war-whoop, *alalê* or *eleleu*. In order to stay in formation, soldiers tried not to run until they came within the reach of enemy missiles, at about 200 yards; experienced fighters might manage to restrain themselves until they were at a mere 100 yards distance (Xenophon, *Hellenica* 4. 3. 17). Spartan hoplites did not run at all, but advanced at a steady pace, singing marching hymns to the music of pipes. They wore garlands, as one would in a religious procession, at least up to the point where they halted to perform, much later than anyone else and deliberately within sight of the enemy, a pre-battle blood sacrifice (Xenophon, *Constitution of the Spartans* 13. 8; Plutarch, *Lycurgus* 22). There were practical advantages to this: music kept the soldiers in step (Thucydides 5. 70) and a last-minute halt for sacrifice provided a chance to dress the ranks again. But the religious dimension should not be denied. The show of discipline which caused many opponents to run without offering any resistance was all the more unnerving for suggesting that the Spartans saw themselves as serenely advancing to the ritual slaughter of the enemy.

The most illuminating evidence for the nature of classical infantry combat is found, ironically, in a historical novel, *The Education of Cyrus*, a vehicle for Xenophon's ideas about military practice and leadership (see p. 135). The story's Persian hero faces the army of a formidable Asian coalition, drawn up thirty deep, but makes his own phalanx merely two deep, on the grounds that only the first two ranks of any army are actively involved in the action (6. 3. 21–3; 4. 17). The rear ranks evidently did not join combat, but merely encouraged their comrades and stood ready to take their place. The front-line action described in Xenophon's novel consisted of a peculiar combination of pushing and fighting, which clearly reflects the Greek style of combat. While the two-deep Persian army easily routs everyone else, they are slowly driven back by the Egyptians, whose superior equipment and tactics in many ways mirror those of Greek hoplites: their large shields, 'leaning against their shoulders, assisted them in the pushing', and so,

joining together their shields, they advanced and pushed. The Persians, who supported their shields with their hands only, could not resist, but retreated step by step, while they struck and were struck. (7. 1. 33–4)

What is happening here is clearly what is often represented in Greek art, too: the shield is carried at a slope, the top tilted towards the body and the bottom pointing away from the body towards the enemy (see Fig. 4). When hoplites, or Xenophon's Egyptians, push, they evidently do so with their left arms only, forcing the lower rims of their shields against the shields of their opponents in order to unbalance them and force them back. At the same time, they deal blows with the spears or swords in their right hands.

In this context, one cannot take too seriously the 'joining' or 'locking' of shields, which also features in classical battle narratives, most explicitly in Thucydides' observation that every hoplite 'brings his unprotected side as near as possible to the shield of the man drawn up on his right and believes that density of formation is the best protection' (5. 71. 1). The density implied by Thucydides' 'as near as possible' depends on how much room hoplites needed to wield their weapons, and we have Polybius' expert opinion that a soldier using a cutting or thrusting weapon as well as a shield required at least six feet of space in every direction (18. 30. 6–9). Most scholars would object that the hoplite shield by its very nature demands extremely

Figure 4 This bronze statuette of a hoplite, dedicated at the sanctuary of Zeus at Dodona, reveals how the shield was held. The right hand originally held a spear which pointed towards the ground at roughly the same 45° angle as the shield.

close ranks, on the assumption that the hoplite stood squarely behind it and in effect used only the right half of his shield, extending the left half to provide cover for a comrade close beside him in the ranks (see Fig. 5*a*). In fact, however, a hoplite, in order to wield his spear or sword with any force at all, would have to adopt a *sideways-on* stance in combat and by doing so automatically placed himself behind the *middle* of his shield (see Figs. 4, 5*b*). The shield thus did not extend unnecessarily far to the left, nor did it fall short on the right, and it was no less suitable for open order combat than for dense formations.

Soldiers in the front line, then, fought essentially as individuals against individuals, with some assistance from the men in the second rank, but only moral support from comrades further back. What was distinctive about hoplites was not so much the density of their formation as their *cohesion* in keeping the line, rather than charging or retreating as the~~~~ ~~~~ ss to engage in *extreme* ~~~~ gainst-shield.

~~~~ ight equally last the best ~~~~ ghting with hands and ~~~~ army broke, battle was ~~~~ ps to rally and charge ~~~~ ides 4. 43. 3). But often ~~~~ ther was broken by the ~~~~ netimes cut short pur- ~~~~ ably in much disarray. ~~~~ ling and capturing as ~~~~ he retreat. The victory ~~~~ after, the troops gath- ~~~~ he enemy first turned. ~~~~ ormed and all present ~~~~ *ica* 4. 3. 21). The dead ~~~~ led when the enemy ~~~~ urn, thereby formally

d not give up after a ttack the city itself. ition of any form of

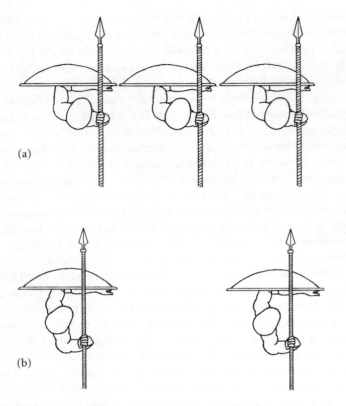

Figure 5 Diagrammatic presentation of the hoplite rank: (*a*) as often envisaged, and (*b*) as it more probably was.

settled and civilized life by Thucydides (1. 2, 5, 7–8). Yet there was a feeling that ideally a city ought to rely on the bravery of its soldiers, not on the protection of its walls: Sparta proudly did without city-walls throughout the classical period.

The main siege tactic for most of the classical period was the blockade. The besiegers surrounded the city with a fortification—anything from a simple ditch or palisade to a double brick wall with battlements and towers—while the besieged tried to keep their supply lines open by constructing cross-cutting counter-walls, by sallies against the siege works, and by covert provisioning expeditions. Even if these defensive measures were unsuccessful, it would take a long time before supplies ran out. Once the harvest had been brought in, a city with a largely agricultural population would have food for a year, and stocks were often made to last longer still by an early evacuation of women, children, slaves, and men unfit for service. A city might hold out for over two years, as did Thasos, Potidaea, and Plataea.

Given the length and cost of blockades, besiegers made every attempt to take fortifications by assault. Until the early fifth century, this was a matter of putting up scaling ladders or constructing a siege mound against the city-wall while bombarding the battlements with javelins, arrows, and stones. We first hear of battering-rams, long known in the Near East, being used by Greeks during the Athenian attack on Samos in 440. Other common assault techniques were mining and setting fire to the defences by means of incendiary missiles and even an early form of flame-thrower (Thucydides 4. 100). Two key innovations of the early fourth-century were heavy artillery and mobile, multi-storied siege towers, designed to provide troops with an elevated position close to the city wall from which to fire missiles or lower gangplanks onto the walls. Heavy artillery, generically called catapults (*katapaltai*) and first mentioned in 399 (Diodorus 14. 42. 1, 43. 3), was the most significant invention. By the middle of the century at the latest, a range of different catapults had been developed which, using twisted sinew or rope, exploited the principle of torsion to propel massive arrows and stones over great distances. The range of artillery was further increased by installing it in siege towers. This was countered by ever more massive defensive walls and towers, often incorporating artillery positions. Brick superstructures would no longer do, and it soon became the norm to have double walls with all-stone inner and outer faces, bonded by a rubble fill, with increasingly elaborate defensive structures around the gates.

Many, perhaps most, cities and forts were ultimately taken as a result of treason. The rivalry between political factions was so intense that patriotism often took second place to the interests of individuals and groups, and the gates were opened to foreign armies in exchange for support against opponents at home.

Sieges were the most demanding form of warfare known to the Greeks. Attackers and defenders needed to be continually on guard, working in shifts for months or years on end, under harsh and always worsening conditions. The besiegers suffered heavy casualties in every assault, while the besieged were forced to call on the services of the old and young who were normally excused military duties. When it came to house-to-house fighting within the walls, even women joined in, climbing onto the roofs of their houses to hurl roof tiles at the enemy (compare pp. 112–13).

Naval warfare

The trireme dominated naval warfare to the almost total exclusion of other types of warship. Although it had sails, it was primarily a rowing ship, powered by its many oarsmen; these, and the rest of the crew, were squeezed into a vessel just over 120 feet (37 m.) in length and about 20 feet (6 m.) wide, which left very little space for storage or amenities. The trireme was fast (7 knots per hour) and highly manoeuvrable, but at the cost of having a short range: it had to make land at every meal-time and every night, since it could not carry enough supplies and had no room for cooking or sleeping on board.

Warships played their part in naval blockades, despite being ill-suited to this role. The wood of the trireme's hull rotted easily and it was essential that the ships were regularly taken into dock and dried out, which was impossible during a lengthy siege. In the absence of modern surveillance technology, it was in any case extremely hard to control any stretch of water effectively, except in narrow straits. The trireme's speed made it rather more suitable for use in launching attacks against enemy territory. Maritime raids could exploit the element of surprise more easily than incursions by land: warships could rarely be spotted as long in advance as invading armies, and the crew could disembark, pillage and burn, retreat to the ships, and disappear again before their victims could muster any resistance. Athens practised these tactics on a particularly grand scale, sending fleets of as many as 100 ships to sail round the Peloponnese and make a series of lightning raids. The disadvantage of using triremes was that they carried few soldiers: a fleet of 100 ships, with up to 17,000 rowers, meant an infantry force of a mere 1,000 hoplites and 400 archers. Naval expeditions planning more than brief raids accordingly brought along additional forces and supplies in vessels converted to troop-, horse-, and grain-carriers.

The use of so much manpower to transport so few fighting men was less inefficient than it might seem, since the oarsmen did not sit waiting for the hoplites to return, but themselves joined the raiding.

The sources do not say so explicitly, but every so often mention the light-armed involved in raiding, who can only be the rowers. On a few occasions, rowers were provided with light wicker shields so that they could fight an infantry battle (Thucydides 4. 9. 1, 32. 2; Xenophon, *Hellenica* 1. 2. 1). That ancient authors barely mention any of this is not surprising: as rowers *and* light-armed, these men carried a double stigma.

To prevent an enemy from landing, to contest his control of a stretch of sea, or indeed to challenge for the title of 'thalassocrat' (ruler of the sea), one would have to meet him in a pitched naval battle. In preparation for combat, triremes deployed in a single line opposite the enemy. Arranging the ships in two or more lines, or forming a circle of ships with the sterns in the centre and the prows facing outwards, were defensive tactics adopted only by those who felt inferior in manoeuvring skill (Xenophon, *Hellenica* 1. 6. 31; Thucydides 2. 83. 5). What Thucydides called the old style of fighting at sea, still practised by Corinth and Corcyra in his day, was effectively an infantry battle fought from the decks. Once within close range, the warships lay still while their marines launched missiles and tried to enter and seize control of the nearest enemy vessel (Thucydides 1. 49. 1–3). The more modern style relied on ramming tactics, and here the manoeuvrability and speed of the trireme really came into their own. The sharply protruding lower part of the trireme's prow was sheathed with bronze to form a heavy, pointed ram, and the task of the crew was to outmanoeuvre an enemy vessel so as to approach it from the flanks, row towards it at ramming speed, crash through its timbers, and quickly back water to pull out again. The buoyancy of triremes was such that they would not sink, but of course the damage done to the hull and the oars, not to mention the loss of life and limb among the crew, would render a rammed vessel useless. The attacking ship was in danger not only of being itself disabled by the impact, but, if it did not extricate itself quickly enough, of being taken over by enemy marines climbing across (Herodotus 8. 90).

As in an infantry battle, the forces could try either to break through or to outflank the enemy line (tactics known in naval terms as *diekplous* and *periplous*, respectively). In each case, the result would be to throw the opposing line into disarray and make it easier to ram vessels in the flank, where this would do most damage. When one side broke and fled, it was pursued over some distance. Enemy ships were

seized or disabled, shipwrecked soldiers and sailors were taken prisoner or killed: 'with splintered oars and planks from wrecked ships
they beat them and broke their backs, as if they were tunnies, or fish
caught in a net; moans and shrieks sounded across the sea' (Aeschylus,
Persians 424–8). The prows of captured ships might be cut off to be
dedicated in commemoration of the victory. Finally, the victorious
fleet raised the *paian* again and set up a *tropaion* on the nearest island
or headland. The recovery of the dead and shipwrecked was even
more difficult at sea than on land, since the bodies would drift and
sink, and adverse weather might prevent rescue or salvage operations.
Men must often have clung to pieces of wreckage, cursing their
commanders for taking so long to come to the rescue, and drowned
before help arrived (Xenophon, *Hellenica* 1. 7. 11).

The economics of warfare

In the archaic period, the cost of campaigns had been borne largely
by private individuals, but wars came to be increasingly funded by the
state, and their outcomes depended more and more on the size of the
belligerents' treasuries.

The dependence of land-based warfare on private funds in some
respects continued well into the classical period. Hoplites were
obliged to provide not only their own arms and armour, but their
own bedding and a few days rations of bread, cheese, onions, or salted
fish. By the time the food ran out, the army should have reached
enemy territory where the soldiers could sustain themselves by plunder. A man finding himself short of equipment or money depended
on neighbours, rather than the state, to help him out (Lysias 16. 14, 31.
15). As for naval expeditions, the archaic penteconter warship appears
to have been provided by private shipowners. Even some triremes
were privately owned, and manned at the owner's expense, as late as
the Persian Wars (Herodotus 5. 47; 8. 17, 47). The limitations of this
economic basis are obvious: very few individuals could afford the cost
of building and manning a ship as large and complex as the trireme,
and not many men could afford to go abroad as soldiers at their own
expense for more than a few weeks. Hence early fleets were small, and
many campaigns were short: the Spartans' sixth-century siege of

Samos and their longest invasion of Attica during the Peloponnesian War both lasted only 40 days (Herodotus 3. 56; Thucydides 2. 57. 2).

Developments in other states are hard to trace, but the turning-point in Athens came in 483, with the decision to spend public revenue from the silver mines on building 100 or 200 triremes and creating a state-owned navy (Herodotus 7. 144; [Aristotle] *Constitution of the Athenians* 22. 7; see p. 172). Since rowers and marines were not normally subject to a compulsory levy, they had to be offered pay, or at least subsistence, as an inducement to serve. The normal rate was at first two, later three, obols per day, which amount-ed to a subsistence income; for lengthy and remote expeditions a double rate of a drachma a day applied. The introduction of pay for hoplites and their servants (Thucydides 3. 17. 3) at the same rate as rowers soon followed, perhaps in the mid-fifth century. When cavalry were established, they too received pay, as well as a state loan towards the cost of buying and feeding a horse. Pay for mercenaries and allies continued, of course, at the same rates as citizens: normally 3 obols (Thucydides 5. 47. 6), sometimes a drachma (Thucydides 7. 27. 2).

The introduction of naval and other military pay made possible larger and longer expeditions and sieges than ever before, which in turn created a need for additional public expenditure. Provisioning could not be left entirely to private initiative when great distances and long periods of time were involved: thus, for the Athenian expedition to Sicily, in addition to the provisions available from private traders, the state provided 30 ships carrying grain, as well as craftsmen and equipment for the construction of siegeworks (Thucydides 6. 44. 1). The navy needed continual, costly maintenance work and new construction; its expansion also required expensive new harbour facilities, including ship-sheds in which to haul up the ships for drying-out and repairs. As sieges became longer and technology more sophisticated, expenditure on engines, artillery, and fortifications spiralled.

The scale of expenses is best illustrated by some of the figures we have for Athens. Around 450, the Athenian treasury contained 9,700 talents of silver. By 431, this amount had sunk to 6,000 talents, depleted by amongst other things the nine-month siege of Samos, which had cost more than 1,200 talents (Fornara 113). Over the next two-and-a-half years, the siege of Potidaea swallowed up another 2,000 talents, which, combined with other military commitments, brought the reserve so low that emergency war taxes had to be raised (Thucydides 2. 13. 3, 70. 2). If even Athens at its richest struggled to find funds for its campaigns, one can imagine how constrained by a lack of money were the war efforts of other states.

Among major sources of funding other than taxes, perhaps the most important was plunder. Sometimes wars could pay for themselves—in one instance through the capture of merchant ships, fishing boats, and passenger ferries (Xenophon, *Hellenica* 5. 1. 14–24). Captives and cattle seized were usually sold on the spot by the army's booty-sellers (*laphyropolai*). Alternatively, prisoners of war might be ransomed, a more laborious yet more profitable process (see p. 142), since a standard ransom of 200 drachmas was a sum which few slaves would fetch. Despite some success stories, booty was by nature an unpredictable source of funds, and by no means always sufficient. The main alternative was to draw on the wealth stored in temples. It was customary to dedicate a tithe (*dekatê*) from spoils at a chosen sanctuary, and there were many occasions on which valuable dedications, public or private, were placed in temples or their treasuries. States might 'borrow' from these funds, vowing to replace them as soon as possible. Such 'loans', however, never offered more than a temporary solution.

The same is true of a final source of money which, when available, often proved decisive: subsidies of Persian gold. From the start of the Peloponnesian War, both Spartans and Athenians tried to persuade Persian governors and generals to bankroll their expeditions, despite the feeling of some that it was undignified to suck up and pay homage to barbarians. When in the later phases of the war the Spartans finally did obtain large Persian subsidies, their navy grew at a staggering rate at the expense of Athens', with dramatic consequences for the outcome of the war (see p. 194). That erratic personal favours from Persian governors and members of the Persian royal family could have such an enormous impact on the balance of power in Greece highlights how weak an economic basis underpinned Greek warfare. From the middle of the fourth century onwards, Athenians were sufficiently aware of this problem to produce a series of proposals and reforms aimed at improving the structure of the state's finances. In the end, however, not even Athens could compete with the economic resources of the new power on the international stage: Macedon.

The transformation of classical warfare

The discipline and courage cultivated by Greek hoplites made them highly effective soldiers, much sought-after as mercenaries. The skill of Greek sailors and rowers was equally outstanding. The city-states of Greece nevertheless shrank to a very minor force in international relations after 338 because their weaknesses were no less striking. The hoplite's amateur ideals inhibited the development of professional standards of soldiering, while their contempt for all non-hoplite forms of warfare led to the marginalization of cavalry and light-armed, as well as the social and political marginalization of naval personnel. Violent rivalry between and within states prevented the creation of anything more than temporary coalitions, and exacerbated the structural shortage of economic resources.

It was obvious even to the Greeks themselves that their city-states could attain significant power only if they joined forces, and in the fourth century idealists tried to forge a spirit of Panhellenic unity against the Persians, while politicians worked to create new entities such as the Olynthian and Arcadian Leagues, much larger than city-states and much more integrated than conventional alliances. But these attempts were overtaken by developments elsewhere. The economic and military power of Macedon had been growing since the late fifth century, but in the 350s, Philip II's military successes unified a greater territory than ever before, and also brought him gold mines producing an annual revenue of 1,000 talents. By 338, he could muster some 30,000 infantry and 2,000 cavalry, an army which matched in size the combined forces of all the Greek city-states ranged against him (Diodorus 16. 8. 6; 85. 5–6). Philip put his soldiers through intensive training 'before they were at war', often exercising them in all-day marches in full gear (Polyaenus 4. 2. 10). Moreover, he improved the efficiency of his troops by allowing only the cavalry to keep personal attendants: the infantry had to carry their own equipment, and provisions for thirty days. A centrally organized baggage train consisted of one man for every ten soldiers to carry 'a flour mill and tent ropes' (Frontinus 4. 1. 16). These changes enabled Philip's armies to move at speeds which amazed and terrified his opponents. They also made possible the adoption of a new style of infantry combat.

Philip invented 'the density and equipment' of what became known as the Macedonian phalanx (Diodorus 16. 3. 1–2). In the densest Macedonian formation, the *puknosis*, each man occupied a mere three feet (90 cm.) of space, both in width and in depth. This was possible because the Macedonian shield was smaller than the hoplite shield, and because each soldier, instead of wielding a spear or sword, used both hands to hold a long pike (*sarissa*) steady in front of him. Each man's *sarissa* projected 15 feet (4.5 m.) in front of him, so that even the weapons of the fifth rank reached a few feet beyond the front line. In a typical sixteen-deep formation, this left eleven rear ranks unable to engage directly, and these held their pikes raised diagonally above the heads of the others (Polybius 18. 29. 2–30. 9). It took a great deal of collective training to hold together such an extremely tight formation in battle, but so long as the Macedonian phalanx stayed intact it presented a wall of spears that Greek hoplites in their looser order were unable to penetrate.

The emphasis on cohesion, close combat, and courage in standing one's ground which Greek and Macedonian infantry warfare shared should not obscure the fundamental differences. On the one hand, we have the gentlemanly hoplite, training at his leisure in the gymnasium, depending on his servant for all daily needs on campaign, and fighting essentially as an individual, albeit within a cohesive formation. On the other hand, we have the Macedonian infantryman, a full-time soldier, rigorously trained, self-sufficient on campaign, and equipped in such a way that he can fight only as part of a unit. Athens went some way towards bridging the social and cultural gap between these types of fighting men by reforming ephebic training, but the gulf between Greeks and Macedonians remained wide.

Whether more radical military reform in Greece would ultimately have made a difference so long as the city-states remained divided is doubtful. They simply did not have the resources of Macedon, the Persian Empire, or the kingdoms created after the conquests of Alexander the Great. Herodotus' judgement on the Thracians proved, ironically, a fitting epitaph for his fellow-Greeks. 'If they were ruled by one man, or united amongst themselves, they would in my opinion be invincible and by far the most powerful of all nations. But there is no way for them to bring this about. It is not going to happen, and that is why they are weak' (5.3).

Political conflicts, political debates, and political thought

Josiah Ober

Introduction: civil war in Corcyra, 427 BC

In a few harrowing pages of terse prose, Thucydides describes the unravelling of the great city-state, Corcyra, in a traumatic civil conflict (*stasis*). The conflict was exacerbated by the Peloponnesian War, the protracted struggle between imperial Athens and Sparta's Peloponnesian League (see pp. 185–94). Corcyra had made a defensive alliance with Athens after losing a naval battle to Sparta's ally Corinth. After the alliance was struck, certain Corcyraeans, who had been taken prisoner by the Corinthians and had come to favour the Peloponnesian side, returned to Corcyra and began to agitate against the Athenian alliance. When the former prisoners of war were unable to pass the requisite legislation in the Corcyraean assembly, they tried another tack and indicted Peithias, a Councillor and the leader of the pro-Athenian Corcyraean democrats, on a charge of treason. Constitutional politics enter the story at this point: the conflict over foreign alliances was intimately connected to a conflict between factions advocating rival political programmes for Corcyra: democrats striving for a constitution that would make all native male Corcyraeans, including labourers and farmers of small plots, into full citizens, versus oligarchs who sought domination for a few relatively wealthy property-holders.

Peithias' oligarchic opponents failed in their prosecution; Peithias was acquitted, and he retaliated with a ploy that underlines the role of class antagonism in Corcyrean politics: he charged five of his wealthiest opponents with an act of impiety: illegally cutting saplings, for use as vine-stakes on their private estates, from a tract of state-owned sacred land. Upon being convicted and faced with enormous fines for their act of impiety, Peithias' opponents fled to a temple, claiming sanctuary. Unable to pay their fines despite their great wealth, they were presumably stripped of their ordinary legal protections as citizens, but as suppliants in a temple they were under the protection of the gods. The men in the temple soon learned that Peithias intended to enforce the full penalty and that he was also seeking to extend the scope of the Athenian alliance. They rallied their supporters, burst into the Council Chamber, and murdered Peithias and 60 other Councillors. The stasis had begun in earnest and the stakes were high: the victors would decide what alliances Corcyra would make (Athenian or Peloponnesian), what constitution Corcyra would have (democracy or oligarchy), and what classes of Corcyraeans would enjoy the privileges of citizenship (all native males, or only the rich).

Peithias' oligarchic opponents called a public assembly and forced through a decree repudiating the Athenian alliance. Next, with the help of the crew of a Corinthian ship, they launched an armed attack on the surviving democrats. The latter took up defensive positions on and around Corcyra's acropolis. Both sides sought assistance from the unfree population, but it was the democrats who successfully recruited the bulk of Corcyra's rural slaves with a promise of freedom. Meanwhile, a small Athenian naval force arrived at Corcyra. Its commander sought to quell the violence, but he was soon confronted by a large Corinthian fleet. The Corinthian ships were forced to retreat in turn upon the arrival of a yet larger Athenian force.

The arrival and departure of outside naval forces added fuel to Corcyra's internal fighting, which became ever more destructive. To forestall a democratic counter-attack, the oligarchs set fire to the buildings around the agora, causing massive loss of property and risking a general conflagration. The fighting soon drew in unexpected sectors of the population. Thucydides highlights the distortions of normal Greek society that the conflict involved when he notes, 'The women also joined in the fighting with great daring, hurling down tiles from the rooftops and standing up to the din of battle with a courage beyond their sex' (3. 74). The stasis climaxed in a paroxysm of killing during which the now-dominant democrats cornered and slaughtered their less numerous opponents:

There was death in every shape and form. And, as usually happens in such situations, people went to every extreme and beyond it. There were fathers who killed their sons; men were dragged from the temples and butchered on the very altars; some were actually walled up in the temple of Dionysus and died there. (3. 81)

Thucydides goes on to say that the stasis in Corcyra was simply the first, and not the worst, of a wave of civil conflicts that shattered many Greek poleis during the long Peloponnesian War.

The drawn-out international war, in Thucydides' view, worsened internal conflicts:

In times of peace and prosperity cities and individuals alike follow higher standards . . . but war is a stern teacher; in depriving people of the power of easily satisfying their daily needs, it brings most people's minds down to the level of their actual circumstances. (3. 82)

The two sides at Corcyra were defined by their preference for a great-power alliance (Athens vs. Sparta), by their support for a specific system of government (democracy vs. oligarchy), and by their economic class (poor vs. rich). But the original issues became blurred as the violence escalated. Thucydides points out that each side advertised the justice of its own position by means of attractive slogans: 'on the one side, political equality for the masses, and on the other side the safe and sound government of the aristocracy'. But behind these slogans Thucydides detected a brutal lust for self-aggrandizement:

they were deterred neither by the claims of justice nor by the interests of the state; their one standard was the pleasure of their own side at that particular moment and so . . . They were always willing to satisfy the hatreds of the hour. (3. 82)

Thucydides' Corcyra narrative concentrates on the doings of citizen men of military age, but it also shows how violent internal struggles drew in women and slaves, persons classical Greeks ordinarily expected to be neither citizens nor warriors: the civil conflict also became deeply entangled with aspects of the polis life that might not, at first glance, seem political: law, religion, and economic interests.

Thucydides points out to his reader how, under the conditions of civil war, the various category distinctions that sustained the polis in more peaceful times—rich and poor, free and slave, male and female, religious and secular, just and expedient, public and private—were at once proclaimed with special vehemence in words and suffered utter collapse in practice. It was only when the ordinary social rules were suspended, and political consensus shattered, that the unitary polis was revealed in all its diversity: the interests of the citizen men were seen to be inextricably bound up with those of women and slaves; religion, politics, and law appeared as part of a single system, driven by some deeper impulse. Coming to grips with that cryptic impulse became a central concern of Greek political thinkers.

Thucydides' account suggests that the driving passion behind the struggle was political, in the fundamental sense of deciding who would have the power to establish the rules by which society would be structured and who would have a share in its governance. The ultimate stake in the Corcyraean conflict, as in other Greek civil wars, was the composition of the citizen body: the key to the question 'Who will rule?' lay in deciding 'Who will be allowed to be an active, participatory citizen?' Who would gain the right to stand forth publicly and proudly, at the centre of society, as its rightful masters? Would it be the heads of a few wealthy and well-born families? Or should the privileges and duties of citizenship be extended to a wider segment of the citizen body? And if so—how much wider? To all landowners? All soldiers? To craftsmen and traders? To landless day labourers? At what point would the expansion of the citizenship threaten the basic categories and distinctions on which Greek culture was predicated— and so foster revolution? What were the ultimate social boundaries— gender? residence? birthright?—beyond which citizenship simply could not be imagined? This complex set of questions had been raised, in theory and practice, early in archaic Greek culture. It was never definitively resolved, despite the oceans of blood spilled in civil conflicts and the pots of ink spilled by classical Greek political theorists.

Political theory: the sources of conflict and its prevention

In the course of describing another revolutionary situation, this time in late sixth-century Persia, Thucydides' older contemporary, Herodotus, laid out the three governmental options taken seriously by the classical Greeks. Herodotus reports that a small group of Persian nobles, when they had violently overthrown a usurper-junta, sat down to discuss how the Persians ought to be governed. One of them advocated the rule of a privileged few (oligarchy), another the democratic rule of the many (democracy, here called *isonomia*—literally 'equality in respect to legal standing'), and a third the monarchical rule of a single individual. Not surprisingly, in the light of actual Persian political history, Herodotus' imagined Persians ultimately decide that monarchy is best. The terms of the debate clearly have more to do with Greek political thought than with practical Persian politics. The outcome of Herodotus' fictional Persian debate points to a Greek conception that emerged with special force after the early fifth-century wars with Persia and would remain influential through the classical period: the world was seen as divided between slavish 'barbarians', naturally suited to being ruled over by an autocrat, and free Greeks, who willingly accepted the authority of law and custom but refused to accept any single man as their master. Despite the fact that tyranny remained common among the Sicilian Greeks, by the fifth century BC the primary governmental options for mainland city-states of Greece were various forms of oligarchy and democracy. And this meant in principle, a choice between the rule of some segment of the propertied classes or the rule of the entire native adult male population (the *demos*).

As Thucydides' depiction of revolutionary Corcyra suggests, deciding whether political claims based on property-holding were more or less legitimate than claims based on regional residence and native ancestry was among the most intractable political problems faced by the classical Greeks. Just as Herodotus' Persian debate would lead us to suppose, the Greek political debate tended to be carried out in negative terms. Since there were only two legitimate options, discrediting one's opponent was tantamount to establishing legitimacy for one's own political preference. The oligarchs pressed their claim by contending that democracy was the self-interested rule of a large faction defined only by lack of wealth—that of 'the poor'. In the view of the oligarchs the worst of these were wage labourers, dependent upon a paymaster; their characters were thought to be corrupted by the 'slavish' conditions of their employment. Since, in the view of the oligarchs, labourers were not truly free men, they were thought to be incapable of making independent judgements, and therefore unworthy of participating in political deliberations. Meanwhile democrats asserted that oligarchy meant the rule of the wealthy in their own material and excessively cosmopolitan interests. Those whose loyalty was to their goods could not be true patriots. They preferred the company of their fellow rich men in far-off places to their poorer fellows at home, and they would willingly sacrifice their polis' independence in order to preserve their wealth. In sum, each side claimed that the other side ignored the common good of the polis as a state and as a society. Each claimed that the other was unjustly seeking to gain control over more than its fair share of the state's limited material and political resources.

Thucydides was both a historian and a political theorist. He was well aware of the long history of Greek intellectual debates over political legitimacy, as well as the equally long history of actual political conflicts. As Greek political writers moved between theory and practice, their careful observation of social practices stimulated the development of abstract political philosophy. Thucydides' account of events in Corcyra shows that he understood that economic interests were important in revolutionary activity, but he regarded conflicts between economic interests as an insufficient explanation of the actual course of events. Like many other fifth-century intellectuals, especially the so-called sophists (self-styled instructors in political wisdom, who flocked to Athens in the fifth century), Thucydides was fascinated by the relationship between existing social conventions and inherent human nature. A passage in the Corcyra narrative that may have been added to Thucydides' text by a later editor states baldly that it is precisely in periods of civil war that human nature itself was revealed most clearly, and in all its stark ugliness:

With the ordinary conventions of civil life thrown into confusion, human nature, always ready to offend even where laws exist, showed itself proudly in its true colours: as something incapable of controlling passion, insubordinate to the idea of justice, the enemy of anything superior to itself; for, if it had not been for the pernicious power of envy, men would not have exalted vengeance above innocence and profit above justice. (3. 84)

Whether Thucydides wrote this passage or not, his historical-theoretical argument grimly suggests that when humans are confronted with a potentially unlimited capacity to self-aggrandize, the conventions of civilized life which ordinarily restrained vicious behaviour will be swept away and under these conditions the state cannot survive. Civil conflict finds its logical end in the elimination of the free, independent state, which either destroys itself or leaves itself fatally exposed to external domination by the powerful.

The problem of internal conflict within the polis was a key issue, perhaps the single most pressing issue, for classical political thought. Given that civil war was regarded as an unmitigated evil, how could it be avoided? Or, if it could not be avoided altogether, could its effects be somehow softened? Must internal conflict lead to the death of the polis?

In the *Republic*, Thucydides' younger contemporary, Plato, offered a long, eloquent, and uncompromising answer to the problem of civil conflict and its relationship to human nature. Plato claimed that every existing polis was in fact at least two poleis unhappily coexisting in the same physical space. The rich and the poor were, in effect, 'cities' unto themselves, with their own distinct cultures and values; hostilities between them were as inevitable as they were undesirable. For Plato, then, overt civil war was simply a 'hot' phase in a chronic state of social conflict that would last as long as there could be any question or debate about 'who should be the rulers', and, more radically, for as long as diversity of any sort pertained among the ruling classes.

Plato argued that the social divisions common to every existing polis reflected a profound psychological sickness, what we might today call a schizophrenic division within each individual human psyche. The *Republic* lays the framework for an idealized polis, Callipolis (Beautiful City), based on the idea that true social harmony could only be achieved when persons whose souls were completely free from internal conflict were organized into a conflict-free polis and ruled by those possessing true wisdom. Every resident of Callipolis necessarily accepted the basic premise that each person is fit for only one task. For example, a shoemaker would limit his activity to shoemaking. He would not attend a political assembly in the morning and make shoes in the afternoon (as he might were he an Athenian citizen) because shoemaking and politics were distinct and mutually exclusive activities, to be undertaken by different persons. Plato's Callipolis was not an oligarchy, insofar as oligarchy meant the rule of a propertied class. In Callipolis it is the shoemaker's technical engagement in his craft, not his wealth, that precluded engagement in the political activity of ruling: whether he was a wealthy owner of a shoemaking factory or just scraping by with piecework was immaterial. Callipolis was divided into castes based on vocation, not wealth. A tiny cadre of philosophers served as the rulers. A more numerous caste of warriors, the Guardians, kept order and defended the state against its external enemies. And a mass of free but utterly apolitical producers of goods provided for the polis' material needs and were the society's only owners of private property.

Plato tells us little about the productive caste, but much of the *Republic* is devoted to the rules by which the philosopher-rulers and Guardians were to live their lives, to the epistemological question of absolute knowledge, and to the long and arduous educational programme that would prepare them to fulfil their strictly defined political roles. The most remarkable aspect of the life of Callipolis' ruling élite is its radical egalitarianism, and this egalitarianism crossed gender lines: male and female Guardians were to undertake essentially the same tasks, including military service. There was no private ownership of property among the Guardian class, no marriage, and no family life. Children were raised communally. The Guardians were as indistinguishable from one another as could be. No one possessed anything, house, wife, child, apart from all others. The philosopher-rulers lived by the same social rules and primary upbringing as the Guardians, but they underwent many additional years of specialized philosophical training in order to achieve access to the knowledge that Plato felt was necessary to sustain the society according to its original and unchangeable founding premises.

Plato's ideas of what a proper social order might look like were radical, but not unique. Similar hyper-egalitarian ideas were parodied by the Athenian comedian, Aristophanes, in a play (*The Assembly-women*) presented in c.393, a few years before Plato's masterpiece was written. In Aristophanes' comedy, the women of Athens, frustrated by the unpatriotic selfishness of their citizen-husbands, contrive to take over the government. They immediately institute a regime in which property is made communal and family life abolished. Even access to sexual pleasure is equalized via a measure that required the young and attractive to have sex with the old and ugly before being allowed access to their preferred partners. Aristophanes' witty play challenged its Athenian audience to think about the lack of fit between the political equality guaranteed by democracy, and pervasive distinctions based on class and gender. The women's egalitarian regime sought to remove the underlying causes of selfish self-aggrandizement and thereby eliminate the primary source of civil conflict.

Plato's project went further. His Callipolis was strictly hierarchical and hostile to change in any form; even the tiniest deviation from the perfect orderliness of the unified society could, he supposed, precipitate a downward spiral into a nightmare of dissent and social revolutions resulting in ever-worse forms of government: first a sort of timocracy, then oligarchy, next a democracy and finally the rule of the most vicious sort of tyrant. In order to forestall this downward spiral for as long as possible, Callipolis was sustained by a web of 'noble lies'—a systematic set of fictions disseminated by the rulers. These salutary myths would serve to indoctrinate each member of society and convince him (and her) that change was literally impossible and that all really was for the best in the best of all possible worlds. Only the few rulers with adequate philosophical training could or need know the truth.

Plato's vision of a well-ordered society has seemed to many readers both terrifying and a practical absurdity. Plato's own attempt to put some of his ideas into practice, by training sympathetic Sicilian Greek tyrants to be philosopher-kings, ended in disaster—and very nearly in Plato's premature death. He was, ironically, saved from a conspiracy of his Sicilian enemies by a timely warning offered by lower-class Athenian seamen, men who acted on the strength of their common bond of citizenship with the philosopher who regarded them as unworthy of that estate. A particularly pungent critique of Callipolis came from Plato's own student, Aristotle, who argued that Plato's ideal polis was hopelessly impractical when viewed in the light of natural human impulses. Like Thucydides, Aristotle assumed that accurate understanding of actual human nature, based on careful collection of historical evidence, was the key to genuinely useful political analysis. In his *Politics* Aristotle argued that humans are by nature 'political animals' – by which he meant that they had a natural impulse not only to live sociably in groups, but also to contribute actively to the flourishing of the group by engaging in political life, ideally by 'ruling and being ruled in turns'. Although Aristotle notoriously claimed that children, women, and 'natural' slaves were psychologically unfit to be true 'political animals,' this still left him with a large and socially diverse body of adult males as 'natural' citizens. Confronting the tumultuous constitutional history of the Greek city-states, and Plato's unsatisfactory solution to the problem of civil strife, Aristotle asked whether there might be room for social diversity within a just and stable polis. Could fatal levels of social conflict be avoided without resorting to rigid castes, improbable social practices, and 'noble lies'? Aristotle believed that it was only in a well-regulated polis that humans could achieve their highest ends of engaging in effective political deliberation and philosophical contemplation. And thus, for Aristotle, the stakes were especially high: by destroying polis life, civil war rendered impossible that which made human life worth living.

Aristotle assigned his students to collect comparative political-historical material from around the Greek world. The evidence suggested to him that there were some important similarities among many revolutions, but that civil conflict ultimately arose from a variety of causes. Like his predecessors, Aristotle recognized that conflicts between economic-class interests often motivated revolutionary activism, but, like Thucydides, he rejected class conflict as a monocausal explanation:

For just as in war the crossing of ditches, even if they are very small, splits apart the ranks, so every difference [between people's circumstances and characters], it appears, makes for a factional split. The greatest split is perhaps that between virtue and depravity, then there is that between wealth and poverty, and so on, with others in varying degrees. (*Politics* 1303^{b} 12–16)

But beneath all destructive conflict lay the tendency for men to form interest groups based on the distinctions among them, for those groups to seek to gain more than their fair share of available goods, and their willingness to resort to violence in that undertaking.

Aristotle sketched a broad spectrum of possible regime-types, based on the political dominance of different categories of persons.

But, again like his predecessors, he acknowledged that, for Greeks anyway, the two main types of legitimate government remained oligarchy and democracy. Aristotle argued that both democracy and oligarchy were 'deviant regimes'. Because of their tendency to further the interests of only one part of the population, both oligarchs and democrats deviated from the moderate 'constitutionalism' that Aristotle supposed would result from the political rule of a large and stable middle class. But Aristotle did not regard the very common (perhaps inevitable) tendency toward 'deviance' as necessarily fatal to civil order. Instead of resorting to Plato's all-or-nothing approach to political theory, Aristotle suggested various practical legal reforms and institutional adjustments—including schemes to weight voting and to encourage or discourage participation, elaboration of legal codes, and the promotion of greater levels of trust between classes— whereby the interests of the poor might be better protected under oligarchic regimes and those of the rich under democracies.

Democracy at Athens and its critics

When Aristotle began studying civil conflict and its potentially peaceful resolution, the civil war that raged in Athens in 404, following Sparta's victory in the Peloponnesian War, was available to him as a particularly vivid and enlightening example. A detailed account was offered by the Athenian Xenophon, who had inherited both Thucydides' historical/theoretical concerns (he wrote a continuation of Thucydides' unfinished history of the Peloponnesian War) and Plato's philosophical interests (like Plato he was a follower of Socrates). As Xenophon tells the story, the first stages of the Athenian stasis developed along the general lines of the standard 'Corcyra' scenario. The Spartans occupied Athens with a military force. Under duress, the Athenian assembly was forced to pass legislation turning over effective control of the city to 'The Thirty', a group dominated by extremist Athenian oligarchs led by the soon-to-be notorious Critias, Plato's uncle. Like Plato and Xenophon, Critias was an associate of Socrates. But once in power, Critias and his cronies proved the very anti-type of selfless 'philosopher-kings'. The Thirty murdered democratic leaders and exiled thousands of ordinary citizens. They confiscated property at whim, and ordered the execution of anyone who raised objections. In response, a band of Athenian democrats, aided by anti-Spartan Thebans, rallied at a hilltop stronghold outside the city of Athens. The democrats quickly gained adherents and eventually captured Piraeus. A pitched battle ended in a victory for the democrats; Critias was killed in the fighting. The Spartans, divided in their counsels, declined to support the Athenian oligarchs, and so democracy was restored.

The surviving oligarchs feared the worst: revenge killings, mass exile, confiscation of property. But the denouement proved far from the blood-bath that Thucydides deplored in his Corcyraean narrative. Recognizing that ongoing civil war would leave Athens permanently crippled, the victorious democrats passed a legislative decree declaring a general amnesty for past revolutionary misdeeds. The official policy of 'forgive and forget' was enforced in the re-established people's lawcourts. In a work entitled *The Constitution of the Athenians* (which combines political history with a description of prevailing government institutions), one of Aristotle's students praises this remarkable amnesty:

on this occasion [the democrats] seem to have reacted to their previous misfortunes, both privately and publicly, in a manner more noble and public-spirited than all other people. Not only did they wipe out all prosecutions for past acts, but they paid back from common funds the money that the Thirty had borrowed from Sparta. (40. 3)

The amnesty worked; Athens entered a long period of relative social harmony which eventually allowed the city to regain much of its former military clout and a high level of economic prosperity (see pp. 38, 206).

The amnesty of 403 marked the end of open oligarchic activism at Athens—the comparison between the viciousness of the oligarchs and the generous leniency of the democrats undermined support for would-be anti-democratic revolutionaries. Yet the amnesty did not interrupt the long and distinguished tradition of Athenian political writing critical of democracy. Thucydides, Plato, Xenophon, and Aristotle each have a place in that tradition. Considering the relationship between that long tradition and practical Athenian politics will clarify the background to the bloody stasis of 404, and will also help to explain why it did not escalate into a polis-destroying maelstrom.

The best introduction to the critical tradition is a short tract written a generation before the Amnesty, in the third quarter of the fifth century (c.440–427). Its anonymous author, dubbed by modern scholars 'The Old Oligarch', assumes the persona of an anti-democratic Athenian instructing a sympathetic foreign friend about the peculiarities of his native polis. The Old Oligarch seeks to explain how and why the consistently self-interested behaviour of 'the democratic multitude' has led Athens to a position of international strength. He ironically praises the Athenian demos, which he identifies as a faction consisting of 'the poor and many', for its single-minded and selfish pursuit of its own advantage, and implicitly urges his pro-oligarchic readers, the 'few who are good', to smarten up and behave likewise. The Old Oligarch himself seems to regard successful revolution as next to impossible, given the democracy's capacity to deceive, coerce, or overawe its internal and external enemies. But his conviction that democrats and oligarchs alike would always seek to promote their own factional interests, rather than the good of the state, sets the scene for destructive civil conflicts like Corcyra's.

At least some of the Old Oligarch's fifth-century contemporaries agreed that the democracy should be done away with, and they were less pessimistic than he about their chances for success. The two generations after the popular Athenian revolution of 508/7 had witnessed the extension and elaboration of democratic institutions, and the concomitant development of the political consciousness of the Athenian people. The conservative politician Cimon had sought to strengthen Athens' ties with oligarchic Sparta, but his plans backfired when the Spartans haughtily turned away Athenian military aid in suppressing a revolt by Sparta's subject class, the helots of Messenia (see p. 183). Cimon's political star plummeted. Immediately following this débâcle in 462, a democratic politician named Ephialtes persuaded the Assembly to strip from the Areopagus council certain of its powers of constitutional oversight and to increase the power of the popular courts. Ephialtes was subsequently murdered, but his young colleague Pericles was already rising to prominence as a 'new model' democratic leader, a master orator, skilful general, and innovative policy-maker. Pericles publicly rejected the old style aristocratic politics, which had focused on networking among small bands of trusted friends (the political clubs know as *hetaireiai*). Instead of doing politics in the 'backroom' forum of the private drinking party, Pericles developed a loyal, if informal, mass constituency of ordinary Athenians through speechmaking in the Assembly. The tight little world of the political clubs was increasingly regarded with suspicion by non-élite Athenians, as the primary site of anti-democratic plotting.

Through the middle decades of the fifth century the possibility of changing Athenian government to some form of oligarchy continued to fuel the rivalries among Athens' politicians. In the best known of these confrontations Thucydides, the son of Melesias (probably a relative of the historian, whose father was Olorus), sought to challenge Pericles in the key public forum of the Assembly. Thucydides arranged for wealthy and anti-democratic citizens to sit together, heckle their political opponents, and vote as a block in the Assembly. It was too little, too late. A series of bold legislative initiatives had left the Athenian demos in full control of the governmental apparatus, and the demos was in no mood to be dictated to by the wealthy few. In 443 the Assembly elected to hold an ostracism—a remarkable institution in which the Athenian citizens voted with inscribed potsherds to determine which prominent individual among them should be sent into exile for ten years. The institution itself, which dates back to the foundation of popular rule at Athens, is an eloquent statement about the scope of authority claimed by the demos, in this case to expel a citizen (although no more than one each year) who was guilty of nothing other than political notoriety. In 443 it was the son of Melesias who won the unpopularity contest; his departure from the political scene left the pro-oligarchic Athenians leaderless. The politician Thucydides' failed attempt to challenge democracy in public provides the context for the Old Oligarch's negative assessment of democracy's morality and his pessimism about its probable longevity. After the ostracism of Thucydides the oligarchic movement went underground and some of the political clubs became centres of revolutionary agitation.

Meanwhile, certain intellectuals challenged the implicit premises of democracy. Borrowing the sophists' sharp distinction between nature *(physis)* and custom *(nomos)*, they claimed that the rule of the people was a flimsy social construct, both perverse and artificial in that its laws and customary practices were contrary to basic laws of nature. In a true state of nature, these critics argued, a few strong and intrinsically excellent men would rule a herd of inferior persons.

They would use that herd for their own instrumental purposes, just as a shepherd shears or slaughters his sheep to suit himself. Democracy, they claimed, only continued to exist because the inferior herd, rightly fearing the capacity of the élite few, had managed to trick and coerce them into accepting an understanding of social justice based on a false notion of equality: the assumption that each citizen, despite his individual attainments or lack of them, was of equal political worth, and thereby worthy of an equal vote in the citizen Assembly. Anti-democratic intellectuals opposed this 'arithmetical', one man one vote, conception of equality with a contrary view of 'natural' equality—the idea that each man's rightful share of social and political goods should be determined by his strength and inherent excellence. On this reasoning, democracy was unnatural, and oligarchy, the rule of the strong and excellent (and, it hardly need be said, the wealthy), was what nature intended.

Other fifth-century intellectuals provided arguments in support of democracy. The sophist Protagoras of Abdera, for example, taught that political capacity (unlike physical strength or even intrinsic intelligence) was not in fact the monopoly of a few, but was distributed generally among the human race (or at least among adult, male Greeks). Protagoras developed a form of human-centred pragmatism that rejected the notion that there was any metaphysical truth to be known about matters such as justice or truth. If there was no final 'god-approved' or even 'natural' social order, then existing customs did constitute all the social reality that was accessible to humans, and consequently customs should be taken seriously. If, in Protagoras' most famous slogan, 'man is the measure of all things', then human customs have all the force of 'natural' laws. If democracy worked well in practice by producing various material and psychic goods for the citizens, as, in mid-fifth century Athens it certainly did, then this was evidence that the political capacity that was widely distributed among humans was indeed being aggregated efficiently. The key to Athens' material success in the fifth century was its empire, and the empire was secured by a large and efficient trireme navy (see pp. 92 and 107). The model of the trireme, in which scores of ordinary men worked towards a common end by aggregating their individually puny strength, thereby transforming a mass of timber into a devastatingly effective naval weapon (see above, pp. 104–6), was a fitting metaphor for Protagoras' understanding of democracy. And, as the

Old Oligarch ruefully recognized, the experience of rowing in the fleet decidedly reinforced the lower-class Athenian citizens' sense of their own worth and their collective power.

Political conflict on stage

Serious discussion of political matters was not restricted to intellectual circles. Athenian dramatists reconfigured the ideas of the sophists and other fifth-century thinkers, often in familiar mythic terms, and presented them annually to huge audiences in the Theatre of Dionysus. All Athenian dramatic productions were subsidized by the democratic state, and state officials were responsible for choosing each year's plays. Although Athenian tragedy took account of a great deal more than political theory and practice, there was obviously a close relationship between the civic arena and the tragic stage. Aeschylus' *Eumenides*, Sophocles' *Antigone*, and Euripides' *Ion* (to take just three examples) explored how human nature related to divine will, man-made laws, and traditional custom, and what all this meant for the governance of the polis. Briefly reviewing these three dramatic plots clarifies the ways in which large audiences of ordinary citizens engaged with political-philosophical problems.

The *Eumenides* begins with Orestes, a prince of Argos, seeking sanctuary in Athens. Orestes had murdered his mother to avenge his father. He is pursued by the Furies, grotesque female divinities charged with the punishment of those who have shed the blood of kinfolk. Athens' tutelary goddess, Athena, refuses to grant Orestes sanctuary on her own authority; instead she creates the Areopagus Council as a citizen's court, and bids the Councillors to decide the justice of the matter. Orestes and the Furies present their cases, the jury is polled, and the decision goes in favour of Orestes (although only after Athena herself has cast the tie-breaking vote). Orestes is grateful, and offers a permanent alliance with Argos. The Furies, however, are angry and threaten revenge: the outbreak of a dreadful stasis among the Athenians. But they are eventually persuaded by Athena's skilful rhetoric (and veiled threats) to take up residence in Athens, and to turn their threat of civil conflict into a blessing on Athena's land.

In this play, produced shortly after the Assembly voted to reduce the extra-judicial powers of the Areopagus Council and some 30 years before the revolutionary crisis at Corcyra, we find a set of issues remarkably similar to those highlighted by Thucydides: the threat of stasis, bloodshed among kin, questions about religious authority and sanctuary, women acting like men, the ambiguous scope of law, foreign policy entanglements, and the problematic use of rhetoric. In this play, however, all turns out well in the end: the state is in effect founded rather than destroyed.

Sophocles' *Antigone*, set in Thebes, offers a darker picture of political conflict. Antigone has been forbidden by Thebes' King Creon the right to bury her dead brother, who had sought to overthrow Creon's rule by leading an armed force against Thebes. This sets up a conflict between the demands of traditional religious practice (kin must bury their dead) and the demands of political authority (the king's will is law). Antigone confronts Creon, who responds by asserting both the legitimacy of his authority and the impropriety of a woman speaking publicly about matters of political moment. Creon has his way, and Antigone is sentenced to die for her insubordinate refusal to obey the royal injunction. But Creon's house is shattered in the process; his own son chooses to perish with Antigone rather than live in the world defined by the unanswerable voice of his autocratic father. Whereas modern readers might immediately identify Creon as a villain and Antigone as a heroine, Sophocles' play stubbornly refuses to demonize any of its characters: all act as they feel they must if the polis is to survive. This stark confrontation between political authority and social norms simply cannot be happily resolved. Sophocles' Thebans are not yet fighting a civil war, but the Athenian audience recognized that a city so desperately divided against itself was ultimately doomed.

Euripides' *Ion* initially seems to concern specifically private matters: Creusa, Queen of Athens and (as she supposes) last surviving member of the original earth-born royal Athenian family, has come to Delphi with her non-Athenian husband, Xuthus, to consult the oracle about her infertility. As the audience quickly learns, however, Creusa had previously born a child after being raped by the god Apollo. That son, Ion, spirited away by his father from the cave in which he was born, now lives as a temple servant in Delphi, Apollo's holy seat. In the course of the play, Creusa and Xuthus come to believe that Ion is Xuthus' illegitimate son, and Xuthus eagerly prepares to adopt him as his heir. Creusa, personally affronted and disgusted at the thought of a non-Athenian gaining a place in the royal lineage, seeks to kill Ion. Her plan is foiled through divine intervention, she finally recognizes her son, and agrees to the adoption. Ion comes to Athens, where, as the audience is informed, he will father the entire race of the Ionians.

This play brings to centre stage the issue of citizenship, the myth of autochthony, and Athenian imperial ideology. Through its improbably happy ending, the Athenians can retain their special 'earthborn' status and claim ancestral authority over all Ionians, which is convenient given that speakers of the Ionian dialect made up a large percentage of Athens' imperial subjects. As in the other tragedies considered here, politics, law, religion, bloodshed, foreign policy, and women's problematic role in the polis are very much to the fore.

The annual festival of Dionysus also featured a competition for comedic drama. The plays of Aristophanes, the only classical Athenian comic playwright of whom complete plays still survive, are characterized by their biting social and political satire. In Aristophanes' comic Athens, politicians were invariably corrupt, citizens often venal and excessively absorbed with getting their dinners, jurors interested mostly in amusement and asserting their arbitrary power over hapless litigants, and women overfond of sex and wine. Yet as with tragedy, contemporary intellectual debates and the concern about the fragility of civic unity under the stress of external war were represented by Athenian comedians in dramatic form. Among Aristophanes' masterpieces is *Lysistrata*, a fantasy in which women from across the Greek world decide that they have had enough of the Peloponnesian War, which keeps their husbands away from their beds and families. The women decide to end the war by a sex strike: upon returning home from the year's campaigning, husbands will find unwilling sexual partners. To drive home their point, the women seize the sacred Acropolis of Athens, where they are attacked by a body of aging Athenian hoplites in a comic restaging of the revolutionary uprising of 508/7. The play ends happily, as comedies must, with everyone going home to restored domestic bliss. Yet, as in Thucydides on Corcyra, issues of religious violation and gender-role confusion are mixed up with the problems of external war and civil strife.

Aristophanes' *Clouds* engages a somewhat different theme: the bizarre ideas and practices of 'Socrates the sophist' portrayed as crackpot natural scientist and teacher of useful verbal tricks that allow 'a bad speech to defeat a good argument'. Strepsiades, an ordinary Athenian who has foolishly married an aristocratic woman and is in debt due to the lavish tastes of their son, sends his son to Socrates in the hope that he will learn how to trick their creditors in the lawcourts. But instead the son learns to act according to 'human nature', and to scorn the customs that allowed a father to discipline his son but restrained a son from raising a hand against his father. The play seems to suggest that sophistic doctrines about nature and custom were undermining the paternal authority that was one of the bases of Athenian society. The inter-generational violence and the play's startling ending, a desperate act of preventative arson in which Strepsiades sets fire to Socrates' 'think-shop' with the hapless sophist trapped inside, again recall the deadly serious conflicts of Thucydides' Corcyra.

'Socrates the sophist' was Aristophanes' creation, but he was clearly modelled on the real Socrates, who, by the time of the play's production in 423, was already known for unorthodox behaviour and thought. In his *Apology*, a free version of Socrates' defence speech at his trial in 399 on charges of impiety and corrupting the youth, Plato portrays him as a pungent critic of Athenian ethical norms and political practices, including the widespread participation of ordinary citizens in government that was the defining feature of Athenian democracy. Socrates spent much of his time in the Agora of Athens, discussing ethical questions with any Athenian willing to be subjected to his peculiarly probing conversational style. Socrates had little time for the sophists' notions about nature and culture, and equally little time for popular assumptions about the inherent wisdom of the citizen masses.

Socrates was not concerned with the theory of politics for its own sake, but he made analogies from animal nature that had profound implications for democratic governance. Socrates scornfully dismissed the popular idea that the decisions of 'the many'—as Assemblymen, Councillors, and jurors—helped to educate the youth of the city by establishing appropriate norms of behaviour and setting salutary examples. He suggested on the analogy of horse-training that only a few persons (or maybe just one man) with a highly special set of talents and specialized knowledge, would be genuinely capable of improving the youth. Socrates' preferred analogy for his own role in the city was that of a gadfly, who lit upon his fellow citizens and sought to sting them into a healthy state of intellectual wakefulness.

Socrates himself seems not to have been interested in any revolutionary implications of his discourse, but they were not lost on some of the young men who enjoyed watching him dissect the flawed logic of his interlocutors. The most vicious of the self-styled Socratics was Critias, not only the leader of the oligarchs who seized control of Athens in 404, but a prolific writer on political-philosophical subjects. His grave monument reportedly featured the personification of Oligarchy setting fire to personified Democracy. His epitaph read: 'This is a memorial to those excellent men who, for a short time, restrained the arrogance of the cursed Athenian demos.' It was in part because the Athenians supposed that Critias had learned his evil ways from him, that Socrates was convicted at his trial and executed.

The suppression of Socrates' critical voice is a stain on the record of the Athenian democracy. But it is important to keep in mind the context. By 399 Socrates had been tolerated for a generation. He was not prosecuted in the immediate aftermath of the fall of the Thirty. But by returning to his critical conversations after the democratic restoration, as if nothing had transpired that concerned him in any way, Socrates seemingly refused to acknowledge that his highly public questioning of basic democratic ideals had played a part in precipitating a frightful stasis. By ancient standards, at least, Athenians were remarkably tolerant of critical public speech. But it was a fundamental tenet of the democratic regime that men who chose to speak in public on matters of political moment were responsible for the effects of their speech, whether intended or not. Although Socrates had studiously avoided speech-making in the Assembly, the Agora was a public place; speech in the Agora that had public effects was subject to public censure.

Socrates himself apparently took the point. In *Crito*, a short but extraordinarily rich dialogue, Plato describes how some of Socrates' friends prepared the way for him to escape from prison after the death sentence had been passed. But Socrates refused their offer, claiming that he, a man who abjured doing harm in any form, could not willingly harm the laws of Athens, laws that had done him good by helping provide for his upbringing. He reasoned that by escaping from prison he would be rendering the laws under which he was convicted impotent. By refusing to accept the chance to escape from prison Socrates acknowledged his own willing acceptance of the authority of the Athenian law, even if he was convinced that the law had been misapplied by a particular jury. If his words had inflamed revolutionary oligarchs, Socrates asserted by his acceptance of the death sentence that he was a loyal citizen who would die rather than endanger the legal framework that had sustained his own life.

Spartan oligarchy: the rise and fall of a political ideal

Greeks like Critias, who were hostile to the idea of democracy, tended to look to Sparta as a model state: aristocratic in that it was ruled by the 'virtuous few', and oligarchic in that a relative handful of rulers controlled most of the property. Thucydides the historian was impressed by Sparta's remarkable constitutional stability. He noted that, having survived a protracted stasis in their earlier history, the Spartans retained a single constitution for over 400 years. Despite some superficially democratic features, that constitution was extremely restrictive in that the great majority of native-born males resident in the Spartan home territory of Laconia were denied the chance of citizenship of any sort. Classical Spartan society was divided into three primary classes based in the first instance on birthright: a warrior élite (the Spartiates), free inferiors (the *perioikoi*—'Fringe-Dwellers'), and a large class of serf-like sharecroppers, tied to the soil and permanently subject to institutionalized oppression (the helots). The Spartans had, in the archaic era, annexed the adjacent territory of Messenia and forced the once-independent Messenians into helotage. Thucydides' comment about a long Spartan stasis refers to the fierce struggles which attended the creation of this 'colonial' regime.

What other Greeks most admired about Sparta was the education and discipline of the Spartiate class. The Spartiates called themselves 'the Similars' (*homoioi*). The goal of Spartiate culture was to forge a citizen body composed of men whose individual characteristics were submerged in a group identity based on uniformity, discipline, and military excellence. Young Spartiates were raised in a rigorous state-organized educational system in which they learned to ignore physical discomfort and to depend on the members of their assigned unit. When a Spartiate reached manhood he was initiated into a social/military unit of 'Messmates', and any young man who was not accepted by an established Mess was permanently dropped from the ranks of the Spartiates. He became an 'inferior' and experienced what amounted to social death.

Each Spartiate held a state-assigned plot of land, which was farmed by helots. Although in fact a wealthy Spartiate might own considerable estates in addition to this state-plot, all Spartiates were expected to live according to a strict egalitarian code of behaviour: clothing, food, houses—every aspect of the public and private life of every Spartiate was to be 'similar'. Each Spartiate kept a watchful eye on his compatriots, suspiciously anticipating any deviation from the established norms. Thucydides has Pericles in his Funeral Oration pointedly contrast Spartan regimentation with the relative liberality of Athenian society: 'just as our political life is free and open, so too is our day-to-day life in our relations to each other; we do not get into a state with our next-door neighbour if he enjoys himself in his own way . . . '(2. 37. 2). It was exactly this freedom and openness that 'Laconophile' Athenians like Critias despised.

On the battlefield, as at home, no Spartiate was to stand out in any way from his fellows: the discipline of the Spartan phalanx was the key to Sparta's capacity to dominate its neighbours in the Peloponnese. And those states in thrall to Sparta were expected to toe a strict constitutional line: Thucydides says that the Spartans saw to it that all member-states of the Peloponnesian League 'were governed by oligarchies who would work in the Spartan interest' (1. 19). This overtly politicized foreign policy helps to explain why civil conflicts during the Peloponnesian War were exacerbated by the conflict between the great powers: everyone knew that a state joining the Peloponnesian League would necessarily adopt a Spartan-approved oligarchy. Aristocrats living in democratic cities sometimes aped superficial aspects of Spartan culture—long hair, distinctive 'Laconian' shoes and staffs, and 'Laconic' speech mannerisms. These lifestyle choices signalled their hopes for Spartan help in imposing an oligarchic regime in which the poorer citizens would be disenfranchised.

Sparta, at least as it was imagined by oligarchic visionaries, bears some resemblance to Plato's Callipolis. But beneath the veneer of stability Sparta was permanently and literally at war with itself. Each year the Spartiates formally declared war upon the helot population, a more-than-symbolic measure that allowed any Spartiate to treat any helot as a foreign enemy. The Old Oligarch informs his reader that, quite shockingly in his view, in democratic Athens you were not allowed to strike slaves or foreigners at will. His apparent reference was to the Athenian law forbidding acts of deliberate outrage against any person, whether male or female, adult or child, free or slave. It was very different in Sparta, where individual helots lived with the fear not merely of being struck, but murdered, by their masters. The krypteia—a secret society staffed by young Spartiates in training— transformed the sporadic violence against helots into a ritual. Members of the krypteia would sneak about at night, selecting victims for assassination on the basis of any outstanding attribute, from extraordinary physical stature to overt evidence of ambition. From the perspective of the helot population, at least, the Spartan stasis never ended; helots lived out their lives in a society governed by the rule that the stronger will inflict their will upon the weak by whatever means they can contrive, where killing one's neighbours was an ordinary fact of life: a society that recalls Thucydides' description of human behaviour during a civil war.

Sparta won the Peloponnesian War, and many of Sparta's adherents within the Greek world may have anticipated the dawning of an oligarchic golden age. If so, the reality proved bitterly disappointing (see pp. 199–211). In a gloomy addendum to his work, *The Constitution of the Spartans*, Xenophon wrote the political obituary for a state he had once so admired. Posing the hypothetical question whether the Spartans of his own day were true to their traditions, Xenophon demurs. He points out that many Greeks now castigate the Spartans and seek to prevent their re-emergence as a great power: 'Yet we need not wonder if these reproaches are levelled at them, since it is evident that they obey neither their gods nor their laws' (14. 7).

Monarchy revisited

The decline of Sparta coincided with broader horizons for Greek political writing. Among the most imaginative is Xenophon's *Education of Cyrus*, a fictionalized biography of the founder of the Persian Empire, Cyrus the First, the namesake of the usurper under whom Xenophon served as a mercenary. Xenophon's 'Persian' society owes a great deal to Greek cultural institutions (see above, p. 99). His Cyrus emerges as a very Hellenized king, concerned with distinctively Greek conceptions of morality, justice, and fairness in regard to distribution. Cyrus is portrayed as the worthy leader of a meritocracy, earning his precedence through superior virtue rather than merely by dint of his noble bloodline. But Xenophon's Cyrus is unquestionably a monarch and founder of a great empire. Xenophon's choice of a Persian emperor as the protagonist of his philosophical fiction shows that the old dichotomy of free Greek versus slavish barbarian was now open to challenge, and with it the exclusion of strong monarchy as a serious topic for Greek political thinking.

Xenophon's contemporary and compatriot, the philosophical rhetorician Isocrates, took monarchy seriously and sought to fit an idealized vision of the worthy strong man into the political conditions of Greece. Isocrates wrote a series of open letters to rulers on the fringes of the Greek world, for example to the semi-Hellenized dynasts of Cyprus, Evagoras and his son Nicocles. In these letters Isocrates attempts to square traditional Greek values of citizenship with a tacit recognition that kings ruled over subjects, not participatory free citizens. His argument was that a monarch with the right character might defend individual liberties better than some existing Greek governments. In 346 Isocrates wrote a letter to Philip II, the dynamic king of Macedon who had turned his once-obscure homeland into the most powerful state in mainland Greece (see pp. 109–10, 212–19). Isocrates urged the Macedonian to use his power for the good of the Hellenic world as a whole. He hoped that Philip would unite the factious Greek cities into a confederacy and then turn to the great project of invading Persia. Isocrates believed that only a grand imperialistic project could put an end to the endemic warfare among the Greeks. Moreover, he saw colonial foundations in new-conquered lands of western Asia as a means of permanently exporting the masses of impoverished and stateless Greeks, victims of civil conflicts and external warfare, who seemed to him a threat to civilized life. With the riff-raff shipped off to Asia, Isocrates imagined that a stable 'ancestral' regime, an oligarchy hiding behind the name 'democracy', might be established in his native Athens. There is little reason to suppose that Philip paid much attention to Isocrates, but Isocrates' political letters were directed less to their ostensible recipients than to his fellow Greeks. He hoped to teach them that kingship had a place in the world of the poleis, if not within the government of any particular polis. Given his enduring influence as an educator, Isocrates' writing may have helped pave the way for intellectual acceptance of the new world that would emerge in the wake of the conquests of Alexander (see pp. 219–22)

Conclusions: from destructive political conflict to constructive political debate

Although Isocrates' political preference was oligarchy, his chosen profession, the teaching of rhetoric, depended on the sort of litigation especially characteristic of democracy. The trial of Socrates has helped to give Athenian legal practice a bad reputation, and Athenian political life after the death of Socrates is often portrayed as falling into decline. But in fact forensic conflicts in the people's courts, like dramatic performances in the theatre of Dionysus, played an important role in sustaining a vibrantly democratic political life that lasted well beyond the end of the classical period. Indeed, the courtroom and the theatre had some striking similarities: a litigant, like an actor, benefited from a strong voice, good memory, and stage presence. At least one major Athenian politician, Demosthenes' rival Aeschines, began his career as a tragic actor.

Every Athenian litigant needed to demonstrate to the ordinary men of the jury that he was a paragon of democratic virtue. Those without political ambitions would point to their record of public service and, if wealthy, to their public and private benefactions. Politicians would emphasize the proven value to the state of their policy recommendations. And in all cases, legal disputes provided a forum for the public expression, testing, and refinement of what might otherwise remain only implicit and ill-understood political and ethical values. It is in the rhetoric of the lawcourt that Athenian democracy and the complex set of sometimes contradictory ideas upon which it rested (liberty and equality, free speech and consensus, respect for individual initiative and social conformity) were most clearly revealed, both to Athenian citizens and to modern readers. Political and legal disputes, rather than being destructive to the polis (as Plato had suggested), actually helped to bring the logic of the democratic polis to light.

When they listened to cases Athenian jurymen tested each speaker's self-presentation against their existing standards, but they could also take the opportunity to revise their standards. The courtroom audience was not limited to the several hundred jurymen; major disputes between famous litigants often drew large audiences of bystanders, and thus the Athenian lawcourt took on important extra-legal functions. It was a forum in which citizens could, in effect, present their own complex system of values to themselves, and could decide, almost day by day, whether or not they liked what they saw. The process of value testing and incremental change allowed democratic ideology to respond to changes in the social environment and to external events.

This process of value testing and revision ordinarily remained implicit and beneath the level of consciousness. But an Athenian politician might sometimes use the lawcourt as a platform for presenting a speech that combined the usual legal and ethical arguments with a bolder theoretical meditation on Athenian political ideals. The legal rules demanded that a litigant discourse at some length. Although jurymen were not shy about interrupting any speaker they felt was wandering too far from the point, some litigants were given considerable leeway for digression. If he saw that he had the jury's tacit blessing, a politician might use the occasion of a courtroom battle to present a fresh take on the nature of democratic leadership, the duties of citizenship, distributive justice, or the relationship between political participation and law.

A good example of the use of lawcourt rhetoric to present a 'theory of politics' is Lycurgus' prosecution speech *Against Leocrates*. Lycurgus contends that by fleeing from Athens in the days after Athens lost the decisive battle of Chaeronea to Philip of Macedon (see p. 219), Leocrates had in effect voted to allow the polis to be destroyed. In this speech delivered in the last years of full Athenian independence, Lycurgus developed an austere vision of citizenship as devotion to the good of the polis. The citizen's behaviour must, he suggested, be constrained by civic, religious, and domestic considerations. If every citizen, like Leocrates, chose to leave the polis when it was at risk, the polis would cease to exist. It was only if all citizens were willing to risk their lives and their personal goods for the good of the whole that the polis would survive. If they did take the risks, Athens could flourish and would live up to its exalted ancestral traditions. Lycurgus graced his speech with lengthy quotations from Athenian tragedy, anecdotes from earlier Greek history, and citations of (sometimes spurious) public decrees. He assumes that his audience of jurymen share his conviction that history and drama are sources of ethical instruction and patriotic inspiration.

The context of the speech, delivered in 330, is telling: the period immediately following the defeat at Chaeronea eight years previously had been a very difficult one for Athens. No one knew Philip's plans. Recriminations flew thick and fast, various radical proposals (including freeing the slaves to help fight) were considered and rejected. Some citizens favoured further resistance, others advocated appeasing the Macedonian victor. Athens seemed ripe for civil conflict. But stasis was averted. The citizens united and prepared to resist an invasion that, in the event, did not come. Demosthenes, the architect of the foreign policy that had led to the lost battle, was given the honourable task of delivering the annual oration over the war dead. In the years after Chaeronea Lycurgus became a major Athenian politician, the central figure in a programme of public building and moral reform that helped to define Athenian civic culture. He was also reputedly a student of Plato.

It is possible to detect in Lycurgus' attack on Leocrates' willingness to flee the city certain overtones of Plato's *Crito*, which portrayed Socrates as refusing to harm the laws of Athens by abandoning his polis. And yet the differences between most of Plato's political writing and Lycurgus' one surviving speech are profound. Plato had equated dispute with stasis, and conflicts between citizens with the destruction of the polis. Lycurgus accepts the democratic polis as a space in which fierce debates among the citizens, followed by decisive judgement, can be expected to produce the best outcome for all concerned.

In his depiction of the stasis at Corcyra, Thucydides had emphasized the link between physical violence and the corruption of ordinary language. He pointed out how fine names were attached to reprehensible deeds, and how rhetorical ability was employed to gain the selfish ends of personal revenge and private aggrandizement. Lycurgus' speech, like other Athenian courtroom orations, affirms to the contrary that in democratic Athens rhetorical battles and political disputes could help create an environment in which political life flourished. It shows how political theory could transcend its elite origins and be received in new guise by a discriminating mass audience. The Greek experience of political conflicts between democrats and oligarchs in the fifth and fourth centuries demonstrated the potential brutality of Greek political life. Yet attempts to understand and transcend conflict also resulted in the flourishing of the sophisticated ethical and political thought that became the foundation of much of Western philosophy. Moreover, although oligarchy remained the preference of many élite Greeks, in the classical period and long thereafter, it was democracy that proved most resilient, most successful in moving beyond violent political conflicts to build a culture defined by productive political deliberation.

Private life

James Davidson

The Athenian wit Stratonicus was with some friends in Maroneia, a small city on the northern coast of the Aegean. Take me to any part of the city, blindfolded, he said, and I will still be able to say exactly where we are. 'They duly covered his eyes and led him off. "Where are we, then?" they said some time later. "Opposite the tavern", said Stratonicus, knowing he was bound to be right, since Maroneia had a reputation for being nothing but a collection of public bars.'

The history of private life is enjoying something of a renaissance in the later twentieth century, the field refertilized by the alluvial deposits of anthropology and sociology. It is often opposed to the history of 'states and dates', which looks back to a Greek, Thucydides, as its founder. The great events of political history are often unique and accessible. The facts of private life are much harder to approach, consisting of many minor and obscure events, which only become important when they are extrapolated into broad patterns of behaviour.

It is not that there are no informants. Anecdotal literature was already flourishing in the fifth century, when Ion of Chios described from personal knowledge what famous contemporaries—Sophocles the tragedian, Cimon the general,—were like in private. In the fourth century Stratonicus' jokes were discussed by his contemporary Ephorus, and may have been collected first by Callisthenes, Alexander's historian. Moreover, ancient writers were not shy of generalizing about the way of life in previous centuries or in other cities or among other groups: homosexuality in Sparta and Crete compared with Athens and Persia, the splendour of a Syracusan banquet, the modesty of Milesian women, the shabbiness of the Athenians, their little cups and little dishes, their fondness for cakes, the superstitiousness of Egyptians, the white flabbiness of Persians without their clothes, the fondness of the Maroneians for bars. Critias (see p. 130) compared Spartan drinking customs with examples from all over the Greek world—Attica, Thasos, Thessaly—drawing conclusions about their social and political character, and at the end of the fourth century one philosopher made a survey of *Bioi (Ways of Life)* of various nations, while another wrote a 'Life of Greece' tracing the development of ways of living through Greek history.

It is difficult to know what to do with such gifts. If other Greeks got Stratonicus' joke, then Maroneia's reputation may have been widespread. If it was widespread, perhaps it was true. There are no rules which allow us to evaluate claims about private life. There are, however, a few useful principles. Firstly we can try to assess the possibilities of knowing. The number of bars in Maroneia was discoverable at least, while statements about a closed society like Sparta are necessarily more speculative and sometimes contradictory. We must also, therefore, be awake to patterns of invention. The most banal statements can be motivated by prejudices of various kinds. It was an enemy of democracy, the Old Oligarch, who claimed the Athenians dressed no better than slaves. Pro-Spartans praised Spartan cloaks (camouflage for the blood of battle) and long hair (terrifying and aristocratic), indicating that less sympathetic Greeks might have read different meanings (luxury, effeminacy) into such institutions. Some historians argue that what was said about others reveals nothing of how they were, merely how insiders chose to construct them. If you can see a motive for invention, however, and a pattern in representations, it does not follow that an author is making it up. Perhaps there was some deeper reason, for instance, why Athenians dressed down. Perhaps Persian 'luxury' read differently to Persians.

To get around these difficulties, historians can attempt to discover stable structures which can be used to generalize. Knowledge of geography, climate, crops, and technology might help us deduce what people ate. Structures of education help us deduce the limits of literacy. Greek culture itself can be seen as a network of structures— habitual practices, conventional ways of thinking about the world. Our experience of wine differs from the ancient Greek experience, because they used different grape-varieties, different wine-making and storage techniques, because they drank it heavily diluted with water, because they drank from cups whose different shapes and decoration had cultural significance, because they drank according to a formal set of rules, from the same bowl, in a cramped room, all of which served to knit the drinkers more closely together, because wine was linked to Dionysian exuberance and danger.

Language plays an important role in these cultural frameworks, differentiating, classifying, and connecting. That they divided food into *sitos*, the staple, barley or wheat, and *opson*, almost everything else, might tell us a lot about the experience of eating, for instance. If we can understand what the difference was between a *hetaera* (a courtesan) and a *porné* (a common prostitute), we might learn something about the terms of ancient erotic life. Here too we must be careful, however. Language is not always neutral and sometimes reflects ideology rather than common usage.

Much of our information—laws, rituals, moral precepts—has a normative value, attempting to dictate what is normal or right. Such norms are interesting in themselves and can be used as a guide to behaviour. Our entire knowledge of the life lived in certain cities comes from descriptions of peculiar customs, and almost all our information about Sparta describes a 'system', as if life in Sparta ran like a machine. Some cultures and some parts of culture were more conformist than others, however, and a description of a society in terms of 'rules and roles' rarely gives a realistic picture of how people actually behaved. Laws are sometimes used to restrict a widespread but disapproved practice, or reflect an irrational moral panic. The philosopher Chrysippus claimed shaving was penalized in Rhodes and Byzantium. Nevertheless, he insists, in both cities, all the men, without exception, shaved.

Historians of Greek private life must compare impressionistic evidence for what was with evidence for what must have been and what should have been. In all cases, however, assessing this evidence is never a science and always a matter of judgement. What we cannot escape is a bias to what the sources noticed and represented, but that gaze is an important historical artefact in itself.

The body

The Spartan general Lysander was strolling with the Persian commander Cyrus around the vast park or 'paradise' Cyrus had built for himself at Sardis. Lysander admired the neat rows of plants and trees and offered his compliments to the man in charge of the design. It was me, said Cyrus, flattered. I even did some of the planting myself. Lysander looked at him, running his eye over his splendid perfumed robes, his beautiful necklaces and beads and the rest of the finery he was wearing. 'Does it surprise you?' said Cyrus (Xenophon, *Oeconomicus* 4. 20–4).

The Greeks seem to have been fascinated by the splendid costumes of the Persians and the bodies they concealed. In the early years of the Delian League (see below p. 176) the Athenian general Cimon was said to have stripped his Persian captives, asking his allies to choose the bodies or the clothes. Considering that slave-buyers would not pay much for such effete physical specimens, they picked the clothes, thus missing out on the huge ransoms soon offered by the prisoners' families (see p. 108). Agesilaus found a different lesson in the Asiatic body. Leading the Spartans in war against the Persians once again, in the early fourth century, he made sure his captives were sold naked, thus giving courage to his soldiers who realised from the condition of their flesh that they were really fighting against the equivalent of women (Xenophon, *Hellenica* 3. 4. 19).

The body was the object of intense ideological reflection, a reflection that produced two of the classical world's most conspicuous legacies: athletics and the nude. Poorer citizens got their muscles and tans from agricultural labour. Better-off citizens mimicked their flesh by exercising naked in a gymnasium. Such outdoor activity came to be seen as a sign of being truly masculine, free, and Greek. A sedentary indoor life, on the other hand, led to a white soft physique which brought one close to the constitution of barbarians, artisans, or women. In early vase-painting, Greek men are depicted 'black-figure', symbolic of their darker skin, while women (and womanish men) are shown pale and white. This ideal is not only implicit in the countless images of the naked and well-defined bodies found in sculpture and painting and in the fine muscled armour worn by the rich, but also in the role played by the body in public festivals. Groups of men and boys stripped to represent their city or their tribe in athletics, torch races, 'pyrrhic' war dances, and competitions for *euandria* ('fine manliness'). In Comedy overweight citizens were vilified, and Plato suggests that when a poor man, lean and sunburned, finds himself fighting alongside a rich man, flabby and pale from a life in the shade, he will despise the élite and start agitating for a democratic revolution (*Republic* 556ce). In Sparta, according to Xenophon, it was compulsory to keep in good physical condition, and one source claims that the bodies of the citizens were inspected every ten days; any man who refused to improve his physical condition faced expulsion.

The time of life which was the focus of most attention was the transitional period, which might extend from the onset of puberty to the late twenties. This period, or the decisive part of it, was called *hêbê* (bloom), and young men at this age were called ephebes or *hêbontes* ('in bloom'), usually characterized in painting and sculpture by a fully grown body but no beard. Sometimes the body and its images were talked of as if they were sources of light reaching a peak of brilliance in early manhood and then fading in old age. Reference to the dead as 'shadows' continues this metaphor beyond the grave.

In Athens, at least, adulthood was decided by a physical inspection before the deme, the Council, and a body of jurors. Those who failed were required to rejoin the ranks of boys. This is the age which is commemorated in those archaic statues known as *kouroi* and the famous Hermes by (or after) the fourth-century sculptor Praxiteles, found in the gymnasium at Olympia. On a more down-to-earth level it was also considered an irresponsible age, typified by the character of Pheidippides in Aristophanes' *Clouds*. Young men in their twenties were the backbone of the army, but were excluded from more responsible positions in the city until they had reached the age of thirty (see pp. 63, 64). In Athens, men were admitted to the Assembly at the age of eighteen or twenty, but were not allowed to serve as Councillors, magistrates, or jurors for another ten years. In Sparta men in their twenties were still supervised by the *paidonomos*, the official in charge of boys.

Many sources point to an ambivalence in Greek attitudes to young men. Their beardlessness and, especially for those with aristocratic pretensions, long hair might be seen as feminine, but at bloom-time these signs of youth were startlingly combined with a sudden manifestation of masculine strength. The Athenians vilified men who appeared beardless in comedies, but Alexander approved a beardless image of himself, leading (or following) a new fourth-century fashion and establishing a link, not with feminine weakness, but youthful power, represented in images of Apollo, young Theseus, or Achilles. One story about Achilles encapsulates this juxtaposition of feminine traits and martial energy, telling how his mother, Thetis, attempted to save him from certain death in the Trojan War by disguising him as a girl. Odysseus tricked him by arranging for an alarm to be raised. The young maiden immediately threw off his disguise and seized the weapons nearest to hand.

Dress

Women, in contrast to men, were represented as keeping their bodies hidden from view, and dress is an essential part of female identity and property from the time of the first woman, Pandora. Although some sources claimed that in Sparta and Chios girls not only stripped for exercise, but even wrestled with boys in public, in Athens, at least, respectable women stayed indoors, cultivating a softer and paler flesh sometimes enhanced with the white powder scraped from lead left to corrode in vinegar. In one comedy courtesans are blamed for adjusting their body-shapes too: platformed shoes to appear taller, a band to flatten the stomach, padding to make their hips look bigger. The women who gather to take over the government in Aristophanes' *Assembly-women* have had to resort to subterfuge in order to escape from their husbands, having spent the past few weeks secretly sunbathing and letting their body hair grow, to appear more like men. In court-cases, speakers boast of how unaccustomed their womenfolk are to male visitors, while others stress their reluctance to enter a house when the husband is not at home. Those who did venture beyond the threshold might find themselves accused of adultery and threatened with death. According to the same logic, Aristophanes indicates that women who showed themselves at the door onto the street were seen as temptresses, while others insist that women who entered the men's room *(andron)* to eat and drink in masculine company were automatically assumed to be prostitutes.

Those occasions when women were allowed out, public festivals or funerals, were seen as moments of danger, when looks and stares might be exchanged with potential seducers. Perhaps most allusions to women appearing in public refer to such a context, when the show-off Meidias drives his wife to the Mysteries at Eleusis, for instance, in a chariot driven by white horses (Demosthenes 21. 158), or when Olympiodorus' impoverished sister and niece look with envy at his mistress going out in all her finery (Demosthenes 48. 55).

Some have balked at this apparently un-European practice of seclusion, arguing that it must in reality have been a luxury. Poorer citizens simply could not have afforded to keep their wives indoors all day. As a compromise, we could give more emphasis to those sources which talk of how, rather than whether, women appeared in public. So long as a woman was well wrapped up and inconspicuous, she might escape censure. Aristotle says some classical cities used officials called *gynaikonomoi* to supervise women and to keep them indoors. Like *paidonomoi*, he considers such magistracies characteristic of aristocratic government on the grounds that in poor families women and children are used in place of slaves and must, of necessity, go out. At least one source (Hyperides F14 Blass), however, claims that even in late classical Athens citizen-women caught on the streets in a state of indecency *(akosmousai)* were liable to a 1,000-drachma fine. A late anecdote tells how Socrates' wife Xanthippe refused to wear his cloak when going out to watch a festival procession. 'Don't you see?' he said, 'You are going out to be looked at, rather than to look' (Aelian, *Varia Historia* 7. 10). It is perhaps significant, however, that Xanthippe, like Aristophanes' *Assembly-women*, does not seem to possess a cloak of her own. By contrast women who had a role in ritual—brides, the *kanephoroi* who carried the sacrificial baskets, and the *arrephoroi* who figured prominently in the Panathenaea—were splendidly adorned with fine clothes, gold and jewels, sometimes paid for by public benefactors.

In this context, the act of unveiling carried an erotic charge, and the unveiling of the bride was a critical moment in Athenian weddings, probably taking place while the groom was entertained at a banquet by the bride's family, and followed by the giving of 'unveiling presents', *anakalypteria* see further pp. 154–7. For the bride to eat with the groom and to show her face for the first time must have had a powerful symbolic impact.

Greek clothes were very simple in design. There was a pleated shift, usually sleeveless, called a *chiton*, which might be long or short. A simpler version, attached on only one shoulder *(exomis)*, was associated with slaves. Over the chiton, if you could afford it, a woollen cloak *(himation)* was worn, made from an oblong piece of cloth, usually simply draped around the body, sometimes pinned on one side. Such clothes were essentially shapeless, taking form from the body they veiled, revealed, and enhanced—a complete contrast with the tailored body-suits in which barbarians are often depicted. 'They wear trousers and turbans,' says Aristagoras, seeking Spartan support for the Ionian revolt against Persia, 'that will show you how easy they are to beat'. (Herodotus 5. 49). When Pausanias, the Spartan regent, at the beginning and Alexander the Great at the end of the classical period appeared in Persian clothes, it indicated oriental despotism and luxury. It is significant that when foreign fashions, like the Persian coat called *kandys*, do appear in Athens in the fourth century, it is women who are wearing them.

Since there was so little tailoring, attention focused on the cloth itself. Fragments of ancient textiles indicate great proficiency and variety, and at Brauron women's chitons are distinguished according to material (hemp, linen, *'amorgis'* [silk?], carded wool), colour (yellow—a feminine colour—greens, purple, white), decoration (striped, spotted, bordered, 'decorated', 'highly decorated') and style. Spinning and weaving were women's work and perhaps much cloth was home-spun, although cloth-manufacture was also an important industry in which men too were employed.

In Athens the processing of wool had great symbolic value. A fillet of wool was fixed to the main door of the house on the birth of a daughter, and it was through weaving a new dress for Athena Polias every year that women participated in the Panathenaea. This piece of cloth (probably) is given great prominence on the Parthenon frieze, placed right above the temple door under the pediment that shows the goddess's birth. Indeed, according to the myth of autochthony, all Athenians were descended from a piece of wool, fertilized by Hephaestus, and dropped onto the Attic soil, to produce the child Erichthonius, in whose name both 'wool' *(erion)* and 'earth' *(chthon)* could be heard.

Dress offered clues to wealth, status, and character. Women of the brothel were said to wear transparent cloth, and vase-painters paid great attention to how much of a woman's body was visible beneath her draperies, an indication of her sexual availability and/or the quality of the material. Men too betrayed a great deal about themselves in their clothes. The cloak *(himation)* was the essential man's garment. Both sculpture and texts imply that ideally it was worn with no *chiton* underneath. One type, called *tribon*, was a sign of modesty, poverty, or even Spartan (oligarchic) sympathies, while the *chlanis* or *chlaina* revealed wealth. What differentiated them is obscure, but contemporaries certainly noticed. One character in New Comedy remarks that now he is poor he has lost all his friends. 'It was my *chlanis* not me they used to approach. Now no one speaks to me' (Posidippus 33 K–A). The reverse is true of the just man newly enriched in Aristophanes' *Wealth*. An informer comes sniffing around. 'Where did you get that cloak?' he says, threatening prosecution, 'Didn't I see you yesterday in a *tribon?*' Other items had significance. 'Spartan shoes' were gentlemanly, while *embades* (felt slippers?) were associated with the old and the poor. One Athenian speaker describes how Dicaeogenes mocked a poor relative, because he wore a *tribon* and *embades* (Isaeus 5. 11). Carrying a staff, on the other hand, implied pomposity (Demosthenes 37. 52). Given the importance of appearances in assessing tax burdens in Athens, it is hardly surprising that some were suspected of disguising their wealth, wearing a tatty cloak over a fine *chiton*.

In a speech concerned with the behaviour appropriate to orators (see above p. 59), Aeschines censures Timarchus for leaping around in the Assembly, exposing his flesh, and Cleon was said to be the first to tie his cloak higher, while addressing the public, so that he could move around, gesticulating freely. By contrast, Solon and Aeschines were sculpted with both arms wrapped tightly in the cloak, the way exemplary young Spartans also dressed. Demosthenes, however, claimed Aeschines' cloak reached to his ankles, a 'cloak-dragging' style, perceived as foppish or antidemocratic (Fig. 6; cf. Fig. 10).

Figure 6 The debonair Aeschines in his tunic and cloak needs to be compared to the more austere statue of Demosthenes (Fig. 10).

Diet and health

Alongside this body presented to the world was the interior body, conceived as a unified system of fluids, so that sperm was linked with marrow and brain-tissue, menstruation with nose-bleeds. Our main sources for this body are the treatises ascribed to Hippocrates. It is difficult to say how far their rationalizing ideas about health were shared by the general populace. Other important traditions looked more to the influence of divine powers or to what we would call 'magic'—on at least one occasion the healing-god Asclepius was asked to mend a broken pot—and a doctor's advice had to compete with messages from oracles and dreams. Images of parts of the body in clay or stone have been found at a number of Greek temples, offered in hope of, or gratitude for, a cure. There was a strong trad-ition, however, that medicine originated in the work of gymnastic trainers, and it is likely that from the gymnasium, above all, ideas about health and nutrition spread. Ancient writers on diet talk as if they are experts in an area where almost everybody has some amateur knowledge.

This expertise can be sampled by looking at the second book of the Hippocratic treatise *On Regimen* or the ancient medical writings excerpted by Athenaeus. Long lists of food and wine in many differ-ent combinations, cooked in all manner of different ways, are assessed for their particular 'power': 'moistening', 'drying', 'heating', 'sweet', 'fatty' or, 'strong'. Such lists are not evidence for the normal diet, however, and when experts refer to the qualities of puppy-meat, hedgehogs, and foxes they may be simply showing off. Food influ-enced the body's various 'juices' (humours), characterized in terms of hot and cold, wet and dry, qualities which might in turn be related to the four elements, climate and the seasons, thus linking the body to the environment and the world. There was no settled consensus about which foods had which properties, about the number and importance of different humours or in what ways the biological woman differed from the biological man, although women were gen-erally thought to absorb more moisture from their diet which led to a wetter, wool-like flesh, relieved periodically through menstruation, and women alone were afflicted with various disorders caused by a wandering womb, cured by coaxing the errant organ back into place. Despite their disagreements, almost all medical experts worked according to a theory of balance, taking account also of how the patient had lived in health. Alcmaeon of Croton in the fifth century referred to such balance as *isonomia*, 'equal distribution', connecting the body to the 'body politic'. Disease could be seen as an imbalance or 'monarchy' of one element over the others which might be remedied by its opposite. A clammy disorder, for instance, might be alleviated by eating honey, which had the power to heat and dry. Vomiting, bathing and exercise also had their place in therapy.

When we move from ideas to practices, we are forced to generalize hazardously. Many classical Greeks probably ate only one meal a day, the *deipnon*, which belonged to the evening. Others ate also the *ariston*, often translated 'breakfast', but perhaps better seen as any meal which was not a *deipnon*. It carried negative associations for many authors, and implied, perhaps, daytime drinking. Each meal was formed around another dualism of *sitos*, the staple (barley or wheat), and *opson*, everything else. Plutarch says that in his time children were trained to take bread with the left hand, *opson* with the right. Taking too much *opson* led to a charge of *opsophagia* (unbalanced, indulgent eating).

Because it was more tolerant of drought than wheat, the mainstay of the diet of many Greeks was barley, a cereal the Romans considered chicken-feed. It was with barley that the helots paid their Spartan masters, and the masters made their contributions to the common mess—barley cakes were even used as ballots, to co-opt new members. In 329/8 (a bad year?), tithes offered to the goddesses at Eleusis indicate a barley-harvest more than ten times that of wheat (see p. 28). Barley was usually soaked and toasted before it was turned into porridge or cakes (*mazai*, probably soft, moist agglomerations rather than baked loaves), and a barley-roasting pan was brought by the bride to her wedding. Cereal-preparation, like wool-working, belonged to the sphere of women. The selling and the preparation of meat and fish, by contrast, was normally in the hands of men.

Meat was rarely eaten outside the context of sacrifices, which regularly concluded with a feast, although portions were sometimes taken home or sold (usually only inedible parts were burnt for the gods). The Greek for 'sacrificer', *mageiros*, also means 'butcher', and 'chef'. Sacrifice, an entire city offering many oxen (the most expensive and honorific victims) at an annual festival, a household offering a sheep or a goat to a favourite divinity, an individual pouring out a libation of a little wine, was the central religious practice, accompanied by prayers which directed the gods' favour in particular directions. Like other gifts—of robes, property, or statues—sacrifice continued a relationship with the gods which looked backwards (in thanks) and forwards (in expectation) at the same time. Its effectiveness was measured in personal or communal success, often of a military or material nature, and avoidance of disaster. There was nothing mechanical about this relationship, however. Divine goodwill could be cultivated or jeopardized but never bought.

Because of the importance of communal sacrifice, we can get an idea of how much meat was consumed annually by an average Athenian from sacrificial calendars and the sale of hides, the perquisite, usually, of the priest presiding. Although outsiders considered Athens exceptional for the number of festivals and the quantity of sacrificial victims, even there meat formed a small part of the diet, less than one twentieth, perhaps, of the amount consumed by modern Europeans.

Despite the extraordinary variety we find in medical writers and comic fragments, in most cases it would have been lentils or chick-peas that accompanied the barley cake or bread. Athenian sources treat milk products as a luxury, although cheese appeared on the tables of the Spartan mess and was also associated especially with the more pastoral culture of Sicily. Olive oil, wine and figs completed the diet.

Oikos: household and house

Houses have been excavated at a number of sites all over the Greek world (Fig. 7). The overall impression is of small unimpressive structures, made of mud-brick on stone footings, close-packed in city-blocks with floors of beaten earth. A Greek cityscape of plain, largely uniform, housing and conspicuous marble temples must have produced a graphic image of polis ideology. Demosthenes in the fourth century talks of houses becoming more extravagant, but given the humble standard of domestic architecture generally, only a small degree of embellishment, a couple of pillars by the door, for instance, would have served to make a house look distinguished.

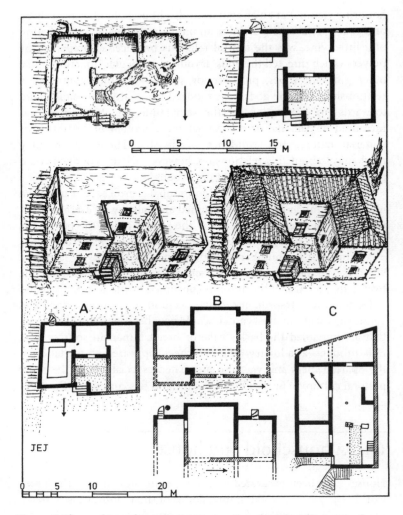

Figure 7 Plan and two alternative reconstructions by John Ellis Jones of a house on the Pnyx hill at Athens (A), with two further house plans.

From the mid-fifth century onwards, a private house or palace provided the backdrop and an 'off-stage' for the majority of Attic dramas, and tragedy, in particular, used the physical image of a house to explore conflicts of loyalty between the polis and the household (*oikos*), or problems of knowledge in perceiving true character through public façade (see p. 195). Euripides' Medea, for instance, is a reasonable character on the outside, but reveals her true ferocity out of sight and indoors, shouting oaths, and rising through the roof in a final bloody triumph. This was an opposition also between male and female spheres, which is one explanation for the prominence of women, who often represent the *oikos* and epitomize privacy, in tragedy's explorations of these relationships.

Although urban settlement was dense, privacy was ensured by architecture. Only a few small windows looked onto the street and the world outside. Light was provided by a small internal courtyard. Literary sources imply that second storeys were not uncommon, reached by a ladder or sometimes a staircase. Many had wells or cisterns for collecting rainwater. It is hard to add much to this bare outline. Few rooms had specific functions, although many houses had a large light room, opening onto the courtyard by means of a verandah or porch, often south-facing. Even the hearth, which plays an important part in household rituals, seems to have been nothing more than a portable brazier, judging from the absence of remains. Household shrines must also have been movable, since sources mention them but few traces survive.

One room is easily identified, the 'men's room' or *andron*, a small squarish space with an off-centre doorway and a raised cement platform around the edge where couches (normally seven) were placed. Here guests were entertained at banquets and drinking-parties *(symposia)*. Despite its intimate size, it was often rather more splendid than other rooms. Floors of pebble-mosaic have been found, and sources talk of frescoes and tapestries. Cups, some of them apparently too large for convenient use, were also hung up as decoration, the round picture (tondo) which often contained a more impressive, shocking, or amusing scene, turned towards the wall, waiting to be discovered by a curious guest. The *andron* was less private than other rooms, often close to the main entrance, with larger windows opening directly onto the street, so that those taking an evening stroll or carrying torches to light the way home after an evening in a bar could hear snatches of music and conversation, or drunken boisterousness, from inside.

Family

An important part of the Greek marriage ceremony was the lead-ing out of the bride to her new home, flanked by the groom and his best friend, in an evening procession with musicians and well-wishers in attendance, the bride's mother carrying torches (Fig. 8). The pro-cession was not repeated for a second wife, and it was a Boeotian custom to burn the axle of the cart in which the bride was brought to mark the finality of the migration. In Athens divorce could, in theory, be initiated by the husband, the wife, or the wife's father, but there is no sign that marriage was taken lightly or seen as a temporary arrangement, and comic playwrights sometimes contrasted the com-placent wife, legally secure, with the vulnerable hetaera who had to 'buy' her lover by pleasing him.

The reference to 'buying' a man is striking, since a bride brought with her a dowry which had to be returned if the marriage ended without issue for any reason. This rule applied even for an adulterous wife whose husband was forced to divorce her, although it might have been difficult, in that case, to reclaim the dowry. Faced with possible financial loss, if he complained, or gain, if he took money from the adulterer instead, husbands sometimes chose the path of lucrative silence. Callias, the richest man in Greece, was said to have paid three talents to his lover's husband to escape the full force of the law. One man who ended up killing his wife's lover, invoking the rarely used Draconian law absolving such murderers, but, predictably, finding himself charged by the victim's family nevertheless, strenuously denies that a plan to extort money went wrong: 'I did not do it for money . . . there was no profit motive at all . . .' (Lysias 1. 4).

Marriages were arranged by parents and betrothal *(enguê)* might have taken place many years earlier, when the girl was still a child. On her wedding-day, especially if she was an heiress, she might still have been as young as twelve or thirteen. Her husband was likely to have been in his late twenties at least. The graves of men and women who died before marriage were marked with vases used in wedding-ritual. The women represented on surviving examples are always young, the men distinctly older.

The husband was often close to the family, a cousin, an uncle, the

Figure 8 A veiled and crowned bride, to whom a small winged figure of Eros (Desire) is offering a garland, being lifted into a wedding chariot on a fifth-century loutrophoros, a pot particularly associated with the nuptial bath and with weddings.

father's best friend. Indeed the law obliged heiresses on their father's death to marry his closest available relative, even if it meant divorcing their current spouse, to keep property intact. Comic poets warned that young wives of old husbands were more likely to slip their moorings and wander into adultery and Chrysilla, who appears as Ischomachus' exemplary young wife in Xenophon's *Oeconomicus*, was still young enough many years later to seduce her daughter's husband (Callias, again) and even bear his child, allegedly.

At betrothal, the bride's father spoke the formula 'I give you this girl for the ploughing of legitimate children', and the idea that marriages were reproductive alliances above all is common. Romantic love between couples is rarely on show, and comic poets often portrayed marriage as a burden to be postponed as long as possible. When, in Xenophon's *Symposium*, a pageant enacting the marriage of Ariadne and Dionysus inspires the bachelors in the company to think of getting married and the married to rush off home to their wives, it is clear the author has a moral agenda. On the other hand, tomb-inscriptions sometimes indicate affection between spouses and it is gods of Love who dominate wedding-scenes and ceremonies.

Demographers note that the practice of marrying girls young often leads to high fertility rates, but mortality rates were also high—at Olynthus about one third of children died before reaching puberty—and there is little sign of anxiety about overpopulation; unwanted pregnancies figure most often in a context not of financial embarrassment, but of shame. In fact historians and philosophers were much more concerned with *oliganthropia* (population-shortage), which Aristotle suggests was the main reason that Sparta failed to recover from her defeat at Leuctra in 371 (see pp. 98 and 207). It is in Sparta especially that we have the most straightforward evidence for measures to promote the family, with confirmed bachelors deprived of citizen-rights and fathers of three or more sons exempted from military and financial obligations. But medical writers too were concerned more to assist conception than to prevent births, and 'Why am I childless?' was a very popular question among visitors to oracles. Among the inscriptions recording divine cures at Asclepius' sanctuary in Epidaurus are several which relate to miraculous births after pregnancies lasting years, sensational demonstrations of the god's power in this important area of anxiety. Children were needed not only to continue the *oikos* and to look after elderly parents but also, crucially, to honour them in death, at the tombs which lined the streets leading from the city-walls, by pouring liquid offerings (choai), wine, water, oil, milk, and honey, or burning food, or little birds, and by tying coloured ribbons around the tombstone. Electra is shown making such offerings at Agamemnon's tomb in Aeschylus' Choephori ('Bringers of choai') and in vase-painting women predominate among grave visitors. In Athens, interestingly, such filial devotion would take them to the Ceramicus, the city's 'red-light' district. The dead could bring benefits or even carry instructions written on lead, requesting Underworld divinities to paralyse enemies. The murdered or 'dead before their time' retained a particular malicious potency.

On arrival at her new home the bride and groom were met by the groom's surviving parents, led to the hearth, and showered with dried fruit and nuts. The wide disparity in age between them meant the bride would be entering a distinctly older family dominated by women, with her mother-in-law still perhaps in her forties and in most cases already a widow. Later writers thought that there had been little respect for parents in classical Greece, because the Greek father lacked the powers of the Roman paterfamilias who could even put his children to death, and a Greek son became legally competent on reaching maturity, but Athenians did at least have an obligation to feed their parents, house them, and tend their graves. If they failed they could be faced with a law-suit for maltreatment. In addition, anyone convicted of dishonouring his parents could be struck off the citizen-lists and was considered automatically disqualified from an archonship, or from the right to address the people. However, we know of no prosecutions for abuse of parents, and the sanctions against such abuse are strikingly political, a feature which is confirmed by Plato, who considers physical abuse of parents characteristic of the 'tyrannical' man. On the other hand, as in most modern European countries, it was very hard to disinherit one's children. In fact it was illegal for a father who had surviving children to make a will at all. On his death the property was simply shared out equally between his sons or, if he had no sons, the men his daughters married.

Slaves

The rest of the household would be made up of female relatives too young or too old to (re)marry, slaves and former slaves, the husband's widowed aunt, his old nurse, perhaps, a few servants. Household slaves were very much a part of the *oikos*, incorporated into the household through the same ritual that welcomed the bride, often participating in household sacrifices. There is evidence that maid-servants established close relationships with their mistresses, sleeping in the same part of the house, sharing domestic space, work, and secrets, much more like personal attendants attached to an individual than household staff. So Aethra, Theseus' mother, who was, according to myth, enslaved to Helen in Sparta, elopes with her mistress to Troy, and the courtesan Neaera (see above, p. 52) kept not only the clothes and jewels she removed from the house of her lover Phrynion but her maidservants too ([Dem.] 59. 46).

A similar pattern can be seen in relations between men and their retainers. Slaves worked alongside their masters to build the Erech-theum, and in Comedy slaves appear as cheeky sidekicks, sometimes helping errant youths outwit their stingy fathers. Slaves in Athens were notorious for their lack of deference. In Plato's *Protagoras* the slave who answers the door at the house of Callias is hardly cringing in his behaviour: fed up with sophistic visitors, he slams the door in Socrates' face. We should be careful of underestimating the brutality which could be meted out to household slaves even in Athens. We hear of citizens of the democracy beating their attendants and threat-ening torture; slave-abuse was a popular form of slapstick on the comic stage. But alongside fear there was trust, an unequal but per-sonal alliance based on mutual interest and close intimacy; the closest modern equivalent might be the relationship between a master and his dog. Xenophon's Socrates actually complains that men are more likely to grieve over the death of a slave than of a friend.

The Old Oligarch sees an economic explanation behind the lack of fear, noting that in Athens slaves working in businesses outside the house were an important source of revenue, which might be threat-ened if slaves were nervous of demanding immediate payment or indiscriminately anxious to please. Together with the freed slaves and the large number of resident aliens who had stalls, they must have lent a distinctly cosmopolitan air to commercial society and allowed suspicions to be raised about the status of the few citizens who traded alongside them (see pp. 49–51).

Moreover mass-enslavement was a not unusual occurrence when a Greek city fell (see p. 81). So it was not only Persians and Asians who found themselves on sale in the market-place, waiting for a last-minute ransom from home, and although Greek slaves were always a minority among the Thracians, Anatolians, and Syrians who made up the bulk of servile bodies, it was always possible for a Greek to hear tales of Aethra enslaved to Helen, or Eumaeus the prince turned swineherd in the *Odyssey*, or to listen to Trojan women contemplating captivity on the tragic stage, or to look at an Olynthian girl enslaved by Philip, or Socrates' friend Phaedo, brought to Athens as a prisoner-of-war, and to think of him or herself.

The Chians were remembered for introducing the slave trade in the first place. By the classical period their estates were thought to employ the highest number of slaves outside Sparta. They were punished for their innovation with revolts, although, at this time, slave-resistance most often took the form of running away, individually or *en masse* (see pp. 38 and 47–8). But the Greeks had little idea how many slaves there were and estimates of their numbers seem greatly exaggerated. The census of Demetrius of Phalerum, for instance, held between 317 and 307, counted 400,000 slaves in Athens. Modern scholars consider even a quarter of this a high estimate. The problem, as the Old Oligarch points out, is that it was not always easy to tell the difference between slaves and the rest of the population. Sometimes, especially if they had tried to escape, they were tattooed on the forehead, and dress, hairstyle, occupation, and accent might raise suspicions, but they did not stand out because of the colour of their skin. Marks of slavery were more subtle than that. The courtesan Callistion notices that a client is scarred with weals. 'Poor thing', she says. 'Where did you get those from?' 'Someone poured hot stew over me', he says, 'when I was a boy.' 'Bull-whip stew, I'll bet', she replies. A comic fishmonger grows his hair long 'for the god', but really it's to cover the tattoo on his forehead. In oratory, the charge that a slave or a former slave is masquerading as a citizen, or alternatively that an unscrupulous character has falsely accused a free person of usurping free status is not uncommon. A Greek's status as a free man was not absolutely secure but something he had to work at. To show himself free by avoiding slavish jobs and slavish relationships and attitudes, avoiding, even, an enslavement to desire, might be the project of a lifetime.

The Old Oligarch contrasts the situation in Athens with Sparta, where, he says, a slave (helot) lived in fear of any citizen. Here and in some other places, Heraclea at the entrance to the Black Sea, Thessaly, Sicily, slaves formed something much more like an oppressed class or group, a conquered nation, who could be released from servitude only by the state, and could not be sold outside the borders of the territory, men treated as cattle perhaps, rather than man's best friend. They were above all agricultural labourers, a self-reproducing population of 'serfs', who probably lived in families with some property-rights, paying a fixed portion of their produce to an individual master who was prevented from extracting more under penalty of a curse. The Spartans, in particular, used this system to subsidize a distinctive way of life focused on military training. In this way the helots supported the militaristic system that oppressed them, feeding the mouths that bit them.

The Spartans were thought to treat the helots with great cruelty. Critias claimed Spartiates always carried spears in case of ambush and even devised special helot-proof keys to protect themselves, and there was a widespread belief that helots hated the Spartans bitterly and were simply waiting for an opportunity to revolt, a particular problem, thought Plato, when slaves shared the same language and national identity. There was a very dangerous revolt in the 460s, although the Athenians who tried to encourage an uprising during the Peloponnesian War were disappointed.

Friendship

Eating and drinking were intimate activities and were used to develop a whole range of relationships in the Greek world. By the same token, neglecting to share a feast indicated an absence of ties, and exclusion from the feasting community meant rejection. Sacrifice was used to seal marriage-bonds, to incorporate wives and children into Athenian phratries at the Apatouria (see p. 75), to demonstrate, and later, in

court, to prove, a father's or grandfather's recognition of his legitimate heir, while, at Sparta, membership of a mess, paid for in barley,
wine, cheese, and figs, was a requirement for membership of the
citizen body. A toast seals the conspiracy of women in *Lysistrata*, and
women seen dining or drinking with men, or handsome youths with
strangers, risked ruining their reputations. On a geo-political level,
truces *were* 'libations' *(spondai)* and sacrifices marked alliances (see p.
79), while ambassadors could be compromised if they were seen
drinking a 'cup of friendship' with a foreign prince.

At private parties it was normal for guests to bring contributions
which they didn't always share (Xenophon, *Memorabilia* 3. 14. 1).
Those who dined *asumbolos* (without contribution), *the parasitoi*,
were placed in a position of dependency and were believed to sing for
their supper in other ways, by assisting their 'keeper' with false testimony, or flattering him, or helping to attack his enemies in law-suits
or brawls, by facilitating his seductions, by sleeping with him, or
simply by entertaining the company with jokes.

Friendship was measured very much in terms of friendly acts,
favours, gifts, in terms of reciprocation rather than sentiment. This
does not mean that affection had no place, rather that friendship was
such an involved relationship that pure, disinterested elements were
impossible to separate or discern. Friends who would do things for
you and for whom you would do things in return were a vital
resource economically, socially, politically, and judicially in the Greek
world. It has been argued that Greece had no equivalent of the
client–patron relationship which was so important to the Romans,
but in Greece as in Rome, some friendships were certainly less equal
than others (see p. 48).

Socializing was not confined to the *andron*, and certain shops, the
barber's, cobbler's and perfumerer's, provided an opportunity for
meeting people and exchanging news (see p. 63). Indeed, those who
avoided them might be accused of misanthropy. Public bars, however,
though popular and ubiquitous, had a reputation as plebeian institutions. In the old days, claims Isocrates, only the most vulgar servants
would go to a bar, but by the fourth century even a man like
Demosthenes might be seen there. He was caught eating *ariston* by
the cynic Diogenes. Embarrassed, he withdrew into the interior. 'You
will still be in a bar', said Diogenes, 'only deeper'. Thasos passed
measures to prevent wine-shops becoming bars, while the fact that

taverns were so popular in Byzantium and Athens revealed the essentially vulgar character of democratic societies. There is an edge to Stratonicus' joke about Maroneia.

Sexuality

No great gulf separated 'friendship' (*philia*) from 'erotic' attachment. Sexuality has for a long time been viewed as an area in which the peculiarity of Greek culture is most marked. Some have argued that 'homosexuality' was a 'pseudo-sexuality' equivalent to adolescent horseplay, 'behavioural' rather than 'psychological', with an emphasis on power and sexual role, 'dominant active' or 'subordinate passive', rather than on the gender of the person to whom one was attracted. Others have argued that homosexuality was a reaction to the seclusion of women or reflects a need for relationships with equals that women could not provide. Still others argue that it was a kind of induction into adulthood, or a hangover from archaic initiation rituals which leave traces in Plato's emphasis on education. Such theories were deployed at first to quarantine the Greeks from homophobic attacks, more recently, to prove the importance of culture in human sexuality. The kind of evidence which is available, however, makes it very difficult to draw definite conclusions about sexual behaviour—an important point in itself. The facts of any particular relationship were always a matter of speculation. There were no illegal sexual acts and no inquisitors to investigate transgression and extract confessions. Sex was much more 'private' before Christian states, nervous of Sodom's fate, made it a matter of central public concern.

There is no sign, however, that Greeks were oblivious to sexual differences between men and women, or that they were seduced by the prospect of performing particular roles rather than by someone's physical (gendered) form. Apart from some dialogues of Plato, moreover, it is difficult to find evidence that women were, somehow, less important sexual partners than men.

In Athens plenty of women plied the streets or worked in brothels. Although they were celebrated in Comedy as safety-valves for discharging excess desire, we should not think that such fornication was socially acceptable. Someone asked Stratonicus why he looked around shiftily as he emerged from the gates of Heraclea. 'It's like coming out of a brothel,' he said. 'I don't want anyone to see me.' Those comic poets were making a satirical point.

At the symposium, women danced and sang and performed on the double-reeded *aulos* (like an oboe or shawm), or lyre, having been hired, sometimes, on the street. Their performances could be elaborate, even creative—Aristophanes claims that Euripides was influenced by 'whore-songs'—and their instruments were not mere props, but they were always assumed to be sexually available and '*aulos*-girl' comes to mean 'cheap prostitute'. Apart from these hired *(mistharnousai)* women, we often hear of hetaeras living in a monogamous relationship with men as mistresses, before, after, or during a marriage to a citizen woman, occasionally as an alternative. Demeas enjoys such a relationship with Chrysis in Menander's *Samian Woman*. The fact that hetaeras, unlike wives, were easily dispensed with, if they ceased to please, seems to have been a major attraction of these relationships.

Transactions between hetaeras and their lovers could be vague. When the hetaera Theodote is questioned about her income by Socrates in Xenophon's *Memorabilia*, she is coy, talking of 'friends' and 'favours'. When Socrates tries to pin her down she is alarmed. Hetaeras did not 'sell' themselves, they received 'gifts'. This blurred arrangement helped to maintain a distance between hetaeras and women who worked in brothels, the *pornai*, obliged to have sex immediately with 'whoever wanted' on payment of a standard fee. The distinction is not merely a question of presentation, but reflects an antithesis between two kinds of relationship: the buying and selling of a sexual commodity, or a more personal 'friendship', based on persuasion, seduction, and reciprocation. This distinction could be slippery, but was critical, nevertheless.

Most of these female roles had male equivalents. There are references to street-cubicles *(oikemata)* occupied by men awaiting clients—Socrates' friend Phaedo was said to have worked in one—and to men hired under contract. Youths performed alongside women in the symposium, and cithara-boys often figure as objects of lust. A character called Misgolas was satirized for this particular passion. By associating with him, Timarchus risked being seen in a similar role.

Love-affairs between citizens are more difficult to pin down. The relationship between the admired youth *(eromenos)* and his, often plural, admirers *(erastai)* might be a rather distant one, realized in pestering, poetry, or stares. Xenophon *(Constitution of the Spartans* 2. 13–14) insists that, at Sparta, relationships between admirers and the admired were as innocent as those between parents and children. He acknowledges that contemporaries find this hard to believe, but he demonstrates, at least, that it was possible to contemplate an 'erotic' relationship in which sex had no part. Moreover he shows that, for some, sex between men was controversial.

Relationships were often pursued at exercise-grounds, which also provide a setting for some of Plato's dialogues. In *Lysis*, Socrates goes there to admire the youths along with Lysis' blushing suitor. In *Charmides*, he is invited to see how Charmides has suddenly blossomed while he has been away. As the boy enters, followed by a whole pack of admirers, he is stunned, as are the younger boys in the room. Socrates thinks Lysis must be young because he has not yet heard of him, and it is the transformation of Charmides that causes so much comment. Along with references to boys 'selling their bloom' this implies that it is the age of *hêbê* that most impressed. Although the Greeks always talked of erotic relationships between men as *paiderastia*, texts provide little evidence of an acceptance, let alone the institutionalization, of sex with pre-pubescent boys. Terms like *pais* or even *paidion* ('baby') are used interchangeably with terms like *neaniskos* (young man) and *meirakion* (youth) to refer to the same person (Lysias 3). Boys were also, if their families could afford it, chaperoned by slaves called *paidagogoi*, and sheltered by laws restricting access to training-grounds.

Socrates complains that youths, predictably, tend to prefer youthful admirers and the fact that Timarchus has been seen with older men lends cogency to Aeschines' accusations of prostitution. Whorish behaviour, surrendering so easily that gifts looked like payments, or to many different men, was condemned, and a man who tried to seduce too obviously risked being labelled *kinaidos*, the homosexual equivalent of the *moichos*, the beautified seducer of women. 'Selling oneself' carried political implications, frequently used as a metaphor for corruption; an Athenian politician convicted of prostitution faced loss of citizen rights—indeed, references to homosexuality in Athens usually occur in a political context. A fine line separated proper from disreputable behaviour, and Plato seems to have concluded that homosexual desire and homosexual relationships carried unnecessary dangers for personal, moral, and political autonomy and should be stigmatized.

At the gymnasium two of the most distinctive features of Greek culture are found side by side, the nude male and Greek Love. 'Beautiful' *(kalos)* also meant 'noble' and 'estimable', and the physical form of a youth 'in bloom' occupied a central place in Greek imagery and imagination. Did so much ideological emphasis on physique and its images 'homoeroticize' Greek culture or was desire submerged in a sea of (other) meanings?

A civic morality

In Athens the ideology of democracy was underpinned by numerous daily practices of equal participation, the sharing out of sacrificial meat through lottery, drinking the same wine in the symposium, the sharing out of the estate equally between heirs or heiresses. An emphasis on isometry, however, can also be seen in the messes of the Spartan oligarchy, or in the uniform housing which characterizes the urban landscape not only of democratic cities. Common assumptions about community, solidarity, and equal participation informed very different political ideologies.

Balance was as important in interpersonal relations as in the individual. In some cases they are impossible to separate. The regulations of the symposium served both to restrain individual excess and to ensure equality between members. An unbalanced individual, like Alcibiades in Plato's *Symposium*, threatened to throw the entire community of drinkers out of kilter, or, like Plato's tyrannical man in the *Republic*, to tip over the entire state. In this sense private life was always political: 'The greatest liturgy one can perform for the city', says the speaker in a fragment of Isaeus, 'is to live day by day a life of discipline and self-control.'

Self-mastery *(enkrateia, sophrosyne)* has long been recognized as the fundamental principle of Greek morality, governing all areas of behaviour, relations with others and with yourself. It was not a question of finding a limit and keeping within it, but the reverse, a continual effort to avoid falling into an abyss of uncontrollable desire,

financial ruin and loss of autonomy. Limitlessness is vividly and hor-
rifically portrayed in literature, and the fall from probity, traced by
Aeschines' Timarchus, or Plato's tyrannical man, is presented as pre-
cipitous. Self-control was a constant effort to maintain balance;
excess a disastrous tipping over.

Myth was full of images of terrifying abysses and infinities. When
Erysichthon dishonoured her, Demeter cursed him with an insatiable
hunger which destroyed his household. At Delphi, the famous motto
'nothing too much', was inscribed and, in his lost painting of Hades
for the Cnidian clubhouse there, Polygnotus showed not only
Sisyphus and Tantalus engaged in endless labours and afflicted with
endless appetites, but Ocnus, who endlessly plaits a rope which is
eaten by a donkey, and water-carriers endlessly filling bottomless
jars. These water-carriers, says Pausanias, represented those who
disdained the Mysteries of Demeter and Persephone at Eleusis,
reminding us vividly that the Greeks called initiates 'fulfilled',
or 'completed'.

An emphasis on beginnings and ends, and an acute awareness of
progress towards completion, of what remained to be done, were
prominent features of rituals and Greek ideas of life and ('untimely')
death and it is not too difficult to link such ideas to the morality of
self-control. Plato uses the image of leaky vessels to describe the
condition of the *akolastoi*, the 'uncontrolled', in Hades, and the same
image could be applied to Erysichthon's unfillable stomach. The Mysteries certainly had 'this-worldly' aspects—Demeter, according to
Eleusinian myth, was mother of Wealth—but they also guaranteed a
better life 'there', in the next world, and, at the very least, these stories
imply metaphysical, eschatological aspects to the Greek horror of
ruination, limitless desire, and loss of self-control.

If the practices of private life informed political ideology, the state
formally and the community informally broke in on personal life at
almost every level. There were the officials appointed in aristocratic
societies to supervise women and youths, and, in Athens, gymna-
siarchs in charge of ephebes, and magistrates to watch *paidagogoi*. By
the late fourth century we even get those laws banning shaving. There
were also more general mechanisms which brought private life under
the public gaze. Sparta's thrice-monthly weight-watching routine
may be apocryphal, but the physical inspection of new citizens and
the numerous 'scrutinies' of Councillors and magistrates in Athens

were all too real. Usually such inspections amounted to nothing, but for a brief period, in the aftermath of the oligarchic revolutions of the late fifth century, they seem to have become more anxious; one candidate feels it necessary to defend his long hair. There were also penalties for squandering an estate and for 'idleness', and any man who got involved in a property dispute would find questions raised about his lifestyle; litigants were not shy of raising an opponent's manner of walking or talking or scowling or carrying a staff. The jurors' gaze paralleled a general gaze which was turned on individuals outside the courtroom, as they walked through the Agora or the streets. Comic authors made jokes about fat men and thin men, those who drank too much or seemed womanish, those who were seen at too many sacrifices or were over-fond of dice.

Normative values could also be transmitted through education, which was divided into music, letters, and gymnastic (Fig. 9). But education was by no means universal and it is probable that less than a third of Athenian citizens could read and write, possibly only a tenth. The inscriptions the democracy produced did not lead to literacy by osmosis, and an ability to write was rarely a necessity. Athens remained an oral culture; the illiterate would not have been significantly disadvantaged. Musical education was perhaps even more exclusive. An ability to play the lyre is a sign of a wealthy aristocratic

Figure 9 Two aspects of education, music and writing, are imagined here on this early fifth-century Athenian red-figure cup.

upbringing. Objections by Plato and others to the innovative and complex 'new music' of the later fifth century arise in part, perhaps, from the perception that professional technicians were taking over what had been a patrician accomplishment and writing music that was beyond amateur skills.

Beyond the basics, there was much rote-learning of the poets, predominantly Homer, increasingly tragedians. Philosophers, like Plato, seem to have worried about the impact on piety and morality of all those gods and heroes behaving badly, but even he concedes that reminding people of the myth of Oedipus (below, pp. 223–5) helps prevent incest, and wonders if myths could be deployed in the same way to discourage homosexuality. However, it was more for detachable snippets of wisdom, rather than because their plays were straightforwardly didactic or their characters exemplary that dramatists were seen as 'teachers'.

Literature also taught the proper use of words, and there is evidence for a normative approach to language in Plato and many other writers, a concern, that is, with true and correct meanings and proper terminology rather than just the current or most widely accepted usage. Discipline was a feature of physical training too. Synchronized movement, dancing in an oblong phalanx, was a feature of tragic choruses and also, probably, pyrrhic dances, and the discipline of working as a single body was a particularly crucial element in the success of a Greek hoplite army or a crew (see pp. 89, 93). Keeping time, on almost all occasions, was facilitated by music, particularly the *aulos*, which was ubiquitous in ancient society, providing rhythms not only for tragedy, comedy, and dithyramb, marching armies and rowing crews (see pp. 91, 98), sacrifices and symposia, but for demolishers of walls and women as they worked.

Conclusion

The historian must be grateful for this intrusive gaze on personal life, but it makes the polis sometimes seem a somewhat totalitarian community, which thought nothing was none of its business and left no room for a truly private life. But the same evidence can lead to an entirely opposite conclusion. The privacy of the *oikos* was fiercely defended by custom and respect for the modesty of women. Without the resources of a police force or a public prosecution service, without central records of births, marriages, deaths, property, and status, the polis had few weapons with which to breach this impenetrable façade (see pp. 64–5). The intensity of the gaze turned on the most trivial aspects of life when they became visible is a sign of the poverty of knowledge, a reflection of how much was unseen. Modern people, despite their vaunted individualism and hard-won rights, live far more highly regulated, state-dominated, homogeneously acculturated, economically interdependent, secure lives.

Moreover, a free Greek was never slavish in his conformity. He was always a voluntary subject and power would be more familiar to him as an internal anxiety rather than as fear of an external authority. If the community was a spectatorship of thirsty eyes, the subject could choose what kind of character to put on show. He was a performer of himself.

The world the Greeks moved in is sometimes presented as black-and-white. But one theme which emerges repeatedly is the fragility of states of being that we take for granted, the indistinctness in areas that for us are quite clear, the effort required to construct difference, to make stark contrasts out of a field of fuzzy grey; what impresses is the energy continually expended in bodily practices and social practices, designed to demonstrate most clearly that one was indeed a decent woman, a good friend, a legitimate heir, a real man, a pious man, a citizen, a true Greek, not an impostor, not a wastrel, not a slave.

The fifth century: political and military narrative

Lisa Kallet

'These ships were the beginning of evils for both Greeks and barbarians.' So Herodotus on the departure of Athenian warships in 498 to help Ionian Greeks revolt from Persian rule (5. 97. 3). Greek history, especially of the Aegean and mainland, of the classical period (*c*.500–336) is intertwined with Persia. The evils that the Athenian ships began were wars: during the fifth and first half of the fourth centuries some Greek city or another was fighting some war or other in perhaps two out of every three years (see p. 82). And like major military engagements in any period, the two 'great wars' that opened and closed the fifth century—the Persian Wars and the Peloponnesian War—had consequences transcending the strictly military and political spheres.

Athens dominates the political and military narrative of the fifth century, to a far greater extent than that of earlier and later periods of Greek history (see pp. 18, 197ff). The reason is not simply the concentration of sources and information from and about that polis; it is also due to the Athenians' creation of the first empire in the west, which gradually affected most of the Greek world (directly or indirectly), and led to the Peloponnesian War.

The Ionian Revolt and the Persian Wars

Greeks had settled in poleis on the coast of Asia Minor from the eleventh to the eighth centuries, but they were not independent, having been conquered in the sixth century, first by Lydians, and then by the Persians; moreover, many still were governed by tyrants (individuals who seized power 'unconstitutionally'). In 499 Ionia, the central region of the coast, revolted from Persian rule but in 494 was brought back into the Persian empire. The episode would have occupied an insignificant place in history but for the fact that the Athenians became briefly involved. While in the Lydian capital of Sardis, Athenians (and Eretrians from Euboea) accidentally set fire to a temple. When King Darius learned of those responsible, writes Herodotus, he vowed revenge and instructed a slave to remind him thrice daily, 'Master, do not forget the Athenians!' (5. 105). The result was the Persian attack on Athens in 490.

The Persian Empire had been pushing west since 514, when Darius crossed into Europe and subdued Thrace and Macedon. But the revenge card was useful for the Persians to play (and was always an acceptable motive for attack): their first stop after crossing the Aegean was Eretria, where they burned temples, sacked the city and enslaved the inhabitants. Then they landed at Marathon in north-east Attica; Athens' victory (with Plataea's help) could not have been predicted, given the Persians' numerical advantage; Herodotus reports that about 6400 Persians died, against 192 (out of 10,000) Athenians. Aeschylus' epitaph celebrated his participation in the Athenian victory without a whisper about his tragic victories, one piece of testimony out of many to the importance of this battle to Athenians.

The Athenians expected renewed attack; it came in 480, led by Darius' son Xerxes; an army and support system crossed the Hellespont and marched via the northern land route, while the fleet—including Ionians—sailed alongside. From the size of the expedition (Herodotus ridiculously estimates five million; the truth is probably closer to 200,000), it was clear that Xerxes intended nothing less than the conquest of Greece; other Greeks besides the Athenians now had reason to fear. The Spartans were committed to resist, though only prodding and threats prevented them from limiting their defence to the Peloponnese. The Athenians could be counted on, and their role would be critical. Their prestige was recent but impressive: the victory at Marathon for the first time made other Greeks sit up and take notice of a city which, during the archaic period, had had minimal impact on the larger Greek scene. But Greek unity was untested, and a mere thirty-one out of around 1000 Greek poleis sent delegates to a council held at the Isthmus of Corinth to prepare strategy and create the Hellenic League, an alliance under the leadership of Sparta, the pre-eminent military power in Greece. In some cases, enmity toward neighbours, not fear of Persia, dictated choice: Herodotus guessed that the Phocians joined in because the Thessalians did not, naughtily adding that had the Thessalians chosen to resist, the Phocians would probably have collaborated.

In summer 480, the League prepared a land and sea defence of the entrance to central Greece, at the pass at Thermopylae, held ultimately by a small force of 300 Spartans under King Leonidas, and off Artemisium in Euboea. When the Persians broke through on land because of an act of treachery and threatened the poleis of central and southern Greece (the naval battle off Artemisium was indecisive), the Delphic oracle told the Athenians consulting it, 'flee, flee to the ends of the earth', subsequently moderating it slightly: 'flee, flee, but if not, take to the wooden walls' (Hdt. 7. 140–1).

The Persian army under Mardonius marched into central Greece, while the fleet sailed alongside. Boeotia promptly 'medized'—the term given to those who collaborated with the Persians. The next stop was Athens. Meanwhile, the Athenians debated whether the 'wooden walls' referred to the walls of the Acropolis, or, as some thought, to their ships. Themistocles supported the latter interpretation and persuaded the Athenians to evacuate the city and to fight the Persians at sea.

Athens had a navy capable of facing the Persians only because of the policy of Themistocles. A few years earlier, he had persuaded the Athenians to use revenue from the silver mines at Laurium to build a fleet of two hundred warships (see pp. 37, 108); its existence was crucial for the Hellenic League's success. Luring the more numerous Persian fleet to fight in the narrows of Salamis, where numbers would not be an advantage, the Greek fleet won. Xerxes took what was left of his fleet and went home.

But Mardonius and his land force were still to be reckoned with, and, in 479, in a battle in a plain at Plataea on the Attic–Boeotian border, the League army prevailed. Meanwhile, the League fleet sailed across the Aegean and defeated the remnants of the Persians off Mt. Mycale; the Wars were over. While the victory was a League achievement, Athens and Sparta, chiefly, were responsible for the successes at Salamis and Plataea, respectively—which meant that Sparta would have to share its position of military pre-eminence among the Greeks with Athens.

Consequences of the Persian Wars

Panhellenism

Before the Persian Wars, Greeks arguably had little sense of identity as Greeks; to be sure they spoke the same language, worshipped the same gods, and shared customs (see pp. 1–2, 18–19). True, their most cherished tradition was the story of a united Greek expedition under Agamemnon that sailed to Troy to recover Helen, the background of Homer's *Iliad*. Yet in a fundamental respect they regarded each other as foreigners and real or potential enemies. The best illustration of Greek disunity is the pitiful size of the Hellenic League.

The experience of the Persian Wars, however, made Greeks regard each other as a homogeneous group which shared fundamental beliefs and values that set them apart from the Persian 'barbarians'. At the core of the new Panhellenic spirit were two things: a commitment to political freedom, *eleutheria*, and an obedience to law, *nomos* (see p. 70), values they saw as opposed to those of the Persians, who, living under an autocratic ruler, and owing absolute obedience, were therefore not free. The words Herodotus puts into the mouth of Demaratus, an exiled Spartan king who took refuge in the Persian court and who served as Xerxes' adviser in the invasion of 480, sum up the ideology. When asked by Xerxes whether the Spartans would stand their ground at Thermopylae against the far more numerous Persians, Demaratus replied, 'Yes, they will, for they are free, though not entirely. For they do have a master over them, Law, and they fear him much more than your men fear you' (7. 104. 4).

Panhellenic ideology was to have a long history (see p. 217). The slogan, 'freedom of the Greeks,' was used and abused over the next 300 years: by Greeks against Persians, by Spartans against Athenians, by the Macedonian king Philip and his son Alexander, and even by the Romans. This underscores the potency of the ideology; cynical, and hypocritical, yes, but with enduring value as a justification for aggression and conquest. And it was crucial in shaping Greek history in the fifth century, as well as for the birth of historiography.

Herodotus and the writing of history

Herodotus was born c.484, between the two Persian invasions. A Greek from the Carian city of Halicarnassus, he had direct experience of what it meant to live under autocratic rule: Caria, like the rest of Asia Minor, was part of the Persian Empire and his city had been ruled by a tyrant, under whom members of his family had directly suffered. He left home as a young man and travelled extensively throughout Asia, Egypt, and the Greek mainland, residing in Athens for some time. In writing about the great conflict between the Greeks and Persians he took the first step toward what would become the genre of historiography; he refers to his work as a demonstration of *historia*, literally 'researches' or 'inquiry.'

Greeks thought of Homer as preserving their 'ancient history' (see p. 5). Nothing of their past could rival the legends of Achilles, Agamemnon, and the other heroes; nothing, that is, until the Persian Wars. Indeed it may have taken an event like the Persian Wars to justify writing an account of human achievement. As Herodotus tells us at the opening of his work:

This is a display of the researches of Herodotus of Halicarnassus, so that neither the deeds of men fade over time, nor the great and marvellous works brought forth both by Greeks and barbarians lose their fame; and especially the reason why they fought one another.

This programmatic statement reveals Herodotus' aims: above all to write about the causes and course of the Persian Wars, but also to preserve traditions about the peoples inhabiting his world; thus the work contains much folklore. He leads up to his main subject by charting the rise of the Persian empire, and includes extensive ethnographies of those who became Persian subjects.

Herodotus' ethnographic sections display an underlying concern with a fundamental antithesis that pervaded the intellectual climate of the time and dominated sophistic literature of the late fifth century, namely, that between custom and nature, *nomos* and *physis* (see above, p. 125). Herodotus explores explicitly and implicitly the question of whether people are disposed toward certain behaviour by nature (*physis*) or by custom (*nomos*), a human construct. Despite his recognition that cultural beliefs and practices were created by humans in a specific cultural context, and therefore are neither given nor absolute, and, by extension, intrinsically neither better nor worse than foreign customs, Herodotus' work reflects the common Greek belief in their cultural and moral superiority over non-Greeks. This brings us back to Panhellenism, a fundamentally chauvinistic outlook which took for granted the superiority of the Greek virtues of freedom and the adherence to law—recall Demaratus' comment to Xerxes.

Herodotus believed that on a deep level the affairs of mankind were controlled by the gods. But his theory of causation was complex, involving coexisting divine and human, long- and short-term causes, as illustrated by his comment on the Athenians' responsibility for the victory at Salamis: 'it was the Athenians who, after the god, repulsed the Persian king' (7. 139. 5). But in trying to answer the big question of why do powers rise and fall that is central to historical understanding of all periods, Herodotus found an answer in a concept, *hybris*, that in his work mingles human and divine elements. Put in a nutshell, wealthy and powerful rulers necessarily strive to become greater; their greatness incites the envy of the gods, and so inevitably leads to their downfall. As Xerxes' uncle, Artabanus, warns the King before he invades Greece, foreshadowing (and not subtly!) the outcome of the Persian Wars:

Do you see how it is the living things that exceed others in size that the god strikes with lightning and will not let exalt themselves, while the little ones do not provoke him at all? Do you see how it is always the greatest houses and the tallest trees that the god hurls his thunderbolts upon? For the god loves to thwart whatever is greater than the rest. Thus a great army may be destroyed by a small one; for once the god feels envy toward the great army . . . it will perish in a way unworthy of itself.   (7. 10)

Herodotus' decision to write about the Persian Wars had a profound impact on historiography. Although the genre as it developed for the most part cast aside the ethnographic and story-telling elements, nevertheless Herodotus had so established war as the proper subject for history, that the Roman historian Tacitus felt compelled to apologize for being forced to write about events other than war.

The Delian League and the creation of empire

The most visible consequence of the Persian Wars was Athens' creation of naval *archê*, literally 'rule,' but usually translated as 'empire'. It presents a fascinating paradox: given the ideology of liberty that was a direct outcome of the Wars, and the Athenians' role as champion of that freedom in the recent struggle, how is one to explain Athens' *archê*, or the fact that many Greeks, to a certain extent willingly, gave the Athenians the means to oppress them? The answer lies in the particular circumstances of the aftermath of the Persian Wars.

With hindsight we know that the Persians would not attempt another conquest of Greece in the fifth century. To Greeks of the Hellenic League in the aftermath of war, however, no such outcome was obvious. The mood at the time would have been a combination of heady self-confidence and fear: self-confidence at having repelled the might of the vast Persian empire, and fear that Xerxes would retaliate, as he had for his father's failure in 490. Greeks living in Asia Minor and on the coastal Aegean islands had the greatest cause for alarm; they had been freed as a result of the wars of 480–79, but their proximity to Persia made that freedom precarious.

Accordingly in spring 478, fifty ships of the Hellenic League set out, liberating Greek cities in Cyprus, and then besieging Byzantium, a Greek city still under Persian control. But the Spartan commander of the fleet, Pausanias, behaved offensively to the Ionians in the League and he was shortly recalled to Sparta to answer charges against him. As Thucydides tells it (on whom, more below), the Ionians, out of hatred toward Pausanias, asked the Athenians to take over the command, and the latter accepted. Herodotus, alluding in passing to the event, says baldly, 'the Athenians stripped the Spartans of the leadership, using Pausanias' behaviour as an excuse' (8. 3. 2).

Thus was born a new military alliance, called the Delian League by modern scholars because its treasury was on the island of Delos, sacred to Apollo. The alliance was to consist of autonomous Greeks with equal voting rights under the leadership *(hegemonia)* of Athens, with a long-term goal of maintaining the freedom of the Greeks from Persia and of retaliation against the Persians. It differed fundamentally from earlier, mostly land-based alliances such as the League of mostly Peloponnesian states under Spartan leadership because it was naval, and this required enormous capital (see pp. 106–7). This explains the unique feature of the League that allowed the Athenians to transform the League into an empire: 'tribute' *(phoros)*, an annual financial contribution paid by most League members (larger communities initially contributed ships instead of money).

Two factors stand out in the transformation. First, it was Athenians who staffed the board of treasurers which received and administered the tribute—despite the fact that their title was 'Greek treasurers' *(Hellenotamiai)*. Athens therefore controlled League wealth. Second, gradually all but three allies (Lesbos, Chios, and Samos) paid money in return for League protection—some ordered to as a result of attempting revolt, others because they resented the long, annual service and arranged to pay money instead—and the navy became increasingly Athenian.

The extent of the economic burden of tribute on the allies is not altogether clear. Assessments were mostly based on local resources, and so mainly on land, with the primary burden falling on the rich. But in the case of cities with busy harbours, port taxes formed at least part of the source of tribute. Given the relative poverty of most Greek poleis, however, any sustained expropriation of local resources must have adversely affected their economic prosperity. The disaffection we find, reflected in revolts and withholding of tribute, may have been due to economic hardship as well as political resistance.

Even if League members were enthusiastic at the beginning, things quickly turned sour. Already in the first few years, League campaigns seemed aimed to a great extent at other Greeks: forcing nonmembers like Carystus, at the southern tip of Euboea, into the League, or, within a few years, fighting against members who tried to secede, as did Naxos. By mid-century, about 150 poleis were under Athens' rule, controlled by various means. Standard procedure after a failed revolt included the taking away of walls and ships, imposition of a military garrison, and payment of money—tribute, in the case of those not tributary at the time, or in some cases an indemnity. Such cities were left with little or no means of defence or potential to unite with other disaffected states. More generally, the Athenians placed a variety of officials in the poleis to ensure loyalty, and in differing degrees impinged on local judicial and political autonomy. For example, allies were forced to come to Athens for suits involving Athenians, a practice that earned the latter the reputation for being litigious (Thucydides 1. 77. 1; Old Oligarch 1. 16).

The Athenians seem to have made no attempt to disguise the nature of the relationship: they spoke of themselves as 'ruling over subjects,' not euphemistically 'leading allies'. A public decree speaks of 'those over whom the Athenians rule', and extant regulations for cities whose revolts had been suppressed, of which the earliest examples date to the 440s, invariably contain the phrase, 'I shall obey the Athenians'—concise testimony of the deprivation of autonomy. Or consider the assertion, indeed, boast, of Pericles, Athens' leading statesman from around 450 until his death in 429, who said, according to Thucydides, 'only in our empire can subjects never complain that their rulers are unworthy' (2. 41. 3). Pericles is probably contrasting Athens with Persia; that he could do so implies that some Athenians did not regard their rule as different in kind from barbarian empires, only better. Whether Pericles himself actually uttered these precise words is less important than the fact that they were thought appropriate to the occasion by a contemporary. Elsewhere, we get closer to the truth, when Pericles and Cleon state flatly: 'we are ruling like a tyrant over cities which do not like it!'

The economics of empire

Our sources, narrative, epigraphic, and archaeological, tell us much about the economics of empire. From tribute the Athenians received about 400 talents of silver annually, known from inscribed stelae recording a required dedication, or quota, to Athena, beginning in 454 when the treasury was moved to Athens (a decision that had larger political and religious significance). But they also deprived cities of their wealth in other ways, for example, by appropriating land and either making it sacred to Athena, to whom rents were then due, or settling on it Athenian citizens who retained their Athenian citizenship but lived and farmed the land of the allied city.

That last example shows how Athenians individually could benefit from empire—the settlers were probably poor citizens, thetes (see p. 61), whose status now improved. Wealthy citizens bought up land in the *archê*, from which they derived income. The increased litigation from the empire benefited Athenian jurors, who received a daily wage (see p. 65), and landlords in the Piraeus. Greeks within the *archê* traded among themselves and with other Greeks, and the Athenians boasted of the luxury imports they received from the east; but those poleis and islands not in the empire could suffer—this may partly explain a dramatic gap in Athenian imports in Crete through most of the fifth century.

So far as they were able, the Athenians created a 'closed sea,' controlling grain imports from the Black Sea through the Hellespont, and levying transit taxes on cargo destined for cities in the empire. As the Old Oligarch states, 'where will a city rich in timber . . . in iron, copper, or flax . . . dispose of its goods without the consent of the rulers of the sea?' (1. 11). Their interest in profiting from trade is best illustrated by their decision during the Peloponnesian War to abolish tribute in favour of a five-per-cent maritime tax imposed throughout the *archê*, on the assumption that it would increase their revenue. The measure probably failed in its objectives, but, like the attempt at some point to impose their own currency and metrological standards on the allies, which aimed at creating a closed economic system, it attests to Athens' acute awareness of the economic potential of *archê*.

It might be easy to regard Athens' allies merely as victims and the Athenians merely as oppressors; but the relationship may have been complex. Thucydides certainly thought so. He suggested that weaker parties in a power relationship voluntarily submit to the stronger out of a desire for material betterment, or, more simply and tendentiously, for profit (the Greek word is *kerdos*, which means 'gain,' and usually carries a negative connotation). Applied specifically to the Athenian *archê*, the allies in 478 probably expected a tangible return, in the form of Persian booty, on their 'investment' of tribute.

The Delian League and Persia

We hear of no League campaigns against Persia in the decade following 478, but the Persians recovered Cyprus around 470. The chronology of the next two decades is controversial, but around 469 a League force under Cimon attacked the Persians at the Eurymedon river in southern Anatolia and destroyed the entire Persian fleet. Further campaigns occurred in the following years and around 459 a League fleet of 200 ships sailed to Cyprus and then to Egypt to help its revolt from the Persian Empire. The revolt failed after six years, and the fleet was almost entirely destroyed. A few years later, Cimon, who had been ostracized after a failed attempt to help Sparta with an internal crisis in 462 (see below), led 200 ships to Cyprus; he died in the course of the campaign, probably in 450, and the fleet withdrew. Further attacks against the Persians stopped. No contemporaries mention it, but in the fourth century it was assumed that Athens had made peace with Persia, the 'Peace of Callias'.

Empire, democracy and culture

Empire and democracy were symbiotic, and each developed in tandem with the other. The 'birth' of Athenian democracy is traditionally placed around 508, with Cleisthenes' reforms; but the form of government labelled *demokratia* evolved gradually, based not on an ideological, but rather on a practical principle that operated in much of the Greek world: those who contributed militarily to the polis should have political rights, or even political power.

The men who won Athens its power in the Greek world were not an élite: they were the hoplites who fought at Marathon, and especially the thetes who rowed in the navy (see pp. 37 and 92). After the Persian Wars greater political power was extended to the demos—the male citizenry—as a whole, so that by the mid-fifth century, the assembly was sovereign and offices in which power and prestige had been previously located were now diminished by being open to the majority of citizens and determined by lot (see pp. 61, 66). Many received pay for their services, including the 500 Councillors and 6,000 jurors, the latter on the proposal of Pericles, who thus promoted the participation and therefore power of the demos. (By contrast, Thucydides [2. 65. 9] refers to government under his leadership as 'democracy in name, rule of the first man in fact').

Aristocratic opposition to democracy can be found through the whole of the fifth century (see pp. 122 ff); so one question is, why was it allowed to develop in this way? One answer immediately suggests itself: the *archê*. The Athenian citizenry collectively wanted the *archê* for the power and wealth it gave to the city, and individuals wanted it for their private prosperity; the price (to élites) was *demokratia*. Thucydides tells us that at its height the sacred treasuries (the traditional repositories of public wealth) held nearly 10,000 talents of silver, much of which must have come from the *archê*. Obviously the Athenians had generated far more revenue than was necessary for the military needs of the Delian League; and their overall wealth gave them the means to spend readily and lavishly at home, in ways that illustrate further the symbiosis between the *archê* and the *demokratia*.

Most conspicuous was a massive public works programme. The Persians had destroyed the temples on the Acropolis and buildings and monuments elsewhere, which the city could now afford to rebuild. The crown was the Parthenon, Athena's temple on the Acropolis (built in marble, not, as normal, limestone), housing a magnificent gold and ivory statue of the goddess, and most of the city's wealth. A marble gateway building of unprecedented scale, the Propylaea, marked the entrance to the citadel. The demos voted and authorized the funds for the programme, which enhanced both their power and prestige and those of Pericles, who had proposed it. His political enemies in Athens attempted to undermine his influence by attacking the extravagance of the monuments. In particular, according to Plutarch (*Pericles* 12), Thucydides, son of Melesias (see p. 124), objected to using money from the *archê* on domestic building projects. He lost the battle, and was ostracized; most Athenians did not agree with him. The nature of the objections suggests that dissent at that time concerned the uses of imperial wealth, not its acquisition (or the existence of the *archê*).

The intertwining of religion, democracy, and empire is reflected in numerous ways: in the dedication of tribute to Athena (and the stelae recording them, set up in front of the temple); in the Great Panathenaea (see p. 76), in which Athens' allies or subjects participated in the procession to the Acropolis; and in the opening ceremony of the biggest Athenian festival of drama, the Great Dionysia (see p. 75) when the annual tribute was carried onto the stage of the theatre of Dionysus, young men whose fathers had died in war were paraded, and public decrees honouring Athenians and foreigners who had benefited the polis were read.

Culture and politics were closely linked on the stage, in tragedies, which reflected concerns and issues affecting the polis, and in comedies, which were overtly political and topical (see further pp. 126, 128).

For example, Aeschylus' *Oresteia*, produced in 458, reflects the recent curtailment of the authority and power of the Areopagus by Ephialtes. Aeschylus uses the stage not to criticize the development of Athenian democracy and pine for the good old days, but to address the theme, among others, of accommodation between tradition and progress in political, judicial, and religious contexts. Sophocles' *Antigone*, performed probably in the 440s—at the time when the Parthenon was being built—highlights issues that reflect that more long-term concern, the relationship between state and divine authority (and family and state), and offers a warning that divine justice will prevail. Sophocles' play and Herodotus' *Histories* share the theme of the dangers of excessive power; both can be read as warnings to Athens.

Drama was a purely Athenian cultural form; but as such it was unusual in terms of the broader cultural and intellectual life of the city. While the Athenians, like other Greeks, jealously excluded foreigners from citizenship, they welcomed outsiders to participate in the cultural life of the city. The building programme required expertise and labour beyond what could be supplied internally, and brought foreign craftsmen, artists, and labourers to Athens to put their talents to work. The city was a magnet for artists and intellectuals from both east and west, who were attracted by its wealth and opportunities to benefit from private and public patronage—the architect Hippodamus of Miletus, who designed the town-plan of Piraeus, the philosophers Anaxagoras from Clazomenae and Parmenides of Elea, the sophists Hippias of Elis and Gorgias of Leontini—so that, with the exception of drama, the cultural and intellectual history of fifth-century Athens is a Greek, as much as an Athenian, phenomenon (see p. 21).

Sparta, Corinth, and Athens, 478–446

It is difficult to extract details about Spartan politics, both because of the lack of Spartan sources and the general secrecy of Spartan internal life. But whatever the truth behind the different, though not necessarily exclusive, perspectives of Herodotus and Thucydides on the transfer of leadership of the Greeks against Persia from Sparta to

Athens, the Spartans did allow the Athenians to emerge and then develop as a rival superpower.

The Spartan retreat after the Persian Wars is in some respects paradoxical and obscure, and in others explicable. On the one hand, Spartan strength and influence had never been higher: its role in the Persian Wars only enhanced its pre-eminent position as leader of the Peloponnesian League; its control of most of the Peloponnese effectively muted its chief rival for power, Argos. On the other hand, Sparta's credit suffered abroad after the Wars, due to individuals like Pausanias, and she became leaderless at home as a result of the vacuum which Pausanias' demise created in one royal house, and the disgrace of the other in 476 when a charge of bribery (to retreat from the conquest of Thessaly) led to King Leotychidas' exile. Perhaps as a result, Argos reasserted itself and attempted to chip away at Spartan control of the Peloponnese. Spartan insecurity is clearly revealed in its behaviour during the revolt of the helots in Messenia in 462: when Cimon and the Athenians showed up to help at the Spartans' request, the Spartans sent them home. The consequences were grave.

The Athenians broke off their alliance with the Spartans (the Hellenic League, still formally in existence) and formed an alliance with Argos, an unambiguous expression of hostility toward Sparta. During the so-called First Peloponnesian War that followed (462–446), Athens allied with Thessaly and expanded its power on land, in Boeotia. Sparta, slow to act unless forced, barely figures in much of the military activity punctuating the conflict. Indeed, to say the war was between Athens and Sparta, or to put inter-polis rivalry and aggression over the next thirty years simply in terms of these two superpowers, is to miss the complexity of regional conflict, in which Athens' relations with Boeotia, but most of all Corinth, occupy the centre; ultimately, it was the threats of Sparta's allies to defect from the Peloponnesian League that were arguably most responsible for the Spartan decision in 432 to go to war in earnest.

Corinth's Homeric epithet, 'wealthy,' was no exaggeration. Its geographical position at the north–south and east–west axes of the mainland brought great prosperity to the city through its harbours on the Corinthian and Saronic gulfs. Corinth and Athens had been friendly earlier in the century, as is shown by Corinth's loan of 20 triremes to Athens in the mid-480s for use in their war with the island of Aegina. Friendship was often based on common enmity and in this case both

Athens and Corinth hated Aegina. But relations between Athens and Corinth soured as soon as Athens allied with Megara in 462, after Megara left the Peloponnesian League following a border dispute with Corinth; they did not improve when Athens gained control of Aegina two years later. This is a fine illustration of the way in which enmities between two poleis, often arising from border disputes, could affect inter-polis relations on a much wider scale (see further pp. 197–9). The Corinthians, not the Spartans, felt most threatened by Athenian alliances and expansion during the late 460s and 450s, for they removed all northern counterweights to Athenian power.

Without Sparta's whole-hearted engagement, there was little real war, and what there was ended in 446 with the Thirty Years Peace. Its terms are not altogether clear, but they required Athens to give up its mainland holdings outside Attica, and stipulated that neither side should enter into armed conflict if one or the other offered arbitration. They may have included a clause of autonomy for the allies of each; but in any case, Athens retained its naval empire.

Greeks in the West

Since the archaic period there had been Greek settlements on the Mediterranean coasts of what are today France and Spain, but the greatest concentration of Greeks in the west was in Sicily and southern Italy. Like Greeks in Asia Minor, the Greeks of Italy and Sicily lived cheek-by-jowl with native peoples, such as the Sicels and Elymians on Sicily. Tension and conflict, as well as vigorous cultural exchange, were the norm; tensions were probably exacerbated by the dense mixture of Ionians and Dorians: Dorian colonies from Corinth, Megara, Crete, and Rhodes existed alongside Ionian settlements from places like Euboea, Samos, and the Ionian coast. Thurii, an Athenian colony established in 444/3 in southern Italy on the site of Sybaris, constitutes a special case in the colonial pattern, since individuals from several poleis, both Ionian and Dorian, joined in the settlement. Among them was Herodotus, who settled there toward the end of his life.

Sicily and southern Italy had material resources unknown in most of mainland Greece, specifically an agriculturally-rich countryside, and, in southern Italy especially, abundant timber. The prosperity of Syracuse and other cities depended on the exploitation of Sicels, who worked the land as serfs, and allowed the emergence of a wealthy agricultural class, sometimes with political results. Sources speak of democracy in Syracuse after the fall of tyranny in 462, but it was far from the Athenian type (which itself was unique); political power was extended to propertied citizens, not to the free landless residents, the equivalent of the thetes in Athens.

The prosperity of the region attracted outsiders. A Carthaginian invasion was defeated by Gelo, tyrant of Syracuse, at the battle of Himera in 480 (the same year as Xerxes' invasion of Greece) but the Carthaginians continued to maintain a presence in western Sicily. Athens' colony at Thurii may have been intended not so much to extend the *archê* as to gain a foothold in an area rich in the timber essential for Athenian naval power—economic, not political, motives, then (though the two are closely related). By the last third of the fifth century if not before, Athenian interest in the region, especially Sicily, had become much more conspicuous, as is seen in her willingness to get involved in Sicilian affairs. This coincided with growing tensions between Athens and Sparta that would result in the Peloponnesian War, the subject of Thucydides' *History*.

Thucydides and the development of a genre

'Thucydides, an Athenian, wrote an account of the war between the Peloponnesians and the Athenians, expecting that it would be great and more worth writing about than previous conflicts.' These words evoke the preface of Herodotus, who much influenced Thucydides, born *c.*460. But Thucydides' *History* (he does not in fact use the word) reveals the development of a genre, and at the same time Thucydides exploits, as does Herodotus, the broader intellectual climate of fifth-century Athens to compose his work: the influences of tragedy and of medical and sophistic writings can all be detected. He restricted his subject rigorously to war (including its social, political, and moral effects), he sought explicitly to refine methods of gathering and assessing information about not only what was done but what was said—a task made easier by the fact that, unlike Herodotus, he was writing contemporary history—and he defined both the purpose of historical writing and the utility of history. 'I shall be satisfied if those who want to examine the clear truth of past events and of similar events that will occur in the future—human nature being what it is—judge my work useful' (1. 22. 4).

Thucydides believed that the constancy of human nature allowed generalization from the particular, hence the lasting value of his history of the Peloponnesian War. Underlying his statement is a fundamental pessimism about human nature (see pp. 11–12). Writing about civil war, he comments, 'many terrible things befell the cities in *stasis* (civil strife), which happen and will always happen, as long as human nature is what it is, though worse or milder and taking various forms, according to the particular circumstances' (3. 82. 2). It is not that commendable portraits of cities or individuals do not appear in his work; the problem, as Thucydides saw it, was that by nature men who can will attempt to exercise power over others—a view expressed by the Athenians in his 'Melian Dialogue' (5. 84–112; see below, p. 192)—and to increase it; but the drive for expansion can lead to collapse. This conception resonates with Herodotus' notion of *hybris*. Both historians share an interest in charting the rise and fall of power; Thucydides' treatment, however, differs in one fundamental respect: human actions and consequences are explicable purely in human terms. To simplify his complex analysis, power develops through man's ability to marshal wealth so as to acquire it, and is exercised and extended by proper leadership and intelligence, along with resources; and power falls, not because of divine envy, but by the inability to combine its ingredients successfully.

Like Herodotus, Thucydides distinguished between types of causes:

As to why [the Athenians and Spartans] broke the peace, I have written first an account of the grievances and disputes, so that no one may ever wonder what specific circumstances produced such a great war. I believe that the real cause of the war, but the one least articulated openly, is that the growth of Athenian power and the fear that it provoked in the Spartans, compelled war to happen. (1. 23. 6)

With these words Thucydides begins his account of the origins of the Peloponnesian War in effect by closing discussion ('so that no one will ever wonder') on its causes. In fact, people have wondered and argued about the causes of the war, and Thucydides' account of them, ever since.

Thucydides' primary concern was why war broke out at all. For him, the 'grievances and disputes' did not have to result in open war, for they did not affect the two superpowers directly. Thus, the war was really caused by the nature of Athens' power and the fear it provoked in the Spartans. His statement on causes and origins is nuanced and polemical. For, in fact, the Spartans were the ones who voted to go to war, and later held themselves responsible for refusing an Athenian offer of arbitration. Thus his claim that the Athenians were the responsible agents is paradoxical.

Thucydides' concentration on the 'grievances and disputes' is a further polemic, this time against the popular opinion (in Athens) that Pericles was responsible for the war by refusing to rescind the Megarian Decree. Passed probably several years before the events of 432, in retaliation for Megara's revolt in 446, the decree barred Megarians from using the harbours of the empire and the Athenian Agora. The decree's impact is unclear, but the evident vigour of the Megarians' attempts to get the decree rescinded, leading to a Spartan ultimatum to the Athenians to do just that or else, and a possible allusion to it in Aristophanes' *Acharnians* of 425, suggest that it was effective.

The Peloponnesian War

The 'grievances and disputes' which led to a Spartan declaration of war concerned two minor incidents, each on the periphery of the Greek mainland. The first, conflict between Corinth and its colony Corcyra over Epidamnus, itself a Corcyraean colony on the Illyrian coast, illustrates the tensions that could exist between colony and mother city over their relationship and obligations. Stasis in Epidamnus led one side to appeal to Corcyra for help. When the Corcyraeans refused, the Epidamnians approached Corinth. The Corinthians agreed to become involved, partly from hatred toward Corcyra for not acting appropriately toward its mother city. Corcyra, determined that Corinth should not interfere in the affairs of its colony, persuaded the Athenians to give military support, though the Athenians insisted on a purely defensive alliance. But in a minor naval battle, the

Athenians and Corinthians clashed, and thus the Athenians, because they fought an ally of Sparta, could be accused of having broken the Thirty Years Peace. In the second incident, Potidaea, in the Chalcidice in the northern Aegean, an Athenian subject but a Corinthian colony, received aid from the Corinthians in a revolt from Athens, and the Athenians besieged the town. (The revolt was quelled, but only after two years.)

These two episodes, like the Ionian Revolt, would have virtually disappeared from history had not greater significance been placed on them, in this case, by Sparta's allies, who intensified pressure on her to bring Athens down. In 432, Spartan envoys issued three sets of ultimatums to the Athenians (see p. 187), but they were clearly pretexts, not serious attempts to reach an agreement, for each was followed by another more serious. The final ultimatum said simply: 'let the Greeks be free and autonomous.' It strains credulity that the Spartans believed the Athenians would seriously entertain it (at least at this time; two years later some Athenians advocated giving up the *archê*). On the other hand, lest we consider the Athenians' offer to arbitrate as completely well-intentioned, we need to recognize that the possession of their *archê* was non-negotiable.

We can see, then, how the minor, local events of 432 were put to use as cards in a much larger game: should the Athenians be allowed their empire? The answer was clear to the Corinthians, Megarians, Aeginetans and other maritime allies of Sparta; but whether the Spartans would have responded as they did without the prodding of their allies—which included threats of withdrawal from the League—is not clear.

It is a mistake to think of Athenian and Spartan attitudes as monolithic, a point which holds for their history as a whole, and which reinforces the claim that war at that time was not inevitable. The Spartan king Archidamus argued that it was premature to attempt war with Athens (it is thus ironic, then, that we give his name to the first ten years' war). But his view was in the minority: the majority were in favour of it, influenced by the opinion of an ephor, Sthenelaïdas, that the Spartans would win. The Spartans, acknowledged as the best hoplites in Greece, whose lives were devoted to intense military training (see p. 86), had not (as far as we know) fought a major battle in 25 years; their vote may be partly explained by eagerness to put their training to use. Likewise in Athens, Pericles urged the

Athenians not to give in to Spartan demands, even if it meant war; Thucydides omits the counter-argument (as usual in the case of Pericles), but it can be inferred from Pericles' remarks that not all agreed.

Thucydides gauges the mood on the eve of war: 'There was tremendous goodwill toward the Spartans, especially as they proclaimed that they were freeing Greece' (2. 8. 4). There is more than a touch of sarcasm in this comment on the Spartans' mission, for Athens' allies soon appreciated the hollowness of the promise: the Spartans did little liberating until 424, and what they did then owed most to the individual energy and initiative of the general Brasidas. Otherwise, when they tried, they failed. Another general, when presented with a ripe opportunity to effect revolts in Asia Minor in 427, instead butchered innocent Ionians; 'an odd way to free Ionians' was the sarcastic comment this drew from those accompanying him. Spartan behaviour after their victory in the Peloponnesian War shows most clearly their interpretation of liberation, when they placed garrisons and military officials in Ionian cities, and subsequently handed them over to Persia (see below, pp. 199–200).

At the outbreak of war, both sides tried to strengthen their coalitions further. Athens wooed the Macedonian king Perdiccas and the Thracian king Sitalces—acts which demonstrate that they judged their ability to hold onto the northern Aegean cities critical for success, as indeed they were: the north was rich in timber and in silver, two commodities that underpinned their naval power. They also cemented alliances in Sicily and southern Italy; the Spartans also sent requests west to their own allies for money and ships (though in vain; neither ever came). Ironically, both sides sent embassies to Persia for assistance. But the Persians stayed out of the war until its final stage; then their role proved decisive.

The Archidamian War (431–421)

The first stage of the war provides an instructive case-study in failed strategy and expectations. In his speech before the Spartans in 432, Archidamus posed the crucial questions:

With what are we to fight a war with Athens? With our ships? There we are painfully inferior. With money? There we fare even worse, since we have no public funds and scattered private wealth . . . so unless we can beat them at sea or deprive them of the revenues which support their navy, we shall lose.   Thucydides (1. 80. 4)

Archidamus' words were prophetic (in the short term) and underscored the basic problem: how does a land power win against a sea power? His words assume the superiority of naval power, but that was a minority view, for Thucydides says elsewhere that most people expected the Spartans to win within a few years, given their superiority on land. The failure of Archidamus' words to have a decisive impact, and the judgement of most Greeks, reflect both Greek lack of understanding about the nature of sea power and the resources underpinning it, and a fundamental miscalculation based on ideology as well as economics: the invasion of 480 notwithstanding, most Greeks evidently thought it inconceivable that the Athenians or any Greeks, when faced with an invasion of their territory, would not defend their land and homes (in which case the Spartans would surely win).

Pericles, however, persuaded the Athenians to abandon the countryside, as they had in 480, but this time they moved within the city walls, which since mid-century had been connected to the Piraeus by a set of 'long walls.' In control of the sea, the Athenians would be able to provision themselves by imports; they would allow the Spartans to invade their land and not fight in its defence. Meanwhile they would attack the Peloponnese by sea.

The test case was the first invasion, in summer 431. The Peloponnesian army under King Archidamus reached the borders of Attica and encamped at the deme of Acharnae. As the Spartans hoped that they would be, the Athenians were furious at seeing their land ravaged (especially, not surprisingly, the Acharnians); but Pericles was able to prevent them from marching out to meet the Spartans, only allowing small units of cavalry to keep the Peloponnesians away from the city walls. At the same time, they sent a fleet of 100 ships to the Peloponnese. This was to be the larger pattern of the Archidamian war: Spartan invasions of Attica, followed by Athenian naval raids on the Peloponnese. It was virtually destined for stalemate.

But the war was also punctuated by several important events that gave each side advantages that could have been more effectively exploited. In 430, a plague broke out in Athens, said to have come from Ethiopia. Thucydides, who caught it, describes its symptoms in painful, meticulous detail 'so that it might be recognized if it ever broke out again' (2. 48. 3). Another unintentionally ironic statement, since no modern attempt to identify the disease has been wholly successful. The disease spread rapidly because of the concentration of people in the city, lasted two years (with a brief recurrence in 427), and killed off thousands, including, according to Plutarch, Pericles. The Athenians were unable to prevent Sparta's destruction of Plataea in 429, a city to which they had been so closely tied throughout the century.

A revolt in 427 by most of the cities of Lesbos (one of three islands which retained a navy, and were, strictly speaking, autonomous) was timely: the Lesbians banked on Athens' weakness from the plague and the hope of Spartan help, but the Athenians were able to put it down before the Spartans arrived. Two years later, in a brilliant string of manoeuvres engineered by Demosthenes, the Athenians not only planted a fort at Pylos in Messenia, but even forced the surrender of 292 Spartan hoplites blockaded on the island of Sphacteria. Thucydides commented that nothing in the war surprised the Greeks more than the surrender, for the Spartans regarded capitulation in battle as anathema.

The war could have ended then (at least temporarily), but Cleon—whom Thucydides describes as 'the most violent and persuasive' of Athens' leaders at the time (3. 36. 6)—persuaded the Athenians to reject all peace proposals; the war continued. In the following year, 424, the Spartans struck back when Brasidas marched north and persuaded many Athenian allies in Macedonia and Thrace to revolt, including the important colony of Amphipolis—which the historian Thucydides, the Athenian general in the area, arrived too late to prevent surrendering (he was exiled in consequence). Brasidas' successes hit the Athenians hard, as did the failure, through an error of co-ordination, of an intricate strategy to take control of a number of Boeotian cities on the same day, and the resulting death of nearly 1,000 Athenians at the battle of Delium. Worn down by the years at war, Sparta and Athens signed a peace treaty in 421; that it happened then owes as much to the deaths of Cleon and Brasidas in 422 as to the efforts of the Athenian Nicias, whom, according to Plutarch, people believed to have been 'responsible for the peace, as Pericles had been for the war' (*Nicias* 9).

The Peace of Nicias

The Peace aimed at fifty years; it lasted six. Technically the Peloponnesian War consisted of two ten-year wars interrupted by this peace; but its unpeaceful nature—the continued agitation of the Corinthians, and the battle of Mantinea in 418, which pitted the Athenians and Spartans and their respective allies against each other, among other episodes—led Thucydides to regard the entire period 431–404 as a single war.

Thucydides records that Pericles had warned the Athenians in 431 not to expand the empire while they were at war with Sparta. It has been a subject of great controversy whether the Athenians followed this advice after the statesman died (or even during his life). Most questionable during the Archidamian war was an expedition to Sicily in 427 in response to an appeal from their ally Leontini (whose ambassadors included Gorgias, the sophist), which was at war with the Syracusans. Merely aid to an ally? Thucydides raises doubts when he comments that the Athenians' real reason for helping was to 'prevent the exportation of grain to the Peloponnese and to test the possibility of conquering Sicily' (3. 86).

In 416 the Athenians conquered the Dorian, though neutral, island of Melos, killing the men and enslaving the women and children. Thucydides chooses this episode in the war to illuminate, in his Melian Dialogue, the relationship between human nature and power and the moral dilemma accompanying such power in a world in which freedom has ideological primacy: those who have power will exercise their freedom to extend it, while the desire for freedom will make weaker parties resist. (Contrast his claim elsewhere that weaker parties will willingly submit in the interest of profit.) The unusual dialogue form prevents the reader from being comfortable or satisfied for long with either position; this may be why he uses it, rather than the standard set speech, in which the rhetorical weight would ultimately rest on the last speech.

The most audacious attempt to expand the *archê* came in 415, when the Athenians sent a massive expedition to Sicily. As in 427, they were answering a call for help, this time from their ally Egesta, at war with neighbouring Selinus (an ally of Syracuse). But once again Thucydides provides an ulterior motive: 'the real reason [literally the "truest explanation," the same phrase he used in his statement on the causes of the Peloponnesian War as a whole] for the expedition was a desire to conquer the whole island' (6. 6. 1). Athenians at the time may have recalled another great Greek expedition overseas, to Troy; Euripides' Trojan trilogy was produced in 415.

As always, democratic decision-making cannot be understood without appreciating the role of individual leaders in the process, in this case the young and flamboyant Alcibiades, pitted against the older and more cautious Nicias. Nicias tried vainly to dissuade the Athenians from going, aware of the folly of beginning a major conquest while war at home was simmering. Alcibiades pushed for the expedition, eager for glory and the wealth necessary to sustain a lavish lifestyle, and persuaded the Athenians. Both Thucydides and Plutarch portray Alcibiades as a charismatic, fascinating, and ultimately dangerous figure (from the democratic standpoint). He was immensely popular among the citizens, but at the same time his personal excesses caused unease—what was he after? Tyranny? At least this was the view encouraged by his political enemies.

Shortly before the expedition was to depart in 415, many Herms, pillar-like representations of the god Hermes with erect phalluses that marked and protected boundaries, were mutilated; at the same time, reports came of mock celebrations of the Eleusinian Mysteries in private homes. These religious offences were taken as ill omens for the expedition and threats to the democracy. Alcibiades was accused, but his complicity was unproven. The expedition sailed, under his leadership (as well as that of Nicias and Lamachus), but his enemies took advantage of his absence, played on the Athenians' fear of tyranny, and recalled him to stand trial; en route home Alcibiades fled to Sparta. Thucydides (6. 15. 3–4, compare 2. 65. 11) commented that Alcibiades' removal from the scene did more to hurt the Athenians than any other single factor. An exaggeration, perhaps, but there is some truth to it.

The expedition ended in disaster for the Athenians in 413 after their defeat in a naval battle against the Syracusans, who were aided by the Spartans. The disaster was not inevitable; it resulted primarily from over-extension and failures in judgement, especially Nicias'. As Thucydides put it, 'the Athenians were beaten at all points and altogether; all that they suffered was great; they suffered, as the saying goes, with a total destruction, their fleet, their army, all was destroyed, and few of many returned home' (7. 87. 6). The survivors returned to a polis in crisis, not only because of the disaster. Earlier that year, on the advice of Alcibiades, turned traitor, the Spartans built a fort in Decelea in north-east Attica; they were now a permanent presence and could cause Athens serious economic damage.

The final stage (413–404)

The Spartans now attacked the Athenians with vigour and sustained effort where it hurt: effecting revolts in Ionia and fighting the Athenians at sea. The roles of Alcibiades, Lysander, a particularly able Spartan general, and Persia were crucial. Alcibiades, ejected from Sparta (reportedly for sleeping with King Agis' wife), offered his services to Persia, advising Tissaphernes, a satrap (governor of a district of the Persian Empire) on how to end the war to the King's advantage. But, as always, he looked out for himself: his real desire was to return to his native city. Testimony to his personal power and charisma was his ability in 410 to return to favour and be elected general—astonishing not only because of his double betrayal, but also because of his part in the oligarchical coup of 411 (see p. 59). But, although he won a naval battle against the Peloponnesians, he again fell out of favour and withdrew.

The Spartans finally won through Lysander's abilities as a general and his friendship with Cyrus, the son of the Persian King, who financed the Spartan navy more regularly and fully than it had been. But luck was involved as well: in 404, the Spartans took the Athenian navy by surprise off Aegospotami, on the north shore of the Hellespont, and defeated them. Then they sailed to Athens, blockaded the harbour, and forced the complete surrender of the Athenians.

The Boeotians and Corinthians urged the Spartans to give the Athenians a taste of their own medicine and do to them what they had done to others, notably at Melos; instead the Spartans allowed them to survive, with twelve ships, no city walls, and, it hardly needed to be stated, no *archê*. The historian Xenophon records that the Spartans refused to destroy (literally, 'enslave') Athens because of its role in the Persian Wars; more likely, they saw value in leaving Athens, between Corinth and Boeotia, as a buffer.

Athenian culture during the Peloponnesian War

The near-three-decade conflict exacerbated tensions between public and private, polis and *oikos*, and magnified the impact that individual self-interest had on the larger political and military spheres. Our best evidence for this comes from Athens, but it reflects a broader phenomenon. These tensions occupy centre stage in the theatre. Both tragedy and comedy, in different ways, present a polis in crisis, unable to function properly as a political system or to mediate the competing claims of family and state. The harsh effect of war on the family and criticism of the political structure inform the treatment of myth in Euripides' tragedies (e.g. *Suppliants; Trojan Women)*, by contrast to Aeschylus' focus on the community. It is perhaps no accident that Euripides' masterpiece, the *Bacchae*, least reflects the problems of the polis; he wrote it in Macedon at the end of the fifth century, after leaving his native city.

Aristophanes' comedies regularly include often vicious attacks on politicians, especially Cleon, portraying them as corrupt, self-interested figures. Other plays feature private individuals who take matters into their own hands to do what the polis would not accomplish. Dicaeopolis, the peasant protagonist of *Acharnians* of 425, implements a private peace with Sparta; for him the problem was chiefly the corruption of politicians like Cleon. In *Lysistrata*, produced in 411, after the Sicilian disaster and around the time of the oligarchic coup, the women of Athens seize the Acropolis and withhold sex until their husbands (= the polis) reset their priorities and make peace with Sparta (see p. 128).

Figures on the periphery of politics also come in for attack in Aristophanes. *Clouds* reflects popular, critical attitudes towards the sophists whose teaching of rhetoric was important in a democracy which placed a premium on the ability to persuade (see pp. 128–9). Their emphasis on techniques of argument, caricatured as 'making the weaker argument the stronger', are presented as fostering a sense of moral relativism, a dangerous development in a city in a protracted, devastating war.

Conclusion

The war left the Hellenic world weakened economically in the short term at least, and arguably with a changed perception of the polis. The increase in mercenaries in the fourth century, often, as in the case of the Athenian historian Xenophon, in the service of Persians, is one reflection of the economic, political, and social effects (see pp. 88–90). The war also imparted a lesson: not that *archê* would not work in a world which placed primacy on freedom and independence, but that one had to try to do it better. This lesson is crucial for understanding the history of the fourth century and the success of the Macedonians Philip and Alexander in altering forever the political landscape of Greece. Finally, the decisive role of the Persians in the last stage of the war is fitting: not only did they, in a sense, close as well as open fifth-century Greek history, but their role also set a precedent for the history of the next half-century.

The fourth century: political and military narrative

Robin Osborne

Discerning a pattern

In 395 BC a long-running dispute between Phocis and Locris in central Greece, over border territory and the pasturing of sheep, led to an armed invasion of Locrian territory by the Phocian army. The Locrians turned to their Theban allies for help, and the Thebans invaded Phocis. The Phocians sent an embassy to the Spartans, who agreed to attack Thebes. So began what has become known as the 'Corinthian War', a conflict between Sparta and her loyal Peloponnesian allies on the one hand, and the Thebans, Corinthians, Athenians, and their allies on the other, which was ended by the threat of Persian intervention.

In a sense, the events of 395 seem familiar enough. It had, after all, been action by a third party, Corcyra, that had acted as a catalyst to the Peloponnesian War (above, p. 187). But in other ways the events of 395 reveal a changed world. The reason why Corcyra's approach to Athens for an alliance in the 430s was so important was that Corcyra was a city whose military power had long been far from negligible (Thucydides [1. 13. 4] held that the earliest of all naval conflicts had been between Corinth and Corcyra), whose friendship had long been courted by other powers, and which occupied a strategically vital position controlling the route from Greece to Italy. Athens could not afford to turn down the opportunity of acquiring an ally such as Corcyra, and the Peloponnesian League could not lightly allow Corcyra's might to be transferred to a power about whose ambitions it was increasingly worried. But Phocis and Locris were not like Corcyra; the Locrians had no special resources to offer, and the strategic importance of Phocis, commanding the easiest route north into Thessaly, had no direct bearing on the inter-city tensions of the 390s, which focused heavily on the cities of southern Greece.

Trying to answer the question of why the dispute between Phocis and Locris led to general war brings us up against another feature that separates the history of the later fifth from the history of the fourth century. For better or worse, and most scholars have been happy to believe it is for the better, we have effectively just one account of most of the events of the second half of the fifth century, the account given by Thucydides and copied by later writers. For events of the fourth century we often have more than one independent account, and the accounts are frequently not just different but contradictory. In this case, we have one account in the history (*Hellenica*) which Xenophon wrote as a continuation of Thucydides, covering events from 411 to 362, and which has come down to us intact, and another account in the fragments of a history which probably also took up where Thucydides broke off (and continued to 386), and which is known as the *Hellenica Oxyrhynchia* ('the account of Greek affairs from Oxyrhynchus') because recovered from the rubbish dumps of that Egyptian town. Xenophon (*Hellenica* 3. 5. 3–4) says that the Phocian attack was precipitated by the anti-Spartan leaders at Thebes persuading the Opuntian (i.e. eastern) Locrians to provoke the Phocians; the *Hellenica Oxyrhynchia* (18) says that those Theban leaders persuaded the *Phocians* to attack the *western* Locrians.

When faced with contradictory accounts of the same events, it is tempting to blame the authors of those accounts. Scholars have pointed to the frequency with which the surviving fragments of the *Hellenica Oxyrhynchia* involve quite complicated stratagems to suggest bias there, or to Xenophon's demonstrable errors and simplifications elsewhere to suggest that he is mistaken here too. But the significance of the disagreement between these two writers, both contemporary with the events they describe, goes well beyond the issue of their personal slants or incompetences. In the fifth century the major powers, Athens and Sparta, entered upon offensives and alliances only after open debate, in the citizen assembly at Athens, in their own assembly of Spartiates and then in a council of their allies at Sparta. It was the interests of the major powers that determined the course of events. Here, however, events are being swung by decisions taken by small political units, effectively by tiny numbers of individuals, and on the basis of more or less secret communications. For the first time in Greek history we see a domino effect at work in inter-city relations, where the changed status of a single piece, however unimportant in its own right, sets off a chain of reactions that leads most of the Greek mainland to almost a decade of sporadic warfare. The historian who could reasonably discover the lines of the argument at big meetings in Athens and Sparta, and the decisions taken there, was in no position to know exactly who had said what to whom in the private exchanges between individual influential politicians, particularly when those politicians had no interest in revealing what they had been up to. In the absence of firm information, rumour and speculation become potent political weapons.

Why had Athens' defeat in the Peloponnesian War so changed the nature of inter-city relations? Athens' fifth-century empire had been sustained by the power of the Athenian navy, and Sparta's Peloponnesian League had been increasingly sustained by fear of Athens. The destruction of Athenian power left Sparta's most powerful allies feeling that the League had lost its rationale, and worrying about the power now in the hands of the Spartans, who they considered had taken more than their fair share of the profits of the war. The Thebans unsuccessfully advocated turning Athens' territory into sheep pasture to prevent Athenian human resources being added to Sparta, and then defied Spartan prohibitions on helping the opponents of the puppet government of the Thirty whose installation at Athens was overseen by the Spartan architect of victory, Lysander. The first forty years of the fourth century were to be dominated by Sparta, Athens, and Thebes; the acute contemporary observer at the end of the Peloponnesian War would have had little difficulty in working out what the crucial issues were going to be: could Sparta maintain the dominance that victory had given her? Would Athens recover as a major power? Would Thebes transform herself from being a thorn in the side of Sparta and Athens to being a major independent power?

At the moment of victory the Spartans seem to have had no settled long-term policy. Some Spartans wanted to take over the Athenian empire and run it to Sparta's profit. Details are few and far between in our sources, but garrisons and garrison commanders (who were called 'harmosts') seem to have been quite widely installed, small groups of men willing to collaborate with the Spartans were entrusted with the government of cities which had formerly been democracies under the Athenian empire, and Sparta extracted large sums of money from her new allies. Other Spartans were worried by the implications of this policy: Spartiate numbers were not large (see further below, pp. 206–7), former helots could not always be trusted when away from Sparta, and unpopularity was not something to be readily courted. In 403 the ephors elected at Sparta seem to have all been advocates of a more conciliatory policy: they removed Spartan garrisons and puppet governments and when the king Pausanias was put on trial for effecting such a policy at Athens they voted solidly, and successfully, for his acquittal.

Those who were opposed to Sparta acquiring new commitments far from home did not necessarily believe in relaxing the grip on the old allies of the League. From 402 to 400 Sparta engaged in war with Elis, citing anti-Spartan manipulation of the Olympic games and her formation in 420 of an alliance with Mantinea, Argos, and Athens, and insisting that Elis should allow the other cities in the region to be autonomous. After invading and ravaging Elis Sparta got its way; Elis was left seriously weakened, although still in charge of the Olympic games. Other cities of the Peloponnese waited for their turn: the small city of Phlius in the north-east Peloponnese was pleasantly surprised, in the late 390s, when the Spartan garrison, which it had been forced to call in because of the danger from Corinth and her allies, did not take the pro-Spartan side in an internal conflict or interfere with her constitution (Xenophon, *Hellenica* 4. 4. 15).

The new century saw a new king in Sparta. The accession of Agesilaus to the throne of Agis profoundly affected the course of Greek history, in particular ensuring that relations with Persia were as dominant an element in the fourth century as they had been in the fifth. Agesilaus had ambitions of his own, but he was also influenced by Lysander, one of those who had worked hardest to secure that Agesilaus became king and the great advocate of garrisons and foreign commitments. In 402 Sparta had agreed to support Cyrus in his bid to usurp the Persian throne from his brother on the death of his father Darius, and Cyrus' death in the attempt had left Sparta compromised with the new Persian king, Artaxerxes. The Persian satrap, Tissaphernes, took this opportunity to open hostilities towards the Greek cities of Asia Minor, and Sparta responded to their appeal first by sending troops under, successively, Thibron and Dercyllidas. Then, in 396, following news of further hostile preparations by Persia, Sparta launched a major expedition led by Agesilaus himself.

Agesilaus' expedition gave the other Greeks what they took to be a clear answer to their last outstanding question. The harmosts, garrisons, puppet governments, and ways in which Thibron and Dercyllidas had abused their powers had shown what Spartan intentions were towards the newly liberated cities; the invasion of Elis had shown Sparta's attitude to her old allies; now Agesilaus' expedition to Asia Minor confirmed that Sparta did indeed have expansionist aims. When other cities were invited to contribute troops to the expedition, the Boeotians, Athenians, and Corinthians refused to do so, and when Agesilaus attempted to suggest that his expedition was like Agamemnon's to Troy by sacrificing at the Boeotian town of Aulis, the Boeotian commanders (Boeotarchs) had the sacrifice disrupted (Xenophon, *Hellenica* 3. 4. 1–4).

Mounting grievances, and the opportunity presented by the absence of the more aggressive of the Spartan kings, Agesilaus, with a sizeable army, transformed the mood of the cities. When in 397/6 the Athenian Council secretly dispatched a single trireme to offer support to Conon, the Athenian who was serving as admiral for the Persian fleet, there was an outcry as soon as the event became public, and the Athenian assembly, although in general hostile to the Spartans, was frightened into disowning the action *(Hellenica Oxyrhynchia* 6–7). In the summer of 395, by contrast, the Athenians voted overwhelmingly to join the Thebans in war against Sparta (Xenophon, *Hellenica* 3. 5. 16).

The domino effect of the Phocian invasion of Locris certainly depended on particular historical conditions. The nervousness that Athens displayed over sending help to Conon in 397/6 and her contrasting willingness to join Thebes in all-out war with Sparta in 395 are both products of a world in which Sparta is sufficiently frightening that no city will take an initiative, because of the consequences of isolation, but every city is on the watch for an opportunity to join others if only they will make the first move.

The Corinthian War failed to change those conditions. Sparta failed to co-ordinate a two-pronged attack on the Boeotians, and Lysander was killed in a Spartan defeat at Haliartus in Boeotia (King Pausanias was blamed for not arriving in time, tried and exiled). Despite the poor performance of their allies, the Spartans redressed this with a victory at Nemea in the north-east Peloponnese in late spring 394; later that year Agesilaus, recalled from Asia Minor where he had achieved nothing of moment, was narrowly victorious in a further battle at Coronea in Boeotia. But shortly before this Conon and the Persian satrap Pharnabazos had destroyed Spartan naval power in a battle off Cnidus. Continued warfare in the territory of Corinth led to a political crisis there, which ended with some pro-Spartan Corinthians being killed, others handing over the Corinthian port of Lechaeum to Sparta, and Corinth joining itself to Argos. Violent political conflict focusing on a foreign policy issue was common (above pp. 111–13), but the union of Corinth and Argos in 392 was unprecedented and indicates the unusually high stakes for which the anti-Spartan alliance saw itself as fighting. Peace negotiations in 392 came to nothing, and the theatres of war diversified. The Athenians resumed naval activity in the Aegean, and then in 389, fatally, allied themselves with Acoris who was leading a revolt of Egypt against the Persian King. The Spartan Antalcidas was able to use this action to persuade the Persian king Artaxerxes that the Athenians, not the Spartans, were the real threat to him, and in 386 a combination of the fear that Persia would once more intervene on the side of the Spartans, and a blockade of the Hellespont that was starving Athens, brought about a peace agreement.

A pattern repeated

In the long term the most important feature of the King's Peace, as it is called, of 386 was that it admitted Persian overlordship of all cities in Asia Minor and Cyprus; in the short term what had most effect was the stipulation of autonomy for all other cities. Agesilaus saw to it that, when the Greek cities got together to swear to the Peace, this autonomy clause was interpreted to mean breaking up not just the union of Corinth and Argos but also the Boeotian confederacy (Xenophon, *Hellenica* 5. 1. 32 ff.). At the end of this first round of conflict, Sparta had apparently succeeded in establishing at least a sort of dominance; Athens had managed a limited recovery—she was no longer restricted to a twelve-ship navy—but Thebes was weakened, unable any longer to determine the actions of the other cities of Boeotia. What happened to Thebes is indeed a clear sign that it was Spartan rather than Persian interests that determined the nature of the King's Peace. Only some Spartans, however, will have welcomed the position in which the Peace left Sparta. The opportunity, open in 404 and taken from 400 onwards, of pursuing an expansionist policy in Asia Minor was forgone; Spartan leadership in the Greek world was now to be limited to the mainland and Aegean islands.

Sparta lost little time in showing that, as in 404, she intended to exploit peace to advance her position. In 385 she complained that her ally Mantinea had helped Argos and not been prompt in supporting campaigns; she besieged the city, demolished its walls, and split it up into the four or five villages from which it had been formed (Xenophon, *Hellenica* 5. 2. 1 ff.). In the following year Sparta insisted that political exiles were restored to Phlius and when they complained that their property was not properly restored to them, Sparta besieged that city too and installed a new government. No other city intervened to resist Spartan action, but as they looked on, all must have recalled what Sparta had done to Elis less than 20 years previously.

If the terms of the peace ruled out opportunities for Spartan glory in Asia Minor, there were other areas of Greece which offered comparable opportunities. In 382 envoys came from Acanthus and Apollonia in the Chalcidice to complain of aggression from the city of Olynthus and to warn that the Olynthians were seeking to strengthen their position by alliance with Athens and Thebes. The Spartans consulted their allies, who agreed to assist the campaign against Olynthus on condition that they could substitute cash payments for men. While the full force was being mustered, Sparta sent ahead an advance force of 2,000 made up of freed helots, *perioikoi*, and light troops from Arcadia. Further troops were to follow, and eventually a force led by king Agesipolis, who was accompanied by 30 Spartiate advisers, 'just like Agesilaus going to Asia' (Xenophon, *Hellenica* 5. 3. 8).

As in the 390s, so again in the late 380s, our contemporary sources claim that the pattern of Spartan disciplining of Peloponnesian allies

and promotion of interests abroad was disrupted by the secret Theban initiatives. But, whereas in 395 it was the anti-Spartan leaders who
ensured the escalation of hostilities between Locris and Phocis, in 382
it was, according to Xenophon's account (*Hellenica* 5. 2. 25 ff.), the
pro-Spartan leader at Thebes who approached Phoebidas, the
Spartiate taking a second contingent of troops north for the war
with Olynthus, and persuaded him to take advantage of the
occurrence of the women's festival of the Thesmophoria, to occupy
the Theban acropolis, and secure firm control of Thebes for the pro-
Spartan faction. This grotesque breach of the King's Peace divided
Spartan opinion: Phoebidas was tried, but only fined; at Thebes the
pro-Athenian leader, Ismenias, was tried and condemned to death;
the Spartan garrison remained at Thebes. Elsewhere there was no
division of opinion: Spartan action was seen as an impious outrage
inviting (and in due course receiving) divine vengeance.

General warfare did not immediately follow the Spartan seizure of
the Theban acropolis, but diplomatic initiatives increased in intensity.
Already in the middle 380s Athens had begun to accumulate friends
and allies, offering honours to Hebryzelmis of Thrace in 386/5, tax
concessions to her friends exiled from Thasos, Byzantium, and
Mantinea, and securing alliance with Chios (Harding 29, 31). By the
end of the 380s, to judge from a pamphlet (the *Panegyricus*) written
by the Athenian political commentator Isocrates, those who dreamed
of renewing the Athenian fifth-century empire thought that they
could see a route to its restoration in the unpopularity of Sparta and
the resentment at the way that the King's Peace had conceded control
of the Greek cities of Asia Minor to Persia. Three years later a new
Athenian empire was in existence, and the Greek world was entering
upon another decade of desultory warfare.

In 379, from an Athenian base and with some support from Athens,
the Theban exiles launched an attack on their home city and ousted
the Spartan garrison. Sparta invaded Boeotia and left a garrison at
Thespiae. Open war seemed imminent. Not certain that she was
ready for war, Athens condemned the generals who had helped expel
the Spartan garrison from Thebes, and stepped up her diplomatic
activity, forming alliances with Byzantium and preparing the ground
for a much more extensive network of allies. Sparta responded by
sending envoys to Athens, but while they were there, another
Spartiate, Sphodrias the garrison commander at Thespiae, decided—

perhaps because the Thebans bribed him (Xenophon, *Hellenica* 5. 4. 20)—to march on the Piraeus. He never got there, but his action (for which he was tried, but acquitted (see above, p. 67), stimulated the Athenians to seek alliance with Thebes and to launch a new confederacy 'in order that the Spartans may allow the Greeks to be free' (Harding 35. 9). The Athenians promised that there would be no garrisons, no Athenian magistrates, no tribute, and no taking over of allied land: the old empire without the old abuses.

The history of the 370s is a history of both Athens and Thebes vigorously extending their power, and of Sparta posturing ineffectually in response. Aegean cities, many of which can have had no fear of Sparta but which may have had worries about Persia, joined the new Athenian confederacy in large numbers: the names of more than fifty cities were recorded on the confederacy's charter in the first three or four years. Spartan attempts to resist by force Athens' recruitment of further allies in the Ionian sea in the middle of the decade met with no lasting success, although the Athenians found the financial burden of increased naval activity hard to bear, despite having reorganized their taxation system at home. In Boeotia cities were one by one coerced by Thebes into a new confederacy—or completely destroyed if, like Plataea, they resisted. Sparta kept a permanent garrison in Boeotia, and both Spartan kings led invasions into Boeotia during the decade; they achieved little except ensuring that Theban policy remained single-minded and Theban troops remained well trained: in 375 the Theban general Pelopidas inflicted a clear defeat on troops from the Spartan garrison at Orchomenus.

The King's Peace had been renewed in 375, without serving as any brake on Theban aggression, and in 371, as Thebes began to turn her attentions north to Phocis, a further congress was held in Sparta. Agreement to renew the Peace was reached, but at the last minute Thebes refused to sign unless she could sign for the whole of Boeotia, comparing the way in which Sparta signed for Lakonia, which as well as Sparta contained other cities inhabited by *perioikoi*. Unable to tolerate the Theban claim, Agesilaus excluded them from the peace and diverted the army that was aiding Phocis to attack Thebes. After initially avoiding conflict with the main Theban army, the Spartan king Cleombrotus gave battle at Leuctra in south-west Boeotia, and suffered a major defeat; novel tactics by the Theban general Epaminondas, who massed his troops at one wing, left 1,000 of the army of

Sparta and her allies dead, including 400 of the 700 Spartiates present.

The decades of uncertainty

Of all battles in Greek history perhaps only the battles of Marathon and Plataea in the Persian war (above, pp. 172–3, 174) proved comparable turning-points. Three factors made this battle crucial: it emasculated Sparta, it opened up a policy division at Thebes, and it showed up the unreality of Persian intervention.

Leuctra was not the first defeat that the Spartans had suffered in the fourth century. They had repeatedly proved unable to command the sea—from the battle at Cnidus in 394 to the attempts to expel the Athenian commanders Timotheus and Iphicrates from the Ionian sea in the 370s—and even on land they had suffered a shaming defeat at Lechaeum in 390 and a further defeat by Pelopidas in 375. But Leuctra was the first defeat in a full-scale set-piece battle against heavily armed troops, and, in contrast with the earlier defeats, this time there were massive casualties, and Spartiate casualties at that. The belief in Spartan infantry power had been weakened by episodes such as Cleombrotus' failure in 376 even to try to force his way into Boeotia because of the Theban and Athenian troops holding the passes through Mount Cithaeron (Xenophon, *Hellenica* 5. 4. 59); after Leuctra that belief could no longer be sustained at all.

Casualties in hoplite battles rarely had demographic significance (see above, p. 81). This case was different. Because much of Laconia and Messenia was exploited by helots or *Perioikoi* (above, p. 131), the proportion of the total adult male population of the area ruled by Sparta who were full Spartan citizens was tiny. Figures given by Herodotus for 479 suggest that there may have been seven times as many helots as Spartiates at that time. To make matters worse, the numbers of Spartiates had been in decline since the Persian Wars. Sparta had been reduced almost to panic by the capture of 120 Spartiates at Pylos in 424 (above, p. 191), and it seems that by the 390s Sparta could field only 60 per cent of the numbers put in the field in 479. In the early fourth century the decline seems to have become very much more severe, so that by the time of Leuctra only just over

1,000 Spartiates were regularly available to fight. To lose 400 from such a total was devastating.

Why were Spartiate numbers declining? Sparta had suffered a very severe earthquake in the 460s in which there may have been extensive loss of life, but the immediate effect on Spartan army size seems to have been small, and even if women and children had proved particularly vulnerable, numbers should have stabilized by more than two generations later. Aristotle, writing in the second half of the fourth century, remarks on the high proportion of property at Sparta which was in the hands of women; the right of Spartan women to inherit land, a right denied to Athenian women, may have led to the rich marrying only among themselves and to a concentration of wealth in so few hands that the numbers wealthy enough to support the expenses required of a full Spartan citizen dropped markedly. Literary sources indicate the existence in fourth-century Sparta of a group known as 'Inferiors' *(hypomeiones)*, and impoverished freeborn Spartiates may have been so categorized. At the time of the accession of Agesilaus, a plot was discovered to induce all non-Spartiates (helots, *perioikoi*, the various groups of helots freed to fight alongside Spartiates and under Spartiate commanders, the 'Inferiors') to combine against the Spartiates; it was suppressed, but on this occasion, unlike the occasion in the 420s when 2,000 helots simply 'disappeared', news of the conspiracy could not be suppressed.

Heavy defeat both revealed and exacerbated the problem of Spartiate numbers. Many of Sparta's old allies saw that Sparta was no longer in a position to coerce them; those who had maintained their political positions because they could claim to be friends of Sparta lost their power, and political strife, even political revolution, broke out in many places. The Spartans attempted a military response, and marched against the leading revolutionary state, Mantinea. The Athenians, who had already made an unsuccessful move to reassert the King's Peace with themselves as arbiters, refused to help Mantinea, but the Thebans, when they were invited, saw their opportunity decisively to alter the traditional balance of power, and planned to invade the Peloponnese. Agesilaus withdrew from the territory of Mantinea, but the Thebans led an invasion first of Laconia and then of Messenia, which they liberated from Spartan control, thereby depriving Sparta of a very large productive area and giving her a resolutely hostile neighbour. When the Thebans followed this with encouraging the formation of a new city, Megalopolis—'the Great City'—uniting the numerous small communities in western Arcadia, the geography of power in the Peloponnese had been permanently changed.

The destruction of Spartan power might not have made so much difference to the Greek world had Thebes simply stepped into Sparta's role, but she did not. In part this was a matter of geography: Thebes was not well placed to exercise strong overlordship of the old Spartan allies in the Peloponnese. Boeotia was agriculturally rich but had neither Athens' silver nor Sparta's helots; the heavy infantry who had won Leuctra were Boeotian farmers and that sharply limited their military deployment. There was also a question of politics. Although the dual kingship at Sparta had generally led to alternative policies being on offer, and sometimes to bitter political disputes ending in the exile of a king, the situation at Thebes was yet more unstable, for the annual office of Boeotarch gave no firm base from which to create a long-term strategy. As the architects of an unprecedented Theban predominance, Epaminondas and Pelopidas did enjoy a special status, but even they were taken to court by their opponents, and Thebes got the reputation for long and stormy meetings of its assembly.

If the King's Peace had operated according to the letter, the events after Leuctra would have led to swift Persian intervention in Greece. Instead it revealed the Persian guarantee behind the Peace to be quite empty. Persia had been interested in peace in 386 because she saw it as a route to secure for herself the cities of Asia Minor. Subsequent events had not threatened her position there, and her main subsequent interest in renewals of the King's Peace (e.g. in 375 and 371) was in freeing Greek mercenaries to fight in her own wars (Diodorus 15. 38. 1): Persia spent the whole of 377–373 preparing for war with Egypt. From the end of the 370s Persia also faced a series of satrap revolts; these revolts particularly involved the western provinces of the empire, and rebel satraps made various overtures to Greek cities. The Athenians toyed with assisting the rebels, took advantage of the anti-Persian momentum to expel a Persian garrison from Samos and install a settlement of her own citizens there, and even made an alliance with Strato, king of Sidon in Phoenicia (Harding 40). But when officially approached by the satraps in the late 360s, the Greeks declined to be involved on the rebel side (Harding 57), and the

Athenians were sufficiently nervous to act very smartly when Persia complained in 379 and again in the 350s about assistance to rebels from the generals Chabrias and Chares. Short of such active Greek hostility there was little chance that Persia would interfere against, or for, any mainland power, but this did not prevent Persia remaining on the mainland political agenda, waiting for some power to be once more in a position to exploit on-going Greek hostility to the only foreign power worth opposing.

With Sparta crushed, Thebes unable to assume her mantle, and Persia safely out of the picture, the battle of Leuctra took the lid off Greek inter-city politics. The tensions which in the 390s caused the latest exchange in the long-running conflict between Phocis and Locris to plunge the whole of Greece into war were eased, and the consequences of any internal revolution or act of hostility to a neighbour ceased to be clear. After the battle at Leuctra southern Greece entered a decade of turmoil, as individuals and cities jockeyed for local and regional advantage. The history of some individual cities during this period reveals very clearly the intensity of political life in the city-state.

Sicyon had been an ally of Sparta since the sixth century, and Sparta had intervened directly in her affairs towards the end of the fifth century to ensure an even more securely pro-Spartan oligarchy. Now that Spartan backing was no longer a guarantee of political ascendancy, one Euphron, who had previously exploited Spartan favour, persuaded the Argives and Arcadians to help him install democracy. Euphron then had himself elected as one of five generals and his son made commander of the mercenary troops, and established himself in a position which his enemies regarded as essentially that of dictator (Xenophon, *Hellenica* 7. 1. 44–6). The former oligarchs proceeded to call in the Arcadians against Euphron, causing Euphron to lay claim to his Spartan ties once more and hand over the harbour to the Spartans. The Spartans were unable to retain a grip on the harbour, but the absence of Euphron did not prevent continued disputes between oligarchs and democrats, and Euphron, who had succeeded in raising Athenian mercenaries, took advantage of this to install himself in power in the city as democratic champion once more. All this time there had been a Theban garrison on the acropolis at Sicyon, and, in an attempt to secure its support too, Euphron went to Thebes, only to be murdered there by one of his opponents whom he had once exiled. The Thebans tried and acquitted the murderer, but Euphron was given a public burial in Sicyon and honoured as founder of the city (Xenophon, *Hellenica* 7. 3).

Even before the Theban invasion of the Peloponnese and the liberation of Messenia, Tegea, the Arcadian city nearest to Sparta, over which Sparta had long kept a close eye, began fighting over a new political agenda: should there be an Arcadian league, or federation, or not? When the Tegean council of magistrates initially favoured the status quo, the advocates of federation looked to armed insurrection, reckoning to have popular support and to be able to recruit military help from neighbouring Mantinea (itself in the process of reuniting). Some of those who favoured the status quo were captured and condemned to death, 800 others fled to Sparta (Xenophon, *Hellenica* 6. 5. 2–11). Three years later Tegea was one of the communities providing founders for Megalopolis.

The strengthening of Arcadia as a result of the formation of the Arcadian League led to further tensions. The Arcadians were now in a position to pursue old claims to Triphylia, the region of southern Elis that had been 'liberated' from Elean control by the Spartans in 400. By the middle of the 360s Elis and Arcadia were at war; the Eleans called in Spartan help(!) and Elean democrats joined the Arcadian cause. In the course of a campaign in which the Arcadians were consistently the more successful, the sanctuary at Olympia fell into Arcadian hands. Olympia was a major resource, and some Arcadians were in favour of exploiting its treasures to reinforce their power and to support the costs of the Arcadian League's standing army. The League's officers favoured such use of the treasures, but a movement initiated by Mantinea led to the Federal Assembly voting against it. To protect themselves, the League Officers summoned the Thebans, claiming that only a Theban invasion would prevent the Arcadians from aligning themselves with Sparta; the Federal Assembly countermanded this invitation, and instead sought peace with Elis. Peace was sworn, but the Theban garrison commander at Tegea was persuaded to take advantage of the celebrations to arrest those who had most opposed the League officers. When Mantinea threatened military action in reaction to the arrests, the Theban commander released the prisoners. The Arcadians sent the Theban commander home, calling for his execution, but the Thebans in return accused the Arcadians of treason in making peace with Elis without consultation,

and invaded. In the succeeding battle at Mantinea in 362 the Arcadians were split between the two opposing sides: Tegea and Megalopolis
fought with the Thebans, Mantinea fought with Sparta and Athens
against the Thebans (Xenophon, *Hellenica* 7. 4–5).

The history of Sicyon and the history of the Arcadian cities in the
360s show how enormously the world of the Greek city had changed.
Oligarchy had once meant favouring Sparta and democracy favouring Athens (and vice versa); now there were multiple possible sources
of outside help available (Sparta, Arcadia, Thebes, Athens), none of
which, given the chance to gain friends and influence, asked too many
questions about constitutional arrangements. Foreign policy no longer
mapped straightforwardly onto domestic policy. Opportunism governed the actions of both individuals and cities, and since no one
could expect the situation to stay the same for any length of time, it
was the ability to project a plausible case at a given moment that
came to count for everything—as both Euphron and his assassin
found. Xenophon ended his account of fifty years of Greek history
with the battle of Mantinea, remarking that 'with regard to accession
of new territory, or cities, or power, it cannot be said that either side
was any better off after the battle than before it. In fact there was
even more uncertainty and confusion in Greece after the battle than
there had been previously. Let this, then, be the end of my narrative.
Someone else, perhaps, will deal with what happened later' (*Hellenica*
7. 5. 27).

If anyone rose to Xenophon's challenge their work has not survived, and we are particularly badly informed about events in the
Peloponnese in the fifties. This is not entirely mischance, for if in the
sixties the focus remained in the south, determined by the shadow of
the past, in the fifties it moved decisively north.

The rise of Macedon

Southern Greek cities had a close interest in northern Greece ever
since the Euboean foundation of settlements in the Chalcidice in the
early Dark Age. Athens had taken great pains to establish a base there
in the fifth century, and Brasidas' successful capture of that base,
Amphipolis, in the Archidamian war had caused enormous anxiety

(above, p. 191). Although no decisive action can be attributed to either Macedonians or Thessalians in the fifth century, the potential importance of these areas was recognized in the eagerness of Athens to enlist them as allies.

Neither Macedon nor Thessaly was quite like the city-states of southern Greece. Both controlled large areas of excellent agricultural land. Although long-established towns were at the core of settlement in both regions, in neither place were independent civic institutions highly developed: Thucydides is notably reluctant to call the towns of Macedon 'poleis', and the earliest civic decrees date only from the end of the fourth century. Although the Thessalians elected a single overlord, political power effectively rested with certain families who sought to sustain themselves by forming links outside Thessaly. Family rivalries in Thessaly, and regional rivalries in Macedonia, prevented either region exercising significant or sustained influence beyond its boundaries. In both places there was a tension between an old vague sense of 'national' unity, which could not be mobilized, and a move to imitate the cities of southern Greece, which made effective organisation possible at the expense of destroying unity.

The potential power of these two large regions, and the difficulty of mobilizing it, is well illustrated by the events of the early fourth century in Thessaly. Jason began as the joint ruler of a single city, Pherae, looking to sustain himself with links abroad—in this case with Thebes. Partly through military reform (including land allotments for soldiers), and partly by dint of good luck in finding an outstanding mercenary general to assist him, he managed to extend his control first to the city of Pharsalus and then, in just the years when Thebes was reunifying Boeotia, to other parts of Thessaly, including Perrhaebia on the Macedonian border. Jason's opponents in Thessaly expected the powerful cities of southern Greece to be concerned about his increasing power, and one of them went to Sparta in 375 to ask, unsuccessfully, for intervention. In fact Jason's unification of Thessaly was short-lived; he was assassinated in 370 when making preparations to raise his profile further by taking over the Pythian games at Delphi. Thessaly in the 360s was marked by internal wrangling and outside intervention by the Thebans. Thessalian constitutional structures were sufficient neither to prevent a single individual getting into a position to run the whole of

Thessaly nor to ensure that unity could be maintained other than through the charm and efficiency of such an individual.

The resources of Macedonia ensured that it was never out of the minds of the cities of southern Greece. The mines of the Pangaeum mountain range were extremely productive of silver and gold, and Macedonia was the richest source of the timber that any city aspiring to control of the sea required. Macedonian manpower, too, was such that alliance was preferable to hostility. But the Macedonian record of utilizing its own resources was unimpressive—even after the 'modernizing' policies of Archelaus in the late fifth century, who did more, Thucydides claims (2. 100. 2), to strengthen communications and offensive and defensive provisions than the eight previous kings together. Archelaus' death in 399 was followed by a period of extreme instability. Amyntas III retained power for a long period, but his grip on Macedon was weak, and his death in 369 was followed by further trouble, with a regent, Ptolemy, remaining in power for as long as three years (368–5) only because he was a puppet of Thebes.

The transformation of Macedon in the decade after the death of Perdiccas III in battle against the Illyrians in 360 was not, and could not have been, foreseen at the time, and it, more perhaps than his military successes, is evidence of the extraordinary abilities of Philip II. It is not simply that Philip came to the throne at a moment when Macedon was under severe military pressure, though the threats from Illyria and Paeonia were severe, and in reaction to Perdiccas' support for the independence of Amphipolls the Athenians were offering material backing (3,000 troops) to a rival for the throne named Argaeus. Philip also had to face the long-standing tensions between upper and lower Macedonia, with their contrasting patterns of agriculture and settlement, and between the royal house and would-be independent cities within lower Macedonia, along with the problem of the Greek cities in the part of Macedonia east of the river Axios and their ambitions. Within five years of his accession, Philip had not only beaten back the external threats, he had turned the previously highly regionalized Macedonia into a single political unit whose resources were at the disposal of a single ruler, himself. With a little rhetorical embellishment, Philip's son, Alexander, could be made to describe this double achievement like this:

Philip took you over when you were poor and wandering, many of you clothed in skins, pasturing sheep in the mountains, and fighting badly to protect these from the Illyrians, Triballians, and neighbouring Thracians. He gave you cloaks instead of animal skins and led you down from the mountains to the plains; he made you fit to stand in battle against your barbarian neighbours, no longer trusting in the defences afforded by geography but in your own bravery. He made you dwellers in cities and adorned you with fine laws and customs. (Arrian, *Anabasis* 7. 9. 2)

How did Philip achieve the transformation? He needed to get himself accepted both by the old nobility of upper Macedonia and by the cities of lower Macedonia. His very military success against Paeonia and Illyria created a basis for support, his marriages to Phila and Olympias, princesses from Elimea and Molossia on the borders of Macedon, created strong personal allegiances; the cities of lower Macedonia were allowed a show of civic pride—they could mint their own coins—but lines of power were more formally laid down. Above all, Philip recognized the ambitions of all by expanding the body of Companions, advisers who fought beside the king as cavalry, and created a common purpose for young men of distinguished ancestry from all over Macedonia by creating a new body of Royal Pages. In so doing Philip was building on past practices rather than replacing them; young Macedonians had long proved their worth by displaying their mettle in the hunt, and had been expected to rise through a series of broadly age-related grades until recognized as equals of the best. Philip now ensured that ambition was focused on joining his circle, offering his Companions the sort of equality which displayed itself in a combination of reciprocal services and obedience to the king. To become a Companion of the King was to acquire a standing that depended on personal merit and to enter a position from which influence could be exercised; but the Companions did not comprise a formal council—there was no such thing—and the number of Companions ensured that the relationship between the informal advice Philip was given and the actions he resolved upon need never become clear.

And then there was the army. This rightly comes last, not first, because without secure political control a powerful army would have been as much a threat as an asset. But Philip's army was a tool of unification within Macedonia, as well as the means by which the rest of the world could be threatened. Philip built up the army numbers: in the course of his reign the number of infantry available to him was increased threefold from 10,000 to 30,000, the number of cavalry more than sixfold, from 600 to 4,000. Differential pay rates and the prospect of becoming a professional salaried officer encouraged ambition; estates in newly conquered territories were a final reward. Whether or not these newly numerous troops were newly armed with the 5.5 m. long sarissa or pike, it was certainly under Philip that, used by troops drawn up very deep, this became for the first time an effective weapon (above, p. 110). Similarly it was Philip who made cavalry, who were only important at the margins of classical hoplite battles, a battle-winning force, driving in wedge formation into any breech in the opposing infantry line. These material and tactical innovations were possible only because Philip created an essentially professional, rigorously trained army.

Given the extent of Philip's transformation of Macedon, it is perhaps not surprising that the cities of southern Greece took a long time to realize that he posed a threat to them quite unlike the threat that they had posed to each other. After initial campaigns to deal with the external threats that he faced from all directions on his accession, campaigns which involved some rather tricky diplomacy as well as military action, Philip turned his main attentions to the Greek cities of the Chalcidice and to Thessaly. Invited by the ruling family from Larissa to assist them against the ambitions of their Thessalian neighbour Pherae, Philip contracted yet another marriage; from this base he was able to take advantage of the conflict in central Greece stirred up by Theban aggression and known as the Third Sacred War. Philip scored a massive victory in the battle of the Crocus Field in southern Thessaly in 352; from that point onwards he was master, if not entirely undisputed master, of Thessaly and in a position to put direct pressure on southern Greece. But even after this, when Philip further extended his pressure on the Chalcidice, the Athenian politician Demosthenes (Fig. 10), in urging the Athenians to fight against him, compared him to past dangers faced from other Greek cities.

The conflict between Philip and southern Greece has come to be seen largely through the eyes of Demosthenes. None of the ancient historical works devoted especially to Philip have survived, and the account in Diodorus of the years from the mid-50s to the end of the 40s, although largely culled from fourth-century accounts, does not focus primarily on Philip. Demosthenes' view of Philip survives in the series of speeches given in the Athenian Assembly and lawcourts.

Figure 10 A pensive Demosthenes, whose representation owes much to the iconographic scheme developed to portray philosophers. Contrast Aeschines (Fig. 6).

In the former he tried to persuade the Athenians to take action, first to fight for Amphipolis, then to defend Olynthus, and then, from the end of the 340s, to seek alliances to defend not just Athens but Greece as a whole. In the latter he defended his political record against threats of prosecution. Demosthenes dwells on Athenian failure to devote adequate resources to warfare and to fight for themselves; he stresses Philip's propensity to fight by unfair means, in particular by trickery and bribery, and sets himself up as the champion of Greek freedom against a 'barbarian'. From all this emerges a picture of Demosthenes himself as the champion of the values of the classical city-state and of Greek freedom. The speeches of Demosthenes' opponents, in particular of Aeschines who unsuccessfully prosecuted him, give a rather different picture, suggesting that Demosthenes was far from consistent in his policies, and driven far more by domestic political ambitions, and determination to oppose the policies of others, than by idealism—let alone by good military sense.

Should we regard Athens and the other cities of southern Greece as victims of their own excessive love of liberty, who failed to see soon enough that only together could they stand? Many Greeks did not regard Philip as a threat at all. Some took a pro-Philip line because they expected their own political position to be improved by so doing: Philip was the new Sparta, able to help his friends not just with military power but with money too. Others were happy to see Philip as a Greek, and as a man who could restore Greece to a position in which it could face the real barbarians, and in particular the Persians. The most eloquent expression of this view that has survived comes from Isocrates (above, p. 204). In 346, the year in which the Athenians reached a temporary peace with Philip, he published a pamphlet, the *Philippus*, in which he called on Philip to be the champion of Greek concord and leader of an expedition against the Persians.

The varied reactions to Philip, and to the emergence of Macedon as a political force, bring out well tensions that run through the whole of archaic and classical Greek history. As the first chapter stresses, the politically diverse cities of classical Greece were in important ways the product of a common inheritance. It was, in particular, to the same foundational texts that all Greek cities looked, and upon the same body of myth that they drew. Athenian tragedy does not concentrate on myths local to Athens, and in only a minority of extant Athenian tragedies are actions at or involving Athens at all crucial; not surprisingly the plays were enormously popular outside Athens as well as at Athens itself. The cultural competition visible in the material record of the eighth and seventh centuries is much less visible in the fifth and fourth centuries, when Aristotle, from Stagira in the Chalcidice, could both spend time in Macedonia as tutor to Philip's son Alexander and set up his philosophical 'school', the Lyceum, at Athens. The conflicts between cities that so dominate classical political history have to be seen against this background. Ambitious politicians in Greek cities, who so often chose to call in military intervention, or to use the threat of military intervention, from other cities, show not so much the readiness of Greeks to act treacherously as the way in which the independence and liberty of the individual city could be subordinated to other social, political, or constitutional ideals. Preservation of those qualities which were considered to constitute Greekness—descent, religion, language, and customs—did not depend upon absolute autonomy. Liberty was an important slogan repeatedly used, but its usefulness depended on its always being a call to freedom from a particular oppressor and upon the state of being free never being defined. Discussions of liberty in Aristotle's *Politics* are about the liberty of the individual, not the liberty of the city.

The events of the 340s show Greek cities treating Philip as they had previously treated Athens or Sparta. His actions in southern Greece were almost all in response to local initiatives, whether it was agreeing to lead an Amphictyonic campaign against Phocis in 346, accepting alliance with Argos, Messene, and probably Megalopolis, all afraid of Sparta, in 344, supporting a coup at Elis in 343, or sending increasing assistance to those Euboean cities which were trying to free themselves from Athenian domination. Like Athens and Sparta, Philip was not indiscriminate in offering assistance—he turned down the earliest appeals from Chalcis; when he agreed to help it was because he saw that the advantages of doing so outweighed the disadvantages.

Southern Greece was no more the centre of Philip's concerns in the 340s than it had been in the 350s. He was busy intervening in Illyria and Epirus, where he put Alexander, the brother of his wife Olympias, on the throne. From 342 his military attention was focused eastward, as he finally defeated the Thracian rulers Teres and Cersobleptes and laid siege to Perinthus and Byzantium. All the indications are that by the latter part of the decade, at least, Philip was seeking ways of ensuring that neither his old northern neighbours nor the cities of southern Greece were in a position to demand his military intervention. But the Athenians managed to spread their fear of Philip so far that other cities in southern Greece became prepared to contemplate an alliance against him, and his attack on Byzantium (accompanied by the capture of a fleet of ships carrying grain) was a direct threat to Athens, which had regular need for cereals from the Black Sea.

Although two more years of threats and negotiations followed, war had become inevitable. When it came, the immediate occasion was once more arguments in the Delphic Amphictyony and a call to Philip to lead an attack on Amphissa. Philip's attempt to repeat tactics that had been successful earlier, and to use the presence of his army to concentrate Theban minds on peace, was unsuccessful. Skilful generalship overcame the initial strategic advantages of the opposition, and battle was joined at Philip's choosing at Chaeronea in northern Boeotia in September 338. Philip's cavalry, under the command of his son Alexander, delivered a decisive victory in which enemy casualties were enormous. Philip marched on to the Peloponnese, and in the spring of the following year the League of Corinth was formed. All the signatories were required to enforce, on the basis of decisions made by them all in synod, a new Common Peace. And the first decision Philip had the synod take was to undertake a war to punish Persia for her invasion a century and a half before. The eastern power that had stood in the background of Greek politics through the classical period was now to be tackled head on.

Greece into Asia

The first Macedonian troops crossed into Asia in the spring of 336 under the command of Philip's experienced general, Parmenio. But the campaign against Persia was not to be the crowning of Philip's extraordinary career, it was to be the whole career of his son Alexander, now aged twenty. For in the autumn of that year, at the Macedonian festival of the Olympia, which was being celebrated with particular pomp, Philip was assassinated. His assassin, a young man from the royal bodyguard, was himself killed, and his motivation (personal or political?) must remain unknown. Alexander was promptly presented to, and recognized by, the army as king, all potential rivals were done away with, and the revolts that broke out in Thrace, Illyria, Thessaly, Thebes, and Ambracia were quickly and ruthlessly crushed. In 334 Alexander crossed the Hellespont, never to return to Europe.

Only a map can reveal the staggering scale of Alexander's conquests in the next decade as, defeating Darius III, who had seized the throne only in 336, in three major victories at the river Granicus in 334, at Issus in 333, and at Gaugamela in 331, Alexander took over the Persian empire; he went on outside Persian realms as far as the Punjab before his troops declined to advance further into the unknown. At his death in 323 he was certainly planning action in Arabia, and talk after his death of plans to move west along the north coast of Africa may not be entirely fantastic. This was revenge on the largest scale for the Persian conquest: the Persians had failed to incorporate Greece and Macedonia in the Asian sphere; Alexander made Asia part of the Greco-Macedonian world.

Alexander took over the loose Persian structures and used them to run his new empire. Initially, Persian satraps were replaced by Macedonians and Greeks; after Darius' final defeat he generally used natives as satraps, often confirming in power those who had previously served Darius. Alexander also took over some of the trappings of the Persian monarch, sacrificing to native gods, dressing in Persian clothes, and expecting to be shown the obeisance for which Greeks had long ridiculed the subjects of the Persian king, calling them all 'slaves'. At the same time, however, Alexander planted new Greek cities across his empire. Though the total number founded by Alexander himself has often been wildly exaggerated—as few as half a dozen are securely known to fall into that category—these cities were vitally important. They were important both in themselves—they include Alexandria in Egypt which became a city second in size in the ancient world only to Rome—and because they offered a model followed by Alexander's successors. These Greek foundations showed little sign of 'going native' and clung to their Greek links and Greek culture. They ensured the massive spread of the Greek language, which now for the first time developed a common dialect, and of Greek cultural values. Identity throughout the Near East came to be negotiated with reference to being Greek, and 'Greek' lost the last vestiges of any narrow geographical connotation.

In the history of classical Greece it is more what the Greeks believed about Persia than what Persia did that is important; from Alexander onwards Greek history cannot be told without telling the history of the whole eastern Mediterranean, and beyond. But there was still a history of the small and mountainous peninsula that is Greece today, and arguably the effect of Alexander's activities on that history were minimal. It is true that having a centre of power that was far away and could only act remotely took some getting used to, but the letters exchanged between Greek cities, particularly those in Asia Minor, and Alexander that were published on stone show that Greeks rapidly adapted to the new situation: Alexander's word was no less powerful for all that he could act only through messengers and agents. And cities learned, too, that the man whom Alexander left in charge in Macedon was quite as useful a source of support, and quite as dangerous an opponent, as the absent king.

Events in Greece during Alexander's Asian expedition show how closely the history of the Greek city-state under Macedonian over-lordship related to the history of the classical city-state. Sparta had refused to be party to the League of Corinth, and had not been drawn into the uprisings that followed the death of Philip. But when Persian naval successes in the Aegean in 334/3 suggested that Alexander might yet be defeated, the Spartans made overtures to them. Revolt in Thrace in 331 distracted Antipater, who had been left in charge in Macedon (with an army ever more depleted by Alexander's demands for additional troops), and Sparta chose this moment to launch a wholesale attack. Most of the cities of the Peloponnese were per-suaded to join in, and the Spartans scored some initial successes; but Athens failed to give support, and Antipater crushed the revolt in a battle at Megalopolis in 330 which left 5,000 dead.

Sparta's revolt shows clearly the familiar pattern, in which yester-day's enemy becomes today's friend as the liberator turns into the new oppressor; the epigraphic record from the city of Eresus on the island of Lesbos shows how the negotiation of domestic politics with reference to whatever power might currently be strongest also con-tinued. Eresus seems to have been under the control of a small group of men at the time of Alexander's invasion of Asia Minor. The people of Eresus seem to have taken advantage of Alexander's claims to be liberating the Greek cities in order to depose these rulers. The deposed rulers themselves then went to Alexander and claimed that they had been misrepresented, and Alexander ordered that they be properly tried and that the voting should be by secret ballot. The former rulers were condemned, but the story does not stop there; eight years later their descendants went to Alexander again, and got him to intervene to see that they too were tried, with a view to the restoration of their civic rights. That intervention still did not settle things, and in the last decade of the fourth century the descendants made another attempt to secure their position; but again the people of Eresus were unmoved.

The story from Eresus is comprehensible on its own, but it actually forms part of a larger story. For almost certainly the appeal from the sons of the condemned rulers of Eresus to Alexander was occasioned by his one decision that directly impinged on all Greek cities, his order that cities take back all exiles other than those exiled for sacrilege. Proclaimed at Olympia in 324, this measure was a bombshell, for it covered not simply individual political figures forced out by their enemies, but whole populations that had been displaced, and in particular the Samians who had been removed from the island when the Athenians established a settlement of their own there (above, p. 208). No city was unaffected, for it was not a matter simply of taking back individuals, but of restoring to them property that had been publicly sold. This was the only demand made by Alexander that was universal, applying to all Greek cities. As a demonstration of power it was a masterstroke: no other move could have had the appearance of generosity and the effect of throwing existing regimes into turmoil. What the motivation was is unclear—was Alexander, who himself may have heard more from exiles than from the cities themselves, now so ill-attuned to Greek affairs that he did not see that this way of reducing the number of tedious visitors with sob-stories that he had to listen to would have such far-reaching effects? or was he all too aware of the trouble this measure would cause, and deliberately choosing to keep Antipater busy? If the latter was the motivation, the plan succeeded: the Exiles' Decree ensured that on Alexander's own death ten months later the Greek city-states, led this time by Athens, would make another unsuccessful attempt to revolt. But just as Athens had not joined Sparta in revolt in 331, so now Sparta, Arcadia, and the Boeotians offered no support to Athens. It was, and would continue to be, business as usual among the Greek city-states. What had changed was that the history of the Greek city-states was now only a small part of Greek history.

Epilogue

Robin Osborne

I saw the beautiful Epicaste, Oedipus' mother,
who in the ignorance of her mind had done a monstrous
thing when she married her own son. He killed his father
and married her, but the gods soon made it all known to mortals,
But he, for all his sorrows, in beloved Thebes continued
to be lord over the descendants of Cadmus, all through the bitter designing
of the gods; while she went down to Hades of the gates, the strong one,
knotting a noose and hanging sheer from the high ceiling,
in the constraint of her sorrow, but left to him who survived her
all the sorrows that are brought to pass by a mother's furies.

(*Odyssey* 11. 271–80, trans. Lattimore [adapted])

So Odysseus relates seeing one of its most famous inhabitants during his visit to the underworld. The author of the *Odyssey* expected the story of Oedipus to be well known to those who listened to his work in the seventh century, and he used this short summary to direct that listener's attention to yet another famous wife to compare and contrast with the faithful Penelope patiently waiting for Odysseus' return to Ithaca. In the telling of the story of Oedipus he brings out the features that allow comparison with the *Odyssey*'s own plot—the role of the gods' 'bitter designing', the way that mortals act in ignorance, the living out of the consequences of past actions.

In fifth-century Athens Sophocles took up the Oedipus story again. In *Oedipus the King* he turned the uncovering of mortal ignorance into a gripping detective story: Oedipus is made to discover the truth about himself as he searches for the murderer of the last king, Laius, in order to end the plague that has gripped the city. He discovers not only that Laius, whose widow he has married, was the stranger he himself killed in an argument at a road junction, but also that Laius was his father. His mother, and wife, named Jocasta by Sophocles, hangs herself at this news; Oedipus blinds himself.

The workings of the gods are still important in this play—'O Zeus, what have you designed to do with me?' is Oedipus' cry as he begins to realize that he may have been the killer of Laius. But the cumulative effect of unwitting human actions is made more central than in the Homeric telling: Sophocles puts not just Oedipus and Jocasta under the spotlight but also the slaves, who had been told to expose the baby Oedipus, but did not do so, and who saw to his adoption by the royal family at Corinth. And on top of this is a political dimension: Sophocles draws attention not just to the fact that Oedipus is king, but to the very manner of his rule. In the *Odyssey* Oedipus' story is a distant example of how some mortals are unfortunate victims of the plots of the gods; in Sophocles' play the action has become grounded in a city of which an Athenian could imagine himself to be a member, even though it is by no means a replica of classical Athens, and the characters have become figures rich with familiar human traits.

More or less a century after Sophocles' play was performed, Aristotle analysed tragedy in his *Poetics*. Aristotle was interested in what marks tragedy out from other literary forms, and he was keen both to classify types of plot or sub-plot (recognition scenes, reversals of fortune) and the qualities required of the central figure for that figure to be tragic (that the figure is not perfect). Sophocles' play was for Aristotle an exemplary tragedy, both formally, in terms of unity of action, and in its tragic story. Aristotle lifts the play out of its context within the city-state and looks at it on the page; he has no doubt about the profound effect a play has on those who experience it, but he envisages the theatre audience as a collection of individuals, like the individual reader, rather than as a community of citizens.

What happens to the story of Oedipus reflects and reveals the broader contours of Greek history, and shows why it is Classical Greece that stands at the head of this History of Europe. The Oedipus and Epicaste of the *Odyssey* live out lives that might be the lives of the audience of the poem, their interest lies at the level of personal morality, and it is their fate as individuals that is drawn to the audience's attention. As in the Homeric poems more generally, it is the potential parallels for the lives of members of the audience, and for individuals known to them, that are important. This and other Homeric stories are notable for the limited role played by the magical and for characters' intense emotional investment, but in other respects they are closely akin to stories of such near-eastern epics as Gilgamesh. Sophocles' Oedipus and Jocasta, by contrast, are very far from the world of Gilgamesh. In Sophocles the lives and actions of the two starring characters are the product of numerous separate decisions made not just by them but by those with whom they are involved, and they are lives whose impact is not just upon individuals but upon the whole community. Social and political relationships have become intertwined with personal relationships in a world where human beings can never know the consequences of their action, not because what happens is determined by cruel gods but because complete knowledge is never available. In the hands of Aristotle Oedipus has changed again, as the relationship between the action on stage and the reactions of the audience come under analytical scrutiny. The Oedipus who fascinates Aristotle is neither the man who is the plaything of the gods nor the victim of cumulative and inevitable human ignorance, but the active manipulator of the theatre audience. Aristotle is not concerned to read the play against the cultural context of the Greek city-state at all, but looks for conclusions about drama that are universal. For Aristotle the relationship of Oedipus' character to his fate is important because it can be treated as exemplary of what even a disembedded cultural product can do to those who encounter it. In stepping back to focus on what words do to the people who hear them, Aristotle took up the analysis of speeches made in political meetings and law courts, which the need to understand how decisions could be influenced in democratic cities had inspired in the late fifth century, and applied it to fiction, so placing himself at the head of the western tradition of literary criticism.

The world of the classical city was a world where citizens had so taken charge of their own destinies that the Homeric explanation that 'it was a plot of malicious gods' ceased to satisfy, and where the demand to decide one's own, and others', destiny brought home the inevitability of ignorance and the urgency of finding ways of restricting the damage that ignorance could do. It was a world in which the individual was seen as essentially social, the life of a particular human being actively and inevitably shaped by the community of which he or she was part. It was also a world in which the prevalence of mass debate drew attention to the way in which words do not simply

convey information, they do things, and where analysis and control
of what they do came to be a pressing concern: thinkers managed so
to distance themselves from their own circumstances as to examine
what was going on from the outside, establishing patterns and general
rules.

The Greek city was small and life within it intense. In the archaic
period we see that intensity in the homosocial groups that produced
the poetry of Archilochus, Theognis, and others. In the classical
period the spread of the habit of putting power into the hands of a
wide group of citizens led to the individual life becoming swallowed
up in the life of the wider community, the action of the group being
more than simply the sum of the independent actions of its members.
But the very intensity of city life, and the prominence of the group as
whole and as parts, promoted a self-scrutiny that we cannot find
parallels for in earlier history and which has provided the basis for
our own self-scrutiny to this day. In the thirty-three tragedies written
by Aeschylus, Sophocles, and Euripides that are still extant today, in
the great sculptural programmes of the temple of Zeus at Olympia or
the Parthenon in Athens, in the monumental enquiries into the
recent past that constitute the histories of Herodotus and Thucydides, and in the thirty-five surviving philosophical dialogues of
Plato and thirty-two surviving treatises of Aristotle, the classical city-
state has bequeathed to us a wide-ranging and profound exploration
of what it is to be human, what it is to live in a society in which the
individual is autonomous but also dependent, physically and emotionally, upon others, and in which, without ever fully understanding
the consequences of their own actions, human beings exercise a controlling role over fellow human creatures and over the animal and
plant world.

The reader of Greek tragedy, of Herodotus and Thucydides, of
Plato and Aristotle, or of other surviving works of classical literature,
and the visitor to Greek archaeological sites or to the museums in
Greece or around the world in which the products of Greek sculptural or ceramic workshops are displayed, is struck by mixed feelings
of familiarity and estrangement. So much of western art and architecture, philosophy and literature, both in the past and still today, is
in dialogue with classical Greek culture that a feeling of familiarity is
inevitable. But we have only to face the masked male actor playing
Jocasta, the tragedian Sophocles welcoming a snake to Athens as the

embodiment of Asclepius god of healing, or a water jug with the image of a satyr masturbating, to be conscious that the Greek city was no mirror image of the modern western world.

This book has tried to map out that strange and yet familiar world, to reveal something of the very different reality concealed behind familiar terms, and to make sense of some of the very different cultural values: in short to build a stage on which Greek writers, thinkers, and artists can play effectively to a modern audience. The Greek world described here was not full of men exposed at birth, rescued and brought up by royalty, who had in ignorance killed their fathers, married their mothers, and only discovered the truth when the city they ruled was struck by a terrible epidemic. But it was a world in which crops did fail, in which illness did strike, in which violence did flare up over petty quarrels which no state body would ever investigate, in which individuals did move from city to city and join communities which were quite ignorant of their past, and in which what could not be explained rationally was readily ascribed to the direct and purposive intervention of the gods. We are familiar with the violence, but expect a murder enquiry, know of epidemic, but expect a medical reaction, move more or less freely from place to place, but expect there to be state records. We can still map Oedipus and Jocasta onto our world and can and do put them effectively onto our stage. We can and do, indeed, map the concerns and assumptions of our world onto them, as we have done in putting Oedipus onto the psychiatrist's couch. But if we want to understand what Sophocles was doing, we need to be able to map Oedipus and Jocasta onto Sophocles' world too, and to put them onto the Greek stage.

Classical Greece belongs to the Third World, but to a third world in which there is no first world. The empires of the Near East had wealth and manpower resources no Greek city could imagine, but their economic base was identical to that of Greece, founded on extorting an agricultural surplus and exploiting a limited range of minerals, almost exclusively metals. Massive manipulation of water supplies to provide crop irrigation that cushioned against the vagaries of rainfall did, at various periods, make for a much higher degree of social and political stability in Egypt and Mesopotamia than the Greek world could ever achieve, but during the period of which we are talking this stability was a thing of the past, and Egypt a reluctant and rebellious member of the Persian empire. In times of crisis cities of the Greek mainland received occasional gifts of grain from Egypt and from north Africa, but this was by no means 'aid to developing countries' and there was no scope for accumulated indebtedness.

Greek cities had to expect to cope with an uncertain food supply from their own resources. Having to face the prospect of a meagre harvest was one thing that united rich and poor farmers, and the disapproval of those who chose to invest their wealth other than in land stemmed in part from their opting out of this shared experience. To turn from the land to the sea, and seek a living from trade was not, however, to avoid risk. In addition to the risks a trader always faces of not being able to sell the goods he acquired at a price sufficient to produce a profit, ancient risks of shipwreck and, at some periods, of being intercepted by pirates or forced into the port of another city, were not small. The prices of staple foods fluctuated by a factor of five or more, and the profits to be made were potentially enormous. A similar gamble affected mining: heavy investment was called for, but the vein of silver mined might or might not prove a rich one. The reversals of fortune that Aristotle identified as a basic plot element in tragedy were equally familiar in life. And just as tragedies often do not end with the change of fortune but go on to show how the protagonist and the community of which he or she is part copes with the reversal, so too in life those reversals bound the individual in to the family and community without whose support life itself would be threatened.

Both within city-states and between them there was constantly an issue of whether co-operation or conflict offered the more secure future. Those whom past lotteries had left on top had reason to join together and exclude others from a say in the city's decisions. Often that meant excluding all the poor from political rights; in some cities it meant particularly excluding those involved in trade. Those who had not inherited wealth looked to make up for their lack of personal security by seeking to play a part in the larger whole. In different cities these opposing interests played themselves out in different ways, and although the Greeks themselves talked about democracy and oligarchy as if they were poles apart, in fact political power was distributed in numerous and diverse ways ranging from individual or collective tyranny at one end to active participation from all adult males at the other.

Theorists ancient and modern have focused on the constitutional rules in their classification of city governments, but much the same rules produced different political effects in different circumstances. The size of a city had a fundamental effect upon relationships within it, but so also did the pattern of settlement and the configuration of religious activity. In some cities religious activity focused on a single sanctuary, in others it was split; in some the main focus was out of town, in others within the walls. In some outsiders were regularly attracted to festivities, in others only citizens were allowed to take part. In every city the inhabitants grouped themselves into cult units in various ways, by family, by place, by gender, by their own elective choice: those various groups might work within a culture of co-operation or a culture of conflict. In Athens, the city we know best, we can see how the enormous effort put into the Panathenaea and into the Dionysia, both occurring in the town of Athens itself, together with the institution of processions which linked the city to such distant sanctuaries as Eleusis and Brauron, whose cult groups encompassed non-citizens, made the town the religious focus even when so much cult activity was taking place outside. It can be no accident that the great majority of tragedies put on at the Dionysia dealt with conflicts situated in other cities, and not at Athens itself, playing out Athenian political issues obliquely rather than directly.

Small cities faced stark choices as to whether they exposed themselves to the risk of isolation or to the risk of being engulfed and eradicated by a larger neighbour. Just as conflicts within cities always carried the threat that they would spill out into conflict between cities, so conflicts between neighbouring cities always carried the threat that they would draw in cities further away. When the distorting effect of having two very powerful cities waiting to welcome allies against each other, as Athens and Sparta were waiting in the fifth century, is removed, we see in the early fourth century mainland Greek cities chronically incapable of deciding whether they are better off together or apart, calling in bigger cities or going it alone. Such decisions were not trivial: the choice of external alliance had implications for internal government, and small cities were never free of the threat of total extermination by large neighbours—the history of Plataea in Boeotia, twice razed to the ground by its Theban neighbours, is a case in point here. Only for members of the largest communities was life less than precariousness: even a city as large and recently powerful as Thebes was eliminated by Alexander the Great in 335 after a revolt.

The need for the member of a small city constantly to reassess his own and his city's priorities made for urgent political debate, both practical and theoretical. It also made for an intensity of observation. No citizen was free from scrutiny: where group decisions hung in the balance, and where the individual citizen was constantly reassessing his interests, there was inevitably a climate of distrust. The company people kept, the places they frequented, the clothes they wore, even the way they walked, were constantly reviewed as outward visible signs of inner disposition. Rules multiplied, and so did tests. When Plato makes Socrates suggest that the unexamined life is not worth living, it was not the fact of examination that made this statement unusual but the nature of the examination. For Socrates the examination was not of the outward signs or conformity to rules, although by going barefoot and refusing to seduce Alcibiades he exploited the rules precisely in his keen disregard for them, but of the relationship of life's constant decisions to moral values that could be independently defended.

The life of the individual, for we can hardly talk of *private* life at all, was always life within a group. For most Greek cities we know little of group dynamics beyond what we can surmise from the laws passed in order to regulate them. But for classical Athens we can see how those groups were constituted (every group above the immediate family constituted itself along the same lines as the city itself, with allotted officials in charge and decisions taken at general meetings), we can see them explored on stage in both tragedy and comedy, we can see them in action in politics, and we can see them theorized, both in the popular theory that was constructed in the lawcourts as litigants presented their rival images of the good citizen and in Plato and Aristotle's more esoteric explorations of what it might be to be virtuous.

This book has tried to throw the spotlight on the individual and the group within the city, to build up a picture of classical Greece which gives priority not to the actions of cities, to what the Athenians said or what the Spartans did, but to what it was to be a member, or at least a citizen member, of those communities. It has done so out of a belief that understanding of the cultural products which have become what Greece is to us can only be achieved against the background of the situation of the individual citizen, rather than against a background of glorious Greek victories over Persians, whether in the Greek mainland in the early fifth century or in Asia in the 330s and 320s. It has also done so from the belief that it is an understanding of the culture of the Greek city-state that must stand at the head of every history of Europe, however short. It was the political and social tensions of the Greek city, and the ways in which they were described and analysed, that created the legacy with which subsequent European politics and culture have been in continuous debate. That debate can be traced into the cities of Hellenistic Asia that were created by Alexander's conquests, but what ensured that the debate was the foundation of modern Europe was the way in which it was taken up by Rome. It is with the story of Rome, and in particular the story of Rome from her conquest of and by Greece, that the history of Europe continues.

Further Reading

Readers may find the following books useful sources of further information about the topics treated here.

Sourcebooks

M. H. Crawford and D. Whitehead, *Archaic and Classical Greece: A Selection of Ancient Sources in Translation* (Cambridge University Press, Cambridge, 1983).

C. W. Fornara, *Archaic Times to the End of the Peloponnesian War*, 2nd edn. (Cambridge University Press, Cambridge, 1983).

P. Harding, *From the End of the Peloponnesian War to the Battle of Ipsus* (Cambridge University Press, Cambridge, 1985).

P. J. Rhodes, *The Greek City-States: A Source Book* (Routledge, London, 1986).

General

P. A. Cartledge, *The Cambridge Illustrated History of Ancient Greece* (Cambridge University Press, Cambridge, 1998). An introduction to the whole course of Greek history and to Greek culture, richly illustrated.

J. K. Davies, *Democracy and Classical Greece*, Fontana History of the Ancient World, 2nd edn. (Fontana, London, 1993). A general history of Classical Greece which makes extensive use of extracts from original sources.

E. Fantham, H. P. Foley, N. B. Kampen, S. B. Pomeroy, and H. A. Shapiro, *Women in the Classical World* (Oxford University Press, Oxford, 1994). Covers the Roman as well as the Greek world, with copious quotation of original sources.

S. Hornblower, *The Greek World 479–323 BC*, Routledge History of the Ancient World, revised edn. (Routledge, London, 1991). Particularly full coverage of the Greek world outside Athens and Sparta.

O. Murray and S. Price (eds.) *The Greek City from Homer to Alexander* (Oxford University Press, Oxford, 1989).

A. Powell (ed.), *The Greek World* (Routledge, London, 1995). 27 chapters by different authors ranging widely over Greek history and culture; particularly strong on Greek religion.

Chapter 1

R. Buxton, *Imaginary Greece: The Contexts of Mythology* (Cambridge University Press, Cambridge, 1994). An imaginative approach to the Greeks through their mythology.

J. M. Hall, *Ethnic Identity in Greek Antiquity* (Cambridge University Press, Cambridge, 1997). A ground-breaking and sophisticated analysis of the nature of ethnicity in ancient Greece.

R. Osborne, *Greece in the Making 1200–479 BC*, Routledge History of the Ancient World (Routledge, London, 1996). Uses archaeology, archaic Greek literature, and later Greek tradition to create a picture of what archaic Greece was like.

Chapter 2

M. I. Finley, *The Ancient Economy*, revised edn., ed. I. Morris (University of California Press, Berkeley, 1999). A classic, if much debated, account of the ancient economy.

Y. Garlan, *Slavery in Ancient Greece* (Cornell University Press, Ithaca, NY, 1988). A full treatment of the topic.

P. C. Millett, *Lending and Borrowing in Ancient Athens* (Cambridge University Press, Cambridge, 1991). Puts commercial transactions into their broad social context.

R. Osborne, *Classical Landscape with Figures: The Ancient Greek City and its Countryside* (George Philip, London, 1987). Shows the centrality of the countryside to political, religious, and social aspects of Greek life.

S. von Reden, *Exchange in Ancient Greece* (Duckworth, London, 1995). Uses the insights of economic anthropology and close literary and iconographical analysis to examine the whole range of exchange transactions.

Chapter 3

P. Cartledge, P. Millett, and S. von Reden (eds.), *Kosmos: Essays in Order, Conflict and Community in Classical Athens* (Cambridge University Press, Cambridge, 1998). Explores a wide range of aspects of the Athenian polis as a community.

M. H. Hansen, *The Athenian Democracy in the Age of Demosthenes*, 2nd edn. (University of Oklahoma Press, Norman, 1999). A text book coverage of Athenian democratic institutions.

R. Parker, *Athenian Religion: A History* (Oxford University Press, Oxford, 1996). A detailed chronological account of Athenian cult practices with an important analysis of the trial of Socrates.

S. Price, *Religions of the Ancient Greeks* (Cambridge University Press, Cambridge, 1999). An introduction to Greek religion with an emphasis on archaeological evidence and practices.

S. C. Todd, *The Shape of Athenian Law* (Oxford University Press, Oxford, 1993). A reliable study of Athenian law informed by modern anthropological approaches, including sections on personal relations.

For Sparta see under Chapter 8, below.

Chapter 4

Yvon Garlan, *War in the Ancient World: A Social History* (Chatto and Windus, London, 1975). A classic study of ancient war in its social and cultural context.

W. K. Pritchett, *The Greek State at War*, 5 vols. (University of California Press, Berkeley, 1971–91). Series of exhaustive surveys of ancient evidence for many aspects of war.

J. Rich and G. Shipley (eds.), *War and Society in the Greek World* (Routledge, London, 1993). Interesting collection of articles, covering several topics not fully addressed here.

Peter Hunt, *Slaves, Warfare and Ideology in the Greek Historians* (Cambridge University Press, Cambridge, 1998). Radical new perspective on hoplite ideals and the role of slaves in war.

V. D. Hanson, *Warfare and Agriculture in Classical Greece* (1983; revised edn. University of California Press, Berkeley, 1999) and V. D. Hanson, *The Western Way of War* (Oxford University Press, 1989). Two innovative and influential studies of vital elements of Greek warfare: agricultural devastation and pitched infantry battle.

Hans van Wees, *Greek Warfare: Myths and Realities* (Duckworth, 2000), and Hans van Wees (ed.) *War and Violence in Ancient Greece* (Duckworth/Classical Press of Wales, 2000) seek to challenge many aspects of conventional wisdom about Greek warfare.

I. G. Spence, *The Cavalry of Classical Greece* (Oxford University Press, Oxford, 1993). Thorough study of the organization, uses, and funding of cavalry forces.

J. S. Morrison and J. F. Coates, *The Athenian Trireme* (Cambridge University Press, Cambridge, 1986). Detailed account of naval warfare which makes use of the results of reconstructing a seaworthy trireme, the Olympias.

V. Gabrielsen, *Financing the Athenian Fleet* (Johns Hopkins University Press, Baltimore, 1994). Lucid discussion of the economics of naval warfare.

Chapter 5

C. Farrar, *The Origins of Democratic Thinking: The Invention of Politics in Classical Athens* (Cambridge University Press, Cambridge, 1988). A sophisticated and provocative analysis of democratic theorizing embedded in the thought of Protagoras, Democritus, and Thucydides.

J. Ober, *Mass and Elite in Democratic Athens: Rhetoric, Ideology, and the Power of the People* (Princeton University Press, Princeton, 1989). A lucid and influential exploration of the ideology of Athenian democracy.

J. Ober, *Political Dissent in Democratic Athens: Intellectual Critics of Popular Rule* (Princeton University Press, Princeton, 1998). A thorough survey of the ancient critics of Athenian democracy.

Chapter 6

J. Burckhardt, *The Greeks and Greek Civilization* (HarperCollins, London, 1998). A view of Greek life by one of the greatest modern historians, a wonderful collection of sources, but some very novel conclusions.

J. N. Davidson, *Courtesans and Fishcakes* (HarperCollins, London, 1997). Eating, drinking, and sex in the context of the Athenian democracy.

K. J. Dover, *Greek Popular Morality* (Blackwell, Oxford, 1974). A comprehensive study of moral attitudes in Athenian comedy and oratory.

M. Foucault, *History of Sexuality, ii. The Uses of Pleasure*, trans. R. Hurley (Penguin Books, London, 1985). An important and influential analysis of 'self-mastery'.

R. Garland, *The Greek Way of Death* (Duckworth, London, 1985). A useful study of ideas about death and funeral practices.

R. Garland, *The Greek Way of Life* (Duckworth, London, 1990). A survey of the stages of Greek life and associated rituals.

P. Garnsey, *Food in the Ancient World* (Cambridge University Press, Cambridge, 1999). A study of diet in the ancient world with an emphasis on nutrition.

Helen King, *Hippocrates' Woman* (Routledge, London, 1998). A study of ancient medicine's approach to the female body, and its modern consequences.

A. Stewart, *Art and the Body in Ancient Greece* (Cambridge University Press, Cambridge, 1997). A study of the ideology of physical form.

Chapter 7

D. Boedeker and K. A. Raaflaub (eds.), *Democracy, Empire and the Arts in Fifth-Century Athens* (Harvard University Press, Cambridge, Mass. 1998).

Examines the relationship between the culture of Athens and the political realms of democracy and empire.

A. R. Burn, *Persia and the Greeks*, 2nd edn. (Duckworth, London, 1984). The fullest treatment of the Persian Wars, with a useful updated postscript by D. M. Lewis.

P. A. Cartledge, *Sparta and Laconia* (Routledge, London, 1979). Contains two chapters on the fifth century but with much of relevance in other chapters.

D. M. Lewis, *Sparta and Persia* (Brill, Leiden, 1977). Deals mostly with Sparta and Persia in the fourth century but important for the final stage of the Peloponnesian War.

D. M. Lewis, John Boardman, J. K. Davies, and M. Ostwald, (eds.), *The Cambridge Ancient History, v. The Fifth Century BC*, 2nd edn. (Cambridge University Press, Cambridge, 1992). A comprehensive history of the Greek world in the fifth century from 479.

Russell Meiggs, *The Athenian Empire* (Oxford University Press, Oxford, 1972). A comprehensive treatment of the Athenian Empire and fifth-century political and military history as it relates to the empire.

G. E. M. de Ste. Croix, *The Origins of the Peloponnesian War* (Duckworth, London 1972). Includes discussion of a wide range of issues affecting fifth-century history.

John Salmon, *Wealthy Corinth* (Oxford University Press, Oxford, 1984). Treats the history of Corinth from the Archaic Age to 338 BC, with much on or relevant to the fifth century.

Chapter 8

D. M. Lewis, J. Boardman, S. Hornblower, and M. Ostwald (eds.), *The Cambridge Ancient History, vi. The Fourth Century BC*, 2nd edn. (Cambridge University Press, Cambridge, 1994). A massive and authoritative coverage of the whole Greek world.

P. A. Cartledge, *Agesilaos and the Crisis of Sparta* (Duckworth, London, 1987). The fullest treatment of Sparta's most influential king.

G. L. Cawkwell, *Philip of Macedon* (Faber, London, 1978). A lively treatment of the man responsible for turning Macedon into a major power.

A. B. Bosworth, *Conquest and Empire: The Reign of Alexander the Great* (Cambridge University Press, Cambridge, 1988). Gives a full narrative along with close analysis of the most important historical problems.

Chronology

Date	Political and military events	Cultural milestones
c.507	Cleisthenic reforms mark beginning of democracy at Athens	Competition for tragedies instituted at the City Dionysia in Athens
499–494	Unsuccessful revolt of Ionians against Persian rule	Temple of Aphaea built on Aegina
		Aeschylus' first tragedy produced
490	First Persian invasion of Greece defeated at Marathon	
487	Athenians change to choosing their chief magistrate (archon) by lot	Competition for comedies added to City Dionysia at Athens
481–479	Second Persian Invasion of Greece defeated after battles at Artemisium, Thermopylae, Salamis, and Plataea	Euripides born
	Carthaginian invasion of Sicily defeated at battle of Himera	
478	Delian League formed to continue the fight against Persia	Aeschylus' Persians (472)
469	Greeks defeat Persians at battle of Eurymedon (or slightly later)	Birth of Socrates
		Painted Stoa built at Athens (470–460)
465	Athenians face revolt of Thasos	Aeschylus' Suppliant Women (463)
	Earthquake in Sparta	
462	Ephialtes' reforms mark beginning of radical democracy at Athens	
458	Battle of Tanagra between Athens and Sparta	Aeschylus' Oresteia trilogy
		Temple of Zeus at Olympia completed
454	Athenian expedition to Egypt defeated	Thucydides born
	Treasury of Delian League moved to Athens	
449	Formal or informal peace agreement between Athens and Persia	Parthenon begun (447)

445	Thirty Years' Peace marks end to conflict between Athens and Sparta	Aristophanes born
440	Attempted revolt of Samos from the Athenian empire	
432	Sparta decides to go to war with Athens	Parthenon completed
430	Plague breaks out at Athens Death of Pericles (429)	Euripides' *Medea* (431) Xenophon born
428	Attempted revolt of Lesbos from the Athenian empire	Euripides' *Hippolytus* Plato born (427)
425	Spartan troops on Sphacteria surrender to Athenians	Aristophanes' *Acharnians*
424	Athenians defeated at Delium Brasidas' campaigns in northern Greece	Thucydides exiled for military incompetence
421	Peace of Nicias ends first part of Peloponnesian War	Death of Protagoras Aristophanes' *Peace*
415	Athenian expedition against Sicily	Mutilation of Herms Euripides' *Trojan Women*
413	Athenian defeat in Sicily Athenians replace allied tribute by 5 per cent tax on imports and exports	Aristophanes' *Birds* (414)
411	Democracy overturned at Athens, regime of 400	Aristophanes' *Lysistrata* and *Women at the Thesmophoria*
410	Full democracy restored at Athens	
405	Athenian defeat at naval battle of Aegospotami marks her defeat in Peloponnesian War Dionysius becomes tyrant of Syracuse	Erechtheum completed Aristophanes' *Frogs* Euripides' *Bacchae*
404	Democracy overturned at Athens, regime of Thirty installed	
399	Sparta begins campaign against Persia in Asia Minor	Trial and execution of Socrates
395	Agesilaus attacks Sardis War breaks out between Phocis and Locris	
392	Athenian Long Walls rebuilt Union of Corinth and Argos	Aristophanes' *Ecclesiazusae*
387	Peace in Greece brokered by Persia (King's Peace)	Plato opens Academy
384	Sparta splits up Mantinea Athens allies with Chios	Demosthenes and Aristotle born

382	Spartans seize Theban acropolis	
379	Liberation of Thebes from Spartans	Temple of Asclepius at Epidaurus begun
377	Second Athenian Confederacy formed	
371	Thebans defeat Spartans at battle of Leuctra	
367	Death of Dionysius I of Syracuse, Dionysius II succeeds	Aristotle joins Academy Plato visits Sicily
362	Battle of Mantinea	
360	Philip II accedes to Macedonian throne	Birth of Pyrrho, founder of Scepticism
357	Athenian allies revolt ('Social War')	Theatre at Epidaurus built
352		Mausoleum at Halicarnassus built
349	Philip II attacks Olynthus	Demosthenes delivers Olynthiac orations
347		Death of Plato; Aristotle leaves Athens
346	Athens makes peace with Philip II	Rebuilding of Temple of Apollo at Delphi begins
340	Athens declares war on Philip II	Temple of Athena Alea, Tegea
337	Philip II wins battle of Chaeronea	
336	Philip II assassinated at Aegae	
335	Alexander the Great destroys Thebes	Aristotle returns to Athens
334	Alexander the Great wins battle of Granicus	Choregic monument of Lysicrates built at Athens
331	Alexander the Great wins battle of Gaugamela Sparta attempts revolt against Macedon and is defeated	
330	Demosthenes and Aeschines do battle in court in the *Crown* trial	
327	Alexander invades India	First victory of Philemon, writer of New Comedy
323	Death of Alexander	
322	Lamian war of Greek cities against Macedonia ends in Greek defeat	Deaths of Aristotle and Demosthenes

Glossary

Where technical terms are used in this book they are generally glossed in the text, but the following may be found useful:

agora: the civic centre and market-place: see pp. 49–51.

Areopagus: the 'Hill of Ares' just northwest of the Athenian Acropolis was the place on which a council met which was made up of Athenians who had previously served as chief magistrate (Archon). The Council of the Areopagus chiefly had judicial functions, and after the reforms of Ephialtes of 462 these were largely restricted to homicide cases and certain religious cases.

helot: the Spartans had basic agricultural labour carried out by a subservient population who had no judicial rights and were known as helots. In Laconia itself the helots may have been a native population; in Messenia the local population were turned into helots when the Spartans conquered their territory in the eighth century.

hoplites: soldiers, heavily armed with bronze helmet, bronze or leather breastplate, bronze greaves, and a round shield worn on the left arm, who fought in massed ranks (see especially pp. 84–7, 98–101).

liturgy: rich Athenians were required to perform a variety of public services for the state at their own expense. These services included manning triremes, putting on plays at the Dionysia, and other expenditure related to the proper performance of religious festivals.

metic: a technical Athenian term for a non-Athenian, whether Greek or non-Greek, resident at Athens either permanently or at least for a period of longer than one month. Such a person was obliged to pay a special tax, the *metoikion*, of one drachma a month. The orator Lysias and the philosopher Aristotle are among those whose status at Athens was that of metic.

perioikoi: as well as the Spartan citizens and enslaved helots, there were free residents of Lakonia known as *perioikoi* (lit. 'Fringe-dwellers'). The *perioikoi* lived as self-governing communities but were obliged to fight alongside the Spartans.

polis (plural 'poleis'), conventionally translated 'city-state': see pp. 72–3.

Table of money
6 obols = 1 drachma
100 drachmas = 1 mina
60 minas = 1 talent

Throughout the book all dates given are BC unless otherwise indicated.

List of Ancient Authors

Aelian (*c.*AD170–235). Taught rhetoric at Rome and published compilations of excerpts and anecdotes on a variety of matters, including the historical collection known as the *Varia Historia*.

Aeschines (*c.*397–*c.*322). Actor who became an important politician most famous for his repeated but finally unsuccessful attacks of Demosthenes in the courts.

Aeschylus (525/4–456/5). The tragedian who dominated the Athenian stage for the first forty years of the fifth century. Six tragedies by Aeschylus survive, including the only extant set of three plays performed together at a single festival, the *Oresteia* trilogy made up of the *Agamemnon, Libation-Bearers* (*Choephori*), and *Eumenides*, and performed in 458. His *Persians*, the earliest surviving Greek tragedy, dating from 472, is the only extant example of a tragedy based on recent historical events.

Andocides (*c.*440–390). Athenian orator and politician who was involved in and informed upon the plot to mutilate the Herms in 415.

Aristophanes (*c.*445–after 375?). Comic dramatist whose earliest recorded work is the *Banqueters* of 427 and latest the *Wealth* of 388. The earlier of the eleven surviving plays are extremely topical and all choose political targets; the later plays have more timeless plots and more interest in social problems.

Aristotle (384–322). Born at Stagira, a pupil of Plato, and for several years tutor to the teenage Alexander the Great, Aristotle returned to Athens in 335, where he founded the Lyceum. His work ranged over the entire field of philosophy and science, including logic, biology, literary criticism, and ethics. His *Politics* seems to derive from lectures given by him in the 330s and are rich with allusions to particular political incidents as well as generalized claims about political behaviour. His *Nicomachean Ethics* is concerned with the nature of *eudaimonia*, 'happiness' or 'human flourishing'. Of his *Poetics*, the first systematic work of literary criticism to survive from antiquity, we have only the first book, concerned with tragedy, but it has been immensely influential.

[Aristotle] *Constitution of the Athenians* (*Athenaion Politeia*). This work, largely known from a papyrus purchased by the British Museum in 1888–9 and published in 1891, is the only one of the 158 Constitutions of Greek states compiled under Aristotle's direction substantially surviving. Written in the 320s, it consists of a history of the Athenian constitution down to the end of the fifth century, followed by a description of how the Athenian constitution worked in the later fourth century. The historical section is compiled from earlier written accounts, particularly those by the local historians of Athens known as Atthidographers.

Arrian (*c.*AD86–160). Born in Bithynia, but became a member of the Roman senate and governor of Cappadocia before retiring to Athens. He represented himself as a second Xenophon and wrote about hunting and how to fight wars, as well as an *Anabasis* in seven books describing Alexander's conquest of the Persian empire.

Athenaeus of Naucratis in Egypt (active *c.*AD200). Known for a single work, the *Deipnosophistai* ('Learned Banquet') in which a large number of guests, some with historical names, exchange anecdotes and excerpts from earlier writings. It is for these excerpts from works that are otherwise lost that the work is most valued today.

Demosthenes (384–322). The most famous of all Athenian orators and an influential fourth-century politician. From the late 350s until the battle of Chaeronea in 337 Demosthenes urged the Athenians to resist Philip II of Macedon's expansion of his powers. One of Demosthenes' chief persuasive gambits was comparing the Athenians of the fourth-century with (a rose-tinted view of) their fifth-century ancestors.

Diodorus (active 60–36BC). A native of Sicily, Diodorus wrote a *Universal History* in 40 books which attempted to give a year-by-year account of both Greek and Roman history. For much of his account of fifth-century Greece he seems to have followed the fourth-century historian Ephorus of Cyme. Ephorus organized his history by topic rather than by year, and Diodorus is inclined to include under a single year events that spread across several (he covers almost a decade as a single year at 11. 60–61). At his best he conveys the virtues as well as the vices of his sources, at his worst he garbles even the accounts he has before him.

Euripides (*c.*480–407/6). The youngest of the three great Athenian tragedians, first competed at the Dionysia in the year that Aeschylus died. Eighteen of his plays survive complete, of which the earliest is *Alcestis* of 437 and the latest *Bacchae* written in Macedon in the last year of his life. His plays explore such things as relationships between men and women (as in *Medea* and *Hippolytus*), myths of Athenian origins and identity (as in *Ion* and *Erechtheus*), and the horrors of war (as in *Andromache*, *Hecuba*, and *Trojan Women*).

Frontinus (*c.*AD40–103/4). A prominent general and politician under the Flavian emperors, who illustrated his book on military tactics, entitled *Strategemata*, with examples drawn from Greek as well as Roman history.

Hellenica Oxyrhynchia. The name given to the substantial fragments of an account of Greek history from 410 to the King's Peace of 387/6 preserved on papyrus. The identity of the author is uncertain.

Herodotus (*c*.480–410) is the father of Greek history. His *Histories* provide an account of the Persian Wars prefaced by a long description of the Persian empire. Born at Halicarnassus but from its foundation resident at Thurii, Herodotus seems to have been writing his *Histories* during the Peloponnesian War. See further pp. 174–6.

Hesiod (active *c*.700). Boeotian poet responsible for the earliest extant Greek didactic poems, *Works and Days* and *Theogony*. His name is often coupled with that of Homer by later Greeks and his works had a profound influence on Greek views of the gods.

Hippocrates. The most famous of all Greek physicians and eponym of the Hippocratic 'school' of medicine. Numerous and diverse works on medical topics written in the fifth and fourth centuries are collectively known as the 'Hippocratic corpus'.

Homer. The name by which the author(s) of the *Iliad* and *Odyssey*, and a number of other epic poems, was known in antiquity. These poems belong to an oral tradition which can be traced back to the Bronze Age, and there is much dispute as to exactly what contribution was made by the poet who turned them into the form we have them in, or when that poet lived. Scholars continue to argue about whether or not the *Iliad* and the *Odyssey* were put into their current form by the same poet.

Hyperides (389–322). Athenian politician bitterly opposed to Philip of Macedon. He was highly rated as an orator in antiquity, but we owe our knowledge of his work only to the survival of substantial papyrus fragments.

Isaeus (*c*.420–*c*.340). An Athenian speech-writer who specialized in inheritance speeches and was a teacher of Demosthenes. Eleven or twelve speeches by him survive. He had a reputation in antiquity for 'wizardry and deceit'.

Isocrates (436–338). Although not himself active as a speaker in the Athenian assembly, Isocrates' written orations provide an important commentary on Athenian politics in the fourth century, and he was important enough as a teacher of rhetoric to be attacked by Plato in *Phaedrus*. Isocrates thought that Greek cities should work together, and he urged Philip to lead the Greek states in a campaign against the Persians.

Lycurgus (*c*.390–325/4). Athenian politician responsible for Athenian finances for more than a decade and author of many Athenian decrees. He was active in the courts, bringing prosecutions for corrupt practices, and his speech *Against Leocrates* is one of the clearest expositions of Athenian citizen ideology.

Lysias (459/8 or later–*c*.380). Born in Athens of a Syracusan father, he spent some time resident at Thurii before returning to Athens in 412/11. As a metic Lysias could take no part in the Athenian Assembly, but many of the speeches he wrote for the Athenian courts have a political slant. In his *Funeral Oration* he turns his skill at glossing over inconvenient facts to the service of the encomium of Athens. He is attacked in Plato's *Phaedrus*.

Menander (perhaps 344/3–292/1). The leading Athenian writer of what is known as 'New Comedy', Menander wrote more than 100 plays. He was extremely influential in antiquity and adapted for the Roman stage, but our direct knowledge of his plays derives from a number of surviving papyri.

Old Oligarch, *Constitution of the Athenians*. This short work included among the pamphlets of Xenophon is distinct from them in style. From its historical allusions it has been thought to date from the late 430s or 420s, and it is thus the earliest surviving work of Attic prose. The author, who is often referred to as the 'Old Oligarch', explains, as if to oligarchs outside Athens, how it is that democracy sustains itself in Athens and cannot easily be overthrown. Although it offers little detailed historical analysis the work mentions in passing much that we are not told by other literary sources.

Pausanias (active *c*.AD150). Author of a *Guide to Greece* whose nine books cover the southern and central parts of the Greek mainland. In describing classical remains he includes, as well as archaeological and topographical information, much accurate historical material drawn from both oral and written sources.

Plato (*c*.429–347). Heavily influenced by Socrates, Plato wrote extensively on many aspects of philosophy, casting his works in the form of dialogues in which Socrates is frequently the main participant and in which Plato himself does not appear. Several of the dialogues (*Crito*, *Phaedo*) are set in the context of the imprisonment of Socrates, whose defence speech Plato also wrote a version of (*Apology*). Other dialogues investigate the nature of various virtues, such as courage or justice. Plato's analyses of the state in *Republic* and blueprint for the ideal city in *Laws* have been extremely influential on political philosophy.

Plutarch (*c*.AD50–120). Philosopher and biographer from Chaeronea in Boeotia who also became a priest at Delphi. He himself insists that his *Parallel Lives*, of which we have 23 pairs (normally comprising one Greek and one Roman), are not history, and he is interested in character rather than the analysis of events, but because he was extremely well read these lives are an important source of information. Most of the Greeks whose lives Plutarch writes lived in the fifth or fourth century.

Polyaenus (active *c*.AD160). A Macedonian rhetorician who dedicated a collection of military stratagems (*Strategemata*) to the emperors Marcus Aurelius and Lucius Verus.

Polybius (*c.*200–*c.*118). Born in Megalopolis, Polybius played an important part in resistance to Rome before being taken to Rome as a hostage. In Rome he wrote an account of the growth of the Roman empire from the first Punic war until his own time, of which a substantial part survives. The work is notable for its care and accuracy, its acute analysis, and its criticism of earlier historians.

Posidippus (active *c.*290). Writer of 'New Comedy' whose work survives only in fragments but was adapted for the Roman stage.

Simonides (active 500). Writer of celebratory and commemorative epigrams, some of which survive, and of victory odes and poems for choral performance, which do not. He is chiefly remembered for his epigrams celebrating Greek victory in the Persian wars. Papyrus fragments of a more substantial poem, a 'pocket epic' celebrating the victory at Plataea, have recently been discovered.

Sophocles (*c.*496–406). Athenian tragedian whose first play was performed in 468 and his last in the year of his death. He was victorious at the Dionysia more frequently than either Aeschylus or Euripides and his winning plays include three of the seven which survive (*Antigone*, *Philoctetes*, and *Oedipus at Colonus*), but his most famous play, *Oedipus the King*, did not win first prize.

Theophrastus of Eresus (*c.*371–287). Successor to Aristotle as head of the Lyceum. Among the several works (on plants, on stones, etc.) that survive, the work most useful to historians is *Characters*, which displays acute social observation and is an important source for Athenian social life.

Thucydides (*c.*455–*c.*400). Athenian of aristocratic background with Thracian connections, whose History of the Peloponnesian War in 8 books, with its account in Book 1 of the years between the Persian and Peloponnesian Wars, forms the backbone of all subsequent histories of Greece during this period. See further pp. 185–7.

Tyrtaeus (mid seventh century). Spartan poet, the surviving fragments of whose work are full of allusions to warfare.

Xenophon (*c.*430–*c.*350). Athenian who wrote *Memoirs of Socrates* (*Memorabilia*), an account of a mercenary expedition into the heart of Persia (*Anabasis*), an account of Greek history from where Thucydides breaks off down to 362 (*Hellenica*), and a number of short works on Sparta, military matters, and hunting. Exiled from Athens for fighting against her at Coronea in 394, he spent some time in Sparta, on an estate in Elis and at Corinth before returning to Athens after 362. His historical works combine accurate detail and perceptive analysis with a certain economy with the truth. His *Poroi*, written in the 350s, advises Athens on how to improve her economy.

Inscriptions are cited by editor's name and number from the following collections of translations:

C. W. Fornara, *Archaic Times to the End of the Peloponnesian War.* Translated Documents of Greece and Rome, vol. i (Cambridge, 1983).

P. Harding, *From the End of the Peloponnesian War to the Battle of Ipsus.* Translated Documents of Greece and Rome, vol. ii (Cambridge, 1985).

Inscriptions for which no convenient translation exists are cited from the following collections by abbreviated title:

LSCG: Lois sacrées des cités grecques, ed. F. Sokolowski (Paris, 1969).
SEG: Supplementum Epigraphicum Graecum.

Maps

Map 1 The Greek World

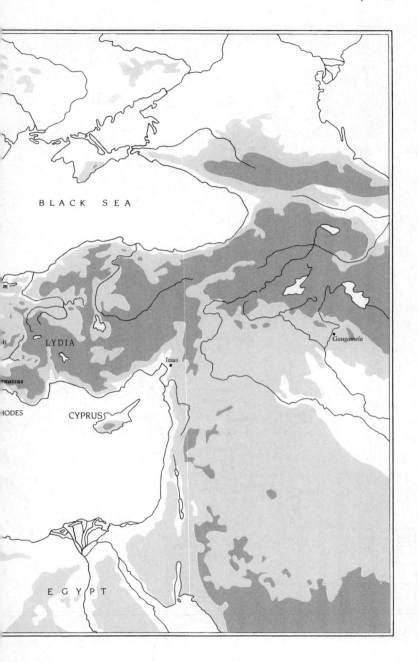

Map 2 Mainland Greece

Index

Asia Minor
  Greeks in 2, 20, 170–1, 176–7, 200,
    202, 204, 221
  Spartan campaigns in 90, 201–2
assembly 1, 9, 58, 74
  at Athens 61
    age for participation in 143
    attendance at 30, 57 62, 72, 118
    frequency of 61, 65
    oratory in 65, 124, 130, 225–6
    pay for 38
    powers of 180
    as court 62
    debates foreign policy 199
    discusses matters of cult 77–8
    makes alliances 112
    rejects action of Council 201
    votes in Thirty Tyrants 121
  at Sparta 66–7, 198–9
  at Thebes 208
Athena 12, 14, 75, 77, 126, 146, 178, 181
  sacred olives of 23–6
Athenaeus 50, 149, 242
Athenogenes 33–4, 46, 50
Athens 111, 174, 185–96, 229
  history:
    archaic temples at 14
    tyranny at 10
    and Ionian Revolt 170–1
    asked to take over resistance to
      Persia 176; see also Delian
      League
    in Peloponnesian War 19, 187–96
    oligarchic revolutions at 26, 33,
      59, 61, 121–2, 130, 167, 199, 238
    surrender of in 404 194
    in Corinthian War 19, 197–203
    and King's Peace 203
    forms new alliances 204; see also
      Second Athenian Confederacy
    in 370s 205
  foreign relations:
    with Alexander 222
    with Boeotia 86, 183, 191, 194
    with Corcyra 111, 112, 187–8, 197–8
    with Corinth 183–4, 194

  with Elis 200
  with Eretria 77
  with Italy 185, 189
  with Macedon 213–19
  with Mantinea 191, 200, 204, 207,
    211
  with Megara 71, 184, 187
  with Melos 186, 192, 194
  with Mytilene 61–2
  with north Aegean 189
  with Persia 17, 20, 108, 171, 172–3,
    176–7, 179–80, 208–9
  with Plataea 71, 191
  with Potidaea 103, 107, 188
  with Samos 57, 103, 107, 208, 238
  with satraps 208
  with Sicily 107, 185, 189, 192–4,
    195, 238
  with Sparta 104, 121, 123, 183,
    186–94, 195, 199, 201, 204–5, 237,
    238
  with Thurii 184–5
society and economy:
  beardlessness in 144
  dependent on imported food 40,
    41, 44, 219
  dress at 145–6, 159
  economy of 23–51
  finances of 56, 66, 107–8, 181
  festivals at 16, 151 (see also
    Dionysia; Panathenaea)
  fondness for cakes 139
  freedom of citizens in 70
  Homeric performance at 16, 19
  homosexuality at 139
  honouring benefactors 44
  obligations to parents at 157
  patterns of residence in 62–3; see
    also Attica; demes
  population of 20–1, 59, 63
  pottery of 18
  silver mines of 36–9, 208; see also
    Laurium
  slaves at 158, 159
  sophists at 116, 158
  taverns in 161–2

music:
    part of education 167–8
    competition in at festivals 74, 76, 77
    new music 168
Mycale, battle of 173
Mycenae 5
Mystery cults 15, 80, 144, 166, 193, 229
Mytilene, Athenian debate over
        punishment of 61–2

nature, as opposed to convention 116,
        124–5, 129, 175
Naucratis 79
Naupactus 77
naval blockages 104
naval warfare 91–3, 104–6
    battle at Salamis 37, 172, 173, 175, 237
    campaigns against Persians 179–80
    battle between Athens and
        Corinthians 187–8
    battle at Cnidus 202, 206
navy, Athenian 91–3, 190, 194
    and democracy 180
    basis of Delian League 177
    and empire 125, 199
    size of 91, 104, 106
    expense of 37, 107
    pay for 41, 92, 107
    funded from silver mines 37, 107,
        172
    training of 93
    use of rowers in land battles 104–5
    in fourth century 38
Naxos 177
Neaera 52–3, 56, 158
Near East:
    influence of 6, 13, 16, 18–19, 103
    compared to Greece 227
neighbours, relations with 24, 26, 27,
        46, 47–8, 106
Nicias, Athenian general 73, 191
    owner of slaves working in
        mines 36, 37
Nicocles, son of Evagoras 134
Nicostratus, neighbour of
        Apollodorus 47–8

nomos, see convention; laws
nude 1, 142, 144, 165

Odysseus 6, 7, 8, 9, 144, 223
Oedipus 223–5, 227
    as role model 168, 224–6
oikos, see household
Old Oligarch 37, 40, 66, 133, 140, 158,
        159, 160, 178, 179, 244
    as critic of democracy 123, 124,
        125–6
oligarchy 53, 58, 70, 111, 132, 228
    advantages and disadvantages of 11,
        115–16
    deviant according to Aristotle 121
    hostile to traders 60
    at Athens 59, 61, 167, 194, 238
    at Sparta 66–9
olives, cultivation of 3, 23, 27
    olive presses smashed in war 97
    as food 151
    non-food uses of 27; see also
        perfume
    sacred 23–6
Olympia 14, 84, 143, 210, 222, 226,
        237
Olympias, wife of Philip II of
        Macedon 214, 217
Olympic games 15–16, 84, 96, 200
Olympiodorus 144
Olynthus 109, 156, 159, 203, 204, 217,
        239
omens, influencing warfare 95
opson 141, 150
oracles 11, 12, 78, 95, 156, 172
oral tradition 5–6, 10–13, 18, 21, 174
oratory, Athenian; see also rhetoric
    as historical source 11, 23–6, 65
    political role of 63, 65, 66, 124, 138,
        225–6
    power of explored in
        tragedy 126–7
Orchomenus 205
Orestes 126
ostracism 66, 124, 180, 181
ox, use of in agriculture 29